# TRADITIONAL KNOWLEDGE SYSTEMS AND ARCHAEOLOGY

With Special Reference to Uttarakhand

# TRADITIONAL KNOWLEDGE SYSTEMS
AND
# ARCHAEOLOGY

## With Special Reference to Uttarakhand

Editors
D.P. AGRAWAL
MANIKANT SHAH
SAMEER JAMAL

ARYAN BOOKS INTERNATIONAL
New Delhi

TRADITIONAL KNOWLEDGE SYSTEMS AND ARCHAEOLOGY

ISBN-81-7305-334-0



First published in **2007** by:
**ARYAN BOOKS INTERNATIONAL**
Pooja Apartments, 4B, Ansari Road, Darya Ganj, New Delhi-110 002 (India)
Tel. : 23287589, 23255799; Fax : 91-11-23270385; E-mail : aryanbooks@vsnl.com

Computer Typeset and Printed in India at
ABI Prints & Publishing Co., New Delhi

*For*

Mohan Upreti

and

Brijendra Lala Daju

# Preface

The United Nations University Proposal defines Traditional Knowledge Systems as follows:

> Traditional knowledge or 'local knowledge' is a record of human achievement in comprehending the complexities of life and survival in often unfriendly environments. Traditional knowledge, which may be technical, social, organizational, or cultural was obtained as part of the great human experiment of survival and development.

When we study Traditional Knowledge Systems of various regions of India, we have to remember that the colonizers systematically exterminated or undermined the local traditional science, technology and crafts of the lands and people they plundered, because of their intellectual arrogance and also to control and appropriate the economic means of production. Western Science created hegemonic categories of science vs magic, technology vs superstitions, etc., which were both arbitrary and contrived, though in ancient Indian culture there was no dichotomy between the *Margi* (Greater Tradition) and the *Desi* (Lesser Tradition). The term 'Traditional Knowledge System' was thus coined by anthropologists as a scientific system which has its own validity, in contradistinction to 'modern' science.

Nader describes the purpose of studying Traditional Knowledge Systems:

> The point is to open up people's minds to other ways of looking and questioning, to change attitudes about knowledge, to reframe the organization of science – to formulate a way of thinking globally about traditions.

History of Science and Technology and Traditional Knowledge Systems are two sides of the same coin. Traditional Knowledge Systems are oral and non-literate, whereas History of Science and Technology is based mainly on literary records. Archaeology provides evidence for both systems of knowledge. In fact, quite often Traditional Knowledge Systems can help to understand the archaeological remains also. A seminar was held in October 2002 at Binsar, near Almora to discuss the problems and the evidence related to the

Traditional Knowledge Systems. We could attract scholars with diverse backgrounds, which enabled us to have an interdisciplinary discussion and perspective. The seminar presented a unique opportunity to discuss different dimensions of Traditional Knowledge Systems and archaeology: ethnographic, architectural, hydrologic, Ayurvedic and other Himalayan medicine systems, informatics, crafts, settlement patterns and even conservation of biodiversity. We had about 22 presentations. Pawan Gupta gave a Gandhian interpretation of the problem of globalization and Traditional Knowledge Systems. C.K. Raju gave a theoretical background of Traditional Knowledge Systems, history, science and culture. D.P. Agrawal explained the importance of Traditional Knowledge Systems and their integral relationship with the elite history of science. In India there was no contradiction between the two traditions: the Greater (*Margi*) and the Lesser Tradition (*Desi*). In fact, the Traditional Knowledge Systems are parental to the greater tradition. The Himalayan medicine system has more than 1,800 medicinal plants; a large number of them entered the *materia medica* of Ayurveda. In fact, the Himalayan medicinal plants and Himalayan medicine must have provided a means of interaction between the Ganga Valley and the Central Himalayas. It is also possible that the rice technology appeared very early in the Central Himalayas as indicated by the complex rituals associated with rice cultivation as also other festivals. Both the hydraulic structures and quakeproof architecture may be useful in understanding secular architectural remains of the area.

Ravi Chopra, the Rawat's, Das, Nirmal Joshi and R.C. Agrawal all emphasized different aspects of traditional architectural technology. Both Jeewan Kharakwal and Diva Bhatt laid stress on the importance of rituals and festivals in inferring ancient agricultural practices. Diva Bhatt explained that a number of cereals are put in the pot to germinate and when they sprout they are put on the head. Rituals of this nature have been connected to the fertility cults and may go back to the Neolithic times. Upreti tried to emphasize the folk science in the folklore. Durgesh and Reema Pant brought in new perspectives of informatics and management sciences to the study of Traditional Knowledge Systems. A number of papers discussed medicine systems in detail – both Ayurvedic and the Himalayan. Roy discussed Ayurveda whereas Tiwari and Pande, and Samant discussed various aspects of the Himalayan medicine system.

As the seminar was held in the sylvan and scenic surroundings of the Mountain Resort with no urban distractions, it provided the participants an opportunity to interact closely and discuss various issues late into the night.

The study of Traditional Knowledge Systems has several merits: it helps develop sustainable and eco-friendly modes of livelihood; it gives us technologies which are cheap and more appropriate; it helps us understand our scientific legacy; it gives us deeper perspective than conferred by the Western Science which seems to assume that all science began with Newton!

Lokvigyan Kendra
Almora

**D.P. Agrawal, Manikant Shah** and **Sameer Jamal**

# Contents

# Acknowledgements

We are grateful to the Infinity Foundation, Princeton, and Indian Council of Historical Research, Delhi, for the financial help which enabled us to hold the seminar. We are also thankful to Lok Vigyan Kendra, Almora and INHERE, Masi, for organizing the seminar. We extend our thanks to R.C. Agrawal, Subhash Agrawal, Diva Bhatt, Krishna Bisht, Ravi Chopra, Rajiv Malhotra, P.C. Pande and C.K. Raju for their active interest and help. A large number of younger colleagues enthusiastically helped us in a variety of ways– we thank them all – Avantika Agrawal, Himal Bhatt, Ritu Gururani, Janki Kandpal, Shekhar Kandpal, Govind Singh, Lalit Tiwari and a host of others whose names cannot be accommodated for want of space. We are also thankful to M.D. Pande and Himanshu Pande for all the help and affectionate hospitality extended to us during the seminar at their Mountain Resort.

# List of Contributors

**D.P. Agrawal**
Lok Vigyan Kendra, East Pokharkhali, Almora-263601.

**Krishna Bisht**
Mahila Haat, 5 Deen Dayal Upadhyaya Marg, New Delhi-110002.

**Ravi Chopra**
People Sceince Institute, 252/1, Vasant Vihar, Dehradun-248006.

**Rishi Das**
People Science Institute, 252/1, Vasant Vihar, Dehradun-248006.

**Nehal A. Farooquee**
G.B. Pant Institute of Himalayan Environment and Development, Kosi-Katarmal, Almora-263643.

**Pawan K. Gupta**
Society for Integrated Development of Himalayas, P.O. Box-19, Hezal Road, Landuar Cantt. Mussourie-248179.

**Hema Joshi**
Department of Botany, S.S.J. Campus, Kumaun University, Almora-263601.

**C.P. Kala**
G.B. Pant Institute of Himalayan Environment and Develoment, Kosi-Katarmal, Almora-263643.

**Jeewan S. Kharakwal**
Department of Archaeology, Rajasthan Vidyapeeth, Udaipur-313001.

**Nirmala Koranga**
Department of Forestry, S.S.J. Campus, Kumaun University, Almora-253501.

**V.N. Misra**
Flat G-2, B Wing, Ganga Park, Pingale Vasti, Mundhwa Road, Pune-411036.

**Malti Nagar**
c/o Department of Archaeology, Deccan College, Pune-411006.

**P.C. Pande**
Department of Botany, Kumaun University, Almora-263601.

**Reema Pant**
Rani Dhara Road, Almora-263601.

**Durgesh Pant**
Department of Information Technology, Kumaun University, Almora-263601.

**Babul Roy**
G.B. Pant Institute of Himalayan Environment and Development, Kosi-Katarmal, Almora-263643.

**Ramashray Roy**
Ranti Deorhi, Madhubani-847211 (Bihar).

**Smriti Kumar Sarkar**
57/2, B.C. Chatterjee St, Belghoria, Kolkata-700056.

**Ila Shah**
Department of Sociology, S.S.J. Campus, Kumaun University, Almora-263601.

**Manikant Shah**
Lok Vigyan Kendra, East Pokharkhali, Almora-263601.

**Rohita Shah**
Department of Botany, S.S.J. Campus, Kumaon University, Almora-263601.

**Shampa Shah**
M-4, Nirala Nagar, Bhadbhada Road, Bhopal-462003.

**Lalit Tiwari**
Homoeopathic Pharmacopoeia Laboratory, C.G.O. Complex-1, Ghaziabad-201002.

**Vibha Tripathi**
22 Sankat, Mochan Colony, Varanasi-221005.

**Alakhnath Upreti**
Pani Odyar, Almora-263601.

**Azusa Yano**
3-2 Oeyama, Goryo, Nishikyo, Kyoto, Japan.

1

# Traditional Knowledge Systems, Science and Globalization

P.K. Gupta

## INTRODUCTION

In this paper I would like to talk about the assumptions of the framework of modern science and modern education; its limitations and how this framework controls and ultimately serves the interests of the market.

## ASSUMPTIONS OF THE FRAMEWORK OF MODERN SCIENCE

### DRISHYA, DRASHTA AUR DRISHTI

One of the basic assumptions of the framework of modern science and the world-view it perpetuates is that there are only two basic entities – the *drishya* (the object or the observed) and the *drashta* (the observer) and that the reality lies in the observed or the object – the *drishya*. This is the principle of objectivity.

We however believe that apart from the observer and the object, there is a third parameter called the *drishti* (vision). The same object is perceived and interpreted in different manner by different people – each according to his or her *drishti*. According to this view, perception is all-important. And most of our experience also collaborates this viewpoint. Ironically, quantum physics also supports this view. Reality no longer remains only in the object– rather reality becomes a construct. The focus shifts to the observer. It is an empowering concept as the observer gets the power to mould his/her perception and play an active role in creating his/her own reality unlike the other world-view where one is merely a passive observer.

## LIMITATIONS OF THE PARADIGM OF MODERN SCIENCE

Although we all perceive through *drishti,* yet as there is no space for it in our present education system, we become oblivious to its presence. Because we take no cognisance of it, we fritter away the power of playing an active role in creating our reality. Because of this mistaken belief (perpetuated by the modern systems and its various instruments) we tend to believe that the reality is out there – in the object alone. Thus, ignoring the presence of *drishti,* limits our perception, making it extremely narrow and we giveaway our power to the outside forces to show us only those which they want us to see. We become disempowered. What is shown to us or what our education system trains us to focus on is only the functional and the instrumental, that which can be seen, touched, heard, tasted, smelled and these too, in a very short, immediate span of time.

The framework of modern science that dominates our lives today creates the illusion that we are "developing a more open mind", "broadening our horizons", "developing a scientific temperament", etc. Actually it is putting blinkers on our eyes. The result is that though the observer feels uncomfortable with the outcomes and experiences a different reality, but he\she is unable to figure out the reasons of it because feelings or experiences do not come under the purview of objectivity.

### Objectives Behind Systems (*Vyavasthas*)

The systems are meant to help people understand and therefore deal with their *sansaar* (their world) and to establish a relationship with the different *ikais* (entities) within that *sansaar*. This world is unique to all of us, and this is the world that we need to deal with and understand deeply with the help of the systems. *Vyavasthas* (systems) are based on *avadharnas/manyatas* (beliefs/ assumptions) and *tarka* (logic or rules). These two are the essential requirements of any system.

In languages there is an assumption regarding the meaning a particular word would convey to the listener, and there is hardly any logic in that. However, each language also has its own unique grammar, which has its peculiar logic. It will be meaningless to compare the grammar of one language with that of another. We can only decide which language is more appropriate for dealing with our *sansaar* at a given point of time, but we cannot compare languages or their grammar in a hierarchical manner.

## Aristotelian Logic

Every system has its logic, which may be different from what we, the educated, have got used to thinking of as logic. We need to appreciate that Aristotelian logic, even though it has appropriated the entire space called logic, is only one form of logic (or *tarka*). Other kinds of logic tend to be discarded by us because we have learned to distrust them and cast them aside as "superstition". This is a trap we must learn to recognize, or we will not be able to restore traditional knowledge to its rightful place. Let me give an example, Dr. Ballal of IIT Mumbai, has studied the traditional methods of iron smelting employed by the Agarias. The iron smelted by the Agarias is of the highest purity, which is difficult to get in the ordinary modern furnace. Ballal and his team wanted to find out the trick. They constructed a similar furnace at IIT under the supervision of an Agaria *karigar* but instead of the bellow they designed a fan to keep the flame going in the furnace. To everyone's surprise this furnace did not produce the required purity of iron. The only explanation for the difference in the quality from the two processes has been traced to the rhythmic pattern of blowing air through the bellows. This does not satisfy the scientific mind, but there seems to be no other explanation. This must be noted that this is perfectly "scientific" as far as the Agarias are concerned.

Every logic (unique to any system, traditional or modern) proceeds in a systematic manner according to the rules as defined by the framework unique to that system. Essentially this logic is based on certain assumptions or *avadharnas,* which are again unique to that system. No system can be constructed without such *avadharnas*. These are the foundations on which the system stands. And *avadharnas* are beyond the dimension of truth.

We cannot apply the criteria of truth or falsehood (superstition) here. The only valid criterion is whether the system works, whether it allows us to deal with our *sansaar* to our satisfaction. If a person actually gets cured through certain *mantras* or what we call *jhad phook,* so be it; but I wouldn't easily reject it as superstition.

## Facade of Modern Science

Modern science gives the impression that it is based on axioms, self-evident truths. The trouble is that thereby, all other systems are dismissed as being based on false assumptions. To quote a few examples, what is a straight line; a point has no dimensions or the shortest path joining two points is a straight line. A straight line on the surface of the earth is not straight. These are mere assumptions. We can only look at the functionality of these assumptions and see if it works. The only yardstick we have is whether the products of the system help us to deal with our *sansaar*.

Modern science only gives one of the many possible explanations of the how, what, why questions that human beings ask. But we need to recognize that there are explanations for explaining physical phenomena around us, which may be equally valid.

### Conflict between *Manyata* and *Anubhav* or *Vastavikta*

In our short experience of twelve years of work in the area of education in Uttaranchal area, we at the Society for Integrated Development of the Himalayas (SIDH) find a lot of conflicts among our people. Conflict between what they have come to "believe" under the influence of modernity, modern science, modern education, development, globalization – call it what you like, and what their experience or reality is. For instance :

| The Belief | The Experience |
|---|---|
| *Padh likh kar naukri milegi, rojgar ke sadhan badhenge* (once educated you will get a job, employment opportunities will increase). | *Padh likh kar ghar ka kaam, kheti bhi nahi hoti, naukri to door ki baat* (once educated people do not want to do household chores, do not carry out agricultural work, not to talk of a job). |
| Globalization would open more job opportunities. | The job market is shrinking, unemployment is on the rise. |
| Literacy has a co-relation with education as if they were synonymous. | A large number of illiterates in our country are truly wise and thus educated. |
| The sex ratio has a direct co-relation with literacy. Figures of Kerala and other states are often cited to establish the co-relation between increasing literacy and survival of females. Without saying so directly, it is imputed that the illiterates are harsher on women. | As India and all its states have become more literate, the sex ratio has gone down. |
| *Chhota parivaar sukhi parivar*. We have chapters to this effect in our textbooks. That in nuclear families children are better looked after, etc. | At least in rural areas, the large or joint families are more prosperous, have less workload on women and children. All dropouts from our schools in last five years were from nuclear families. |

There are many more such conflicts but I have given only a few examples. The point is that the modern system creates these illusions because it has managed to drive our attention away from the reality of *drishti,* thus allowing the powerful to show us what they want us to see (believe), to create our belief systems.

Therefore in the schools run by SIDH, the teachers and students rely very little on textbooks. They are told what the textbooks say and then encouraged to test it for themselves. This decreases the fear that textbooks hold for them. Another activity is the questioning of myths and commonly held assumptions. Various commonly held beliefs are challenged and doubts encouraged.

## Confusion between *Sukha* and *Suvidha*

By not recognizing *drishti, sukha* (the goal) is replaced by only one of the possible means, that which can be seen – *suvidha.* An illusion is created that we are going after the goal, but actually we go only after one of the possible means. Essentially, western society has evolved over the last five hundred years in a manner, which tries to control nature and all its entities, and ultimately tries to control human societies. Perhaps, this is because they do not recognize *drishti* and so, confuse ends (*sukha*) with means (*suvidha*). Hence, all their efforts are directed towards acquisition and control of the material world.

## Homogenization

The phenomenon of globalization (a modern day *avatar* of colonization) is essentially an effort to shape international society in a uniform manner. The idea is to steer it in that direction through various means, and ultimately to control it to serve the larger interests of the dominant power centres of the West. Homogenized societies are easier to control than diverse cultures. Modern science, technology and education are major instruments of such control.

In the globalized world, as the focus is on the object, *sukha* is confused with *suvidha* which becomes the object to be coveted (in the hope of gaining *sukha*). The market becomes the instrument to lure the majority. It is easier to sell jeans to the entire world but not so easy if a company had to sell a *dhoti* in one place, a *pyjama* in another, *sural* in the third and so on. Psychologically sophisticated techniques such as advertising are used for altering people's ends to suit the structure of available means.

## The Illusion of Individual Freedom

By keeping alive the illusion of individual freedom, control is exerted through thought control. For instance, to quench our thirst, we have the illusion of having a choice of drinks – Pepsi, Coke, 7UP, Mirinda, etc. Yet we have hardly any choice in drinking tap water (branded as unsafe), or water from wells, *bawdis* or *naulas* (which have disappeared with the onslaught of modern development) or *sherbet* (outdated and unavailable) or juice from a street-side vendor (again branded as unsafe because human hands touch it). Who puts these ideas in our heads? And even if they are unsafe, why have they become unsafe in the first place? We thus think we have the freedom of choice whereas we are totally at the mercy of the choices made for us by the market.

If we go back in time, we had more control over technologies such as a plough or even a typewriter, and were thus more empowered. We ourselves, or someone close to us (a person from our *sansaar*) could make, repair and control the technology and once invested in, the item would be used and maintained for a very long time. This also avoided the built-in obsolescence of the western markets and waste of natural resources.

Now things are out of our hands. We cannot make a new piece or repair it ourselves. Instead of making us free, it enslaves us. I can no longer repair a computer as easily as I could fix the typewriter. I am forced to upgrade the computer every few years (the span becoming shorter by the day) otherwise I might as well stop using it. Who is in control, the market or me? The power has shifted out of the periphery of my *sansaar* to a place very far away.

## Centre of Power and Disempowerment

The more remote the centre of power, the more disempowered I become. The closer and more visible the power centre, the more empowered I am. We can easily see that in all spheres of our lives we have become less empowered-*sukha* has become a distant dream even though we perhaps may be enjoying many *suvidhas*. Essentially this is because I am becoming less and less in control of my life. By steering the focus of my attention only to the functional aspects, the dominant system has succeeded in making me believe in the neutrality of science and technology. As if technology is neutral!

In a very subtle way, technology moulds our *drishti*. For example, a pedestrian has a certain flexibility of movement – he can pause to look at his surroundings, speak to a passer-by and so on. All entities have a name and a distinct meaning for him. But as soon as he becomes a driver of a fast-moving vehicle, suddenly all entities turn into nameless obstacles that he must avoid, if he is a good driver. Without his knowledge, his *drishti* undergoes a change.

In a globalized world, large, centralized, hierarchical, socio-technical entities eliminate other varieties of human activity. Traditional occupations become difficult, even impossible to pursue as a means of survival. The tragedy is that not merely useful devices and techniques of earlier periods become extinct, but more importantly, the patterns of societies and individual experiences that created these tools are also vanishing along with them.

### Speed and Insecurity in Life

The rhythmic pace of life associated with traditional societies gives a sense of security. The two in fact go hand in hand. However, secure and self-confident people are difficult to dictate and control. So it emerges that increasing the pace of life, which in turn brings with it a sense of insecurity, it is in the interest of those who want to control people's behaviour. So, it is in the interest of the dominant forces to destabilize people from traditional occupations (with their set rhythms of living), and to push them into the cash economy. Here people are forced to lead a fragmented and fast life, ultimately leading to insecurity, which makes them more vulnerable to manipulation and control.

## CONCLUSION

Ideally the scientific temperament is supposed to make us question, broaden our horizons, to make us see multiple perspectives on issues, to broaden our *drishti*. Instead it gives no credence to *drishti* while creating an illusion to the contrary. It makes us see things in almost a unidimensional way, and this blinkered vision is the sign of its control over us. Our children are taught to have an unquestioning belief in anything branded as *scientific*. Our people covet any thing that comes under the umbrella of *development*. How do we get out of this control?

The answer perhaps lies in recognizing that the reality is not "out there" but has to be constructed by ourselves for our own purposes. When we take *drishti* into account, the focus shifts from the object to ourselves, the observer. The focus shifts from the "seen" – the functional, the instrumental – to include feelings and experiences, to the observer. And slowly it dawns on us that we can work to create our own reality by working on our perceptions.

We could then work towards shifting the power centre closer and closer to ourselves, becoming empowered in the process, with the ultimate objective of shifting it within one's own self, when we could hope to be completely at peace – fully empowered. This empowerment will not be at the cost of the disempowerment of the others. Everyone would be able to realize his/her own potential in such a scenario.

# 2

# Traditional Knowledge Systems in Uttaranchal

D.P. Agrawal

## INTRODUCTION

In this paper I discuss the richness and diversity of Traditional Knowledge Systems (TKSs) in Uttaranchal, their relevance to the development of the region today and also try to situate TKS in a wider perspective.

The TKS or folk science of Uttaranchal is very rich in all its various forms: architecture, hydraulics, ethnomedicine, ethnobotany, metallurgy, agriculture, etc. The micro-variations of the ambient harsh environment have been responsible for the extremely rich community knowledge systems and a biodiversity, necessary for sustainability of human life here. Many varieties of plants and animals have originated in the mountains. The mountain people also cultivate many lesser known crops and medicinal plants and this biodiversity is of immense value for the future, for genetics, health and breeding. As these communities are the rich repositories of knowledge, their knowledge would be indispensable in creating and applying sustainable mountain strategies and programmes. Despite the tremendous importance and value of traditional knowledge, especially in the hilly areas such as Uttaranchal, it is at a risk of extinction for various reasons. Hence, it is necessary that we pause and take a note of this alarming situation before it gets too late. This is crucial not only because it may help people to augment their income but also because it will preserve our biodiversity and rich traditional heritage of science and architecture.

## TRADITIONAL KNOWLEDGE SYSTEMS OF UTTARANCHAL

Here I will briefly discuss the richness and potential of the main TKSs of Uttaranchal.

### METAL CRAFTS

Some of these technologies are relevant even today in generating wealth and employment on a very micro level. This will help stem the large-scale migration of hill people to the plains. For example, revival of copper and iron smelting on small scale can generate local employment; so also can cultivation and sale of medicinal herbs without endangering their survival. The tradition of copper technology of Uttaranchal goes back to second millennium BC and that of iron to first millennium BC.

The general perception of Uttaranchal is that it is a backwater and that it has had not much interaction with the Ganga Valley. Recent research however is showing that this area contributed to the early copper and iron technologies which were the backbone of early urbanization of the Ganga Valley. Even a few decades back, stainless steel utensils were made in Lohaghat area of Pithoragarh district. The early copper artefacts show a resemblance to the famous Copper Hoard Culture. Their relevance in today's economic development is that there are reasonably large copper and iron mines in Uttaranchal. They may not be large from the industrial point of view but they could help nourish the traditional artisan. In district Almora alone hundreds of Tamta (traditional coppersmiths in the area who over the period of time have become a caste) families still practise copper smithy. If the government allows small smelting plants at the local mines, they could generate adequate copper for producing utensils for the local demand and handicrafts for national and international markets. Such enterprises can be opened on a cooperative basis and the government could help them by setting up design centres, for designing artefacts so that they could export their products to the rest of the country, and also abroad. Such a small industry would be handicraft oriented and fully sustainable and eco-friendly. The millions of tons of *pirul* (pine needles) which largely get wasted or is a cause of the unwanted forest-fires or of injury to the womenfolk who have to carry fodder and fuel through the forest strewn with pine needles (which becomes the cause of injury as it is very slippery to walk on), could be suitably modified to yield abundant fuel for the smelting purpose. Probably a better plan would be to use them for mattresses, like they use coir.

At present the total requirement (based on a 1994 survey) of the coppersmiths is only 90 tons of raw copper, out of which only 10 tons is supplied by the Brass Corporation of the government. The rest is provided by the scrap dealers who supply inferior metal and hire the local artisans for piece work at miserable rates. It is therefore necessary that they should be allowed to smelt their own copper for their copper wares.

In Askot region (Pithoragarh district) and also in other areas of the state, there are large polymetallic mines but the laws made by the British still come in the way of exploiting such mines even for handicrafts and local need. The British started copper and iron works in this region and learnt the technology and dismantled them in the beginning of the 20th century.

## Traditional *Gharats* and Hydropower

*Gharats* are the traditional cross-flow watermills, which have been used in this region from time immemorial. Now it seems that with a little improvement in their technology they can be made much more efficient and can be used in a very profitable manner for power generation too.

So a major part of the energy requirements by way of power in the hills of Uttaranchal can be met by the modification of the *gharat*s. There are approximately 60,000 *gharats*, each producing on an average about 1.5 kW power, which can be increased up to 5 kW per *gharat* by a little extra technical input. With the increased efficiency levels of these new machines, they can be effectively employed to produce electricity in addition to meeting the mechanical power needs of the people. One cross-flow watermill could produce anywhere between 3-5 kW of power, sufficient to meet the electricity needs of 25-50 households. However, the cost of mills and accompanying machinery to produce power could be around Rs. 15,000. The social and economic benefits arising from the availability of having electricity in these villages would be self-evident.

The Himalayan Environmental Studies and Conservation Organisation (HESCO), an Indian NGO based in Chamoli district, was responsible for setting up the *Gharat* Owners' Association in Chamoli and has been working with them to design and implement simple upgrades for traditional *gharat*s. The improvements have involved lining the open chute with galvanized steel sheet, using a Teflon bush for the top-bearing (at the centre of the bed-stone) and using a fabricated ball-bearing assembly as the footstep bearing at the base of the rotor. About 12 *gharat*s have been upgraded to date in Chamoli district. The component and material costs are about Rs.1,500 and the miller himself undertakes the upgrading work. Increased output of 2-3 times has been achieved with stone speed increasing typically from 70 to 120 rpm. With this upgrade, the millers can grind at least 15 kg of wheat per hour. They traditionally keep 5 per cent of the flour as payment-in-kind, which can be sold for Rs. 5 per kg (or more). Equating income against energy use leads to a value for the energy of Rs. 3.75 per kWh. This is 2-3 times the income that could be earned using the same power to generate electricity, but at a fraction of the investment cost.

The improved *gharat* costs about Rs. 15,000 for all components, including some civil works. The jet of water can be provided either by the traditional wooden chute, or by a PVC pipe with a nozzle. The chute is less efficient, so needs more water to get the same output. If the old wooden chute is used, the cost for only replacing the runner is around Rs. 6,000. These modifications increase the grinding rate to between 15 and 30 kg per hour (Manikant Shah, personal communication).

Improving traditional watermills would benefit:

- Millers and their families whose economic condition will be improved by greater productivity and income-generation.
- Local communities which would stand to benefit from faster and more efficient agro-processing services like a wider range of mechanized crop-processing machinery, crop-drying, irrigation pumping at night, etc. Besides this they shall also be benefited by electrical services (such as evening lighting, or water-heating, battery-charging) via an add-on generator.
- Women, who will have a reduced burden of either manual crop-processing or of hours or days of walking to electric or diesel machines for the purpose.
- Manufacturers, who will have the possibility of producing and selling large batches of simple, standardized equipment.
- Local workshops, which will be needed to supply components and spares, provide repair services or which may choose to develop/copy their own watermill upgrade.
- The environment, by displacing harmful emissions and reducing the reliance on wood-fuel.

## Himalayan Traditional Medicine

The area is endowed with an extremely rich biodiversity. A large number of plants grow here at different altitudes, which have medicinal and aromatic properties. Quite a few of them are used for spices also. The global herbal trade is estimated to be of about $60 billion per year, out of which 7 per cent is cornered by China; India's share is a measly 0.3 per cent. I see no reason why Uttaranchal cannot bag 5 per cent of the total herbal trade which comes to at least $3 billion per year. This in itself is comparable to the GNP of the state.

In the Himalayan medicine system (HMS) there are more than 1,800 plants of potent medicinal value; a bulk of them have been used in the *materia medica* of Ayurveda. There are quite a few medicines which are claimed to cure even incurable diseases (in allopathy) like eczema, cancer, blood pressure, diabetes, balding, leucoderma, etc. If the cultivation and sale of herbal wealth is allowed without endangering their survival, it could prove to be a promising business for the people here. But the State should sell only value added products and not raw herbs.

A number of aromatic plants including rose, lavender and geranium are also being grown in this region. Besides, a variety of spices like big cardamom, cinnamon, bay leaf etc., also grow very well.

Most of the rural population has been tapping minor forest produce but it is sold at a pittance. If this could be canalized through cooperative outlets, this could bring good money to the rural people. The multinational companies have no qualms in over-exploiting the herbal wealth. They look at short term gains; as a result, some of the plants are on the verge of extinction. On the one hand, multinational companies (MNCs) and the West deliberately decry our traditional knowledge, and on the other hand exploit the local plants for their pharmaceutical industry. As they are interested only in making a fast buck, they have driven precious herbs to near extinction. This sort of trade is now officially banned but has now become a lucrative activity for the mafia dons.

## TRADITIONAL KNOWLEDGE SYSTEMS IN A WIDER PERSPECTIVE

It is now recognized that the western criteria are not the sole benchmark by which other cultural knowledge should be evaluated. The British systematically uprooted or undermined the traditional science, technology and crafts of the lands and people they plundered. In Uttaranchal they first encouraged copper and iron production but later on banned it, as they had to export their own finished metal products to India.

Modern science can perhaps be dated to Newton's times, but the TKSs date back to more than 2 million years (which seems to be a forgotten fact in the framework of Eurocentric science), when the early hominid, *Homo habilis,* started making his tools and interacting with nature. Besides, one also finds that generally the history of science is Eurocentric. It typically consists of two phases: First it starts with Greece, neglecting the influences of others upon Greece. Then it "fast forwards" many centuries to the Enlightenment period in Europe around AD 1500, to claim modern science as an exclusively European triumph, by neglecting the influence of others, especially that of India, upon the European Renaissance and Enlightenment.

The British colonizers could never accept the fact that Indians were highly civilized even in the third millennium BC, when the British were still in a barbarian stage. Such acknowledgment would have destroyed the civilizing mission of Europe that was the intellectual premise for colonization.

Even in today's India, entrenched prejudice against TKSs still persists. For example, Indian government today continues to make many TKSs illegal or impossible to practise. Even after Independence, many British laws against TKSs have continued, even though their original intent was to destroy India's massive domestic industry and foreign trade and to replace them with Britain's Industrial Revolution. Today's socially and economically low castes were at one time the guilds of specialized workers that supplied the world with many industrial items. Even in Uttaranchal, the leather workers are not being allowed to practise their traditional trade.

Therefore now it is our duty that we demystify this discriminatory and arrogant mindset of the West (not all and only of those who are geographically located in the west but also of all those who believe in this ideology) and lay it open for the people to understand the hidden agenda of the "opinion makers". Besides this we all know that for the poor, including those of the hills, Westernization and globalization are not the answers. So we have to revive some of the viable traditional technologies. Because:

- Western civilization depends upon inequality – there must be cheap labour "somewhere else", and cheap natural resources purchasable from somewhere, without regard to the big picture of society or ecology. If you ask a Western country to equalize all humanity by opening its borders so that labour may move freely and compete in a global market for jobs, you will get only all sorts of excuses.
- The Western lifestyle drains natural resources and would be impossible for the six billion humans to achieve or for the planet to sustain.
- When Gandhiji was asked whether he would like India to develop a lifestyle similar to that of England, his reply was the British had to plunder the earth to achieve their lifestyle. Given India's much larger population, it would require the plunder of many planets to achieve the same.

## CONCLUSION

We have therefore to study, preserve and revive the TKSs for the economic betterment of the world in a holistic manner. As these technologies are eco-friendly and allow sustainable growth without harming the environment these have a special relevance to Uttaranchal.

## BIBLIOGRAPHY

Agrawal, D.P. 1997. 'Traditional Knowledge Systems and Western Science', *Current Science* 73 (9): 731-33.

——. 1999a. 'The Role of Central Himalayas in Indian Archaeo-metallurgy' in *Metals in Antiquity*, Young, S. *et al.* (eds). Oxford: Archaeopress.

——. 1999b. *Early Indian Iron Technology, Himalayan Contacts and Gangetic Urbanisation*. The Fourth International Conference on the Beginning of the Use of Metals and Alloys *(BUMA-IV)*: 53-58. Japan: The Japan Institute of Metals.

——. 1999c. *Central Himalayan Archaeology and Culture: Challenges and Potentialities*. Rahul Sankrityayana Memorial Lecture. Nainital: PAHAR.

——. 2000. *Ancient Metal Technology and Archaeology of South Asia*. Delhi: Aryan Books International.

——. 2001. 'The Idea of India and its Heritage: The Millennial Challenges', *Man and Environment* 26 (1): 15-22.

——. (in press). *Non-Literate Traditional Knowledge System with Special Reference to Himalayan Folklore*. Shruti Seminar, IGNCA, New Delhi, 18-23 November 2000.

Agrawal, D.P. *et al.* 1991. 'Archaeology of Kumaon: Problems and Prospects', *Man and Environment* 16 (1): 59-63.

Agrawal, D.P. and J.S. Kharakwal. 1998. *Central Himalayas: An Archaeological, Linguistic and Cultural Synthesis*. Delhi: Aryan Books International.

Agrawal, D.P. *et al.*1995. 'Was Kumaon the Source of Early Iron in North India?', *Man and Environment* 20(1): 81-85.

Agrawal, D.P. *et al.* 1997. 'Central Himalayan Folklore (Jagars) in an Inter-Disciplinary Perspective' in *Him Kanti, Archaeology, Art and History*, B.M. Khanduri and V. Nautiyal (eds.). Delhi: Book India Publishing Company.

Agrawal, D.P. *et al.* (in press), *A Multidisciplinary Study of Traditional Knowledge Systems of Uttaranchal*. Delhi: IGNCA.

Atkinson, E.T. 1980. *The Himalayan Gazetteer*. New Delhi: Cosmo Publication.

Badoni, A. and K. Badoni. 2001. 'Ethnobotanical Heritage', in *Garhwal Himalaya: Nature, Culture and Society*, O.P. Kandari and O.P. Gusain (eds.). Srinagar: Transmedia Media House.

Joshi, P.C. 2001. 'In the Lap of the Himalaya: Gandhi's Visit of Uttarakhand', *Economic and Political Weekly* 36 (34): 3301-10.

Joshi, G.C. *et al.* 2001. 'Ayurvedic Medicine Plants of UP Himalaya: Status and Conservation', in *Himalayan Medicinal Plants: Potential and Prospect*, S.S. Samant *et al.* (eds.). Nainital: Gyanodaya Prakashan.

Nader, L. (ed.), 1996. *Naked Science: Anthropological Enquiries into Boundaries, Power and Knowledge*. New York: Routledge.

Pande, P.C. and G.C. Joshi. 2001. 'Cultivated Plants of Kumaon Himalaya Used for Medicinal Purpose' in *Himalayan Medicinal Plants: Potential and Prospect*, S.S. Samant *et al.* (eds.). Nainital: Gyanodaya Prakashan.

Pande, P.C. *et al.* (eds.), 1999. *Ethnobotany of Kumaon Himalaya*. Jodhpur: Scientific Publishers.

Pant, C.C. 1988. 'Mineral Wealth of Kumaon: Prospects and Problems' in *Kumaon: Land and People*, K.S. Valdia (ed.). Nainital: Gyanodaya Prakashan.

Samant, S.S. *et al.* 1998. *Medicinal Plants of Indian Himalaya: Diversity, Distribution Potential Value*. Nainital: Gyanodaya Prakashan.

# 3

# Ecological and Technological Knowledge of Hunter-Gatherers in India

## Some Examples

V.N. Misra and Malti Nagar

### INTRODUCTION

The most distinctive feature of the culture of hunting-gathering communities is their thorough and intimate knowledge of their environment, of wild plants having edible parts like leaves, flowers, fruits, seeds, roots and tubers, of animals both terrestrial and aquatic and of birds. They know the local names of all the wild plants and the season of their flowering and fruiting, of wild animals, fish, and turtles and of birds, which they hunt and trap for food and other purposes. They are fully conversant with the nature of these animals and birds, i.e. whether they move individually or in herds, they are aggressive or shy, they are diurnal or nocturnal, etc. They have devised and manufactured their own hunting, snaring and trapping gear and strategies, which they use with remarkable success.

Here we set out the task of detailing a few selected hunting-gathering communities of Rajasthan and Uttar Pradesh.

### EXISTING DATABASE ON HUNTING-GATHERING COMMUNITIES OF INDIA

Though agriculture started in Indian subcontinent around nine thousand years ago, yet even to this day hundreds of communities continue to live by hunting and gathering in many parts of India, including the forest and hilly terrains as well as the intensively cultivated and densely populated alluvial plains. The documentation of these communities started in the latter part of the nineteenth century by British administrators and later on by amateur Indian anthropologists as well. A number of volumes containing a mine of valuable information on several hundred communities are available. These include the volumes by D. Ibbetson on the Punjab, W. Crooke on the United Provinces of Agra and Oudh (present-day Uttar Pradesh), E.J. Dalton on Bengal, R.V. Russell and R.B. Hiralal on Central India, R.E. Enthoven on Bombay Presidency and E.H. Thurston on South India. A lot of information is also present in district gazetteers and Census reports. In addition, there are publications by amateur as well as professional anthropologists like S.C. Roy, D.N. Majumdar and L.P. Vidyarthi on the tribes of Chhotanagpur district of Madhya Pradesh and Mirzapur district of Uttar Pradesh, C.V. Fuerer-Haimendorf on the Chenchus of the Eastern Ghats, T.B. Naik on the Bhils, K.C. Malhotra and others on the Pardhis of Maharashtra, Z. Cooper on the Kurukhs of Bastar district of Madhya Pradesh, M.L.K. Murty on the Yerukulas and Yanadis of Andhra Pradesh and L.A.K. Iyer on the tribes of Kerala. Further, during the last four decades or so it has become common practice for archaeologists working on Stone Age prehistory to collect data on hunting-gathering communities of the region and as a result, a lot of information is available in Ph.D. theses, especially those completed at the Deccan College, Pune.

We have carried out fieldwork, individually and jointly, among the following hunting-gathering communities:

- Kharwars, Chiros, Gonds and Korwas of Mirzapur district and Kanjars of Farrukhabad district of Uttar Pradesh;
- Van Vagris, Kalbeliyas and Bhils of Rajasthan;
- Maria and Muria Gonds, Korkus, Pardhis and Kuchbandhiyas of Madhya Pradesh; and
- Bondos, Parjas and Saoras of Orissa.

Although all these tribes practise primitive agriculture, they also practise hunting and gathering to some extent to supplement their living sources. In this paper we will confine ourselves only to a few of these communities studied by us.

## KNOWLEDGE BASE OF HUNTER-GATHERERS

### Rajashthan

#### The Van Vagris

The Van Vagris (forest dwellers) inhabit a sparsely wooded sandy terrain in the semi-arid region of Ajmer, Nagaur, Sikar, Churu and Jhunjhunu districts of Rajasthan and the adjoining districts of Haryana. They are totally nomadic and camp for a few days only on sand-dunes away from the villages and towns in small bands of a few families. The strongest bond is between brothers-in-law. The Van Vagris depend almost entirely on meat for their subsistence. Though large prey is now scarce and its hunting is prohibited by law, there are enough small preys like jackal, fox, hare, monitor lizard, partridge and quail that they are never short of meat. The vegetarian component of their diet comes from food, which their women beg from village.

The Van Vagris use a variety of equipment for hunting, snaring and trapping. The tools include gun, spear, long stick, bow and arrow, net *(jaal)*, noose (*pansa*) and iron trap *(kudko)*. The *pansa* is made of multiple string loops, which are tied to small sticks that are buried in the sand or the ground. The gun, spear and long stick are used for hunting fox, jackal, monitor lizard, hare and birds. The *pansa* and *jaal* are used for snaring partridges, and *kudko* for catching hare. Monitor lizard is also dug out from tree hollows. Besides, they use trained hunting dogs for catching hare and other animals. The Van Vagris' skill in shooting birds was demonstrated to us by a young man, Mohanyo near Varangana village, some 12 km south of Didwana town in Nagaur district. A partridge came and sat down on a *babool* tree amidst thick foliage. Mohanyo made several rounds around the tree as if to transfix the bird by magic. He then shot an arrow with such deadly accuracy that the arrow pierced right through the body of the bird. We asked Mohanyo to climb the tree and remove the bird with the arrow inside it, and this he did with remarkable facility. Animal flesh is the staple diet of the Van Vagris and in two hours time they are able to catch and trap enough hares and birds for one day's requirement of the entire family.

### The Kal Beliyas

While the Van Vagris are confined to the semi-arid zone of western Rajasthan, the Kal Beliyas and Bhils are found on both sides of the Aravali hills. The main occupation of the Kal Beliyas is catching snakes and entertaining village people with snake charming. Besides, their women entertain village people with song and dance. But the Kal Beliyas also practise hunting. They hunt small game mainly with the help of sticks and trained dogs.

### The Bhils

The word Bhil is believed to be derived from a Dravidian word which means to pierce. This is indicative of their prowess in wielding the bow and arrow. Even today in the hilly and forest tracts of Rajasthan and Madhya Pradesh, a Bhil never moves without the bow and arrow. In respect to population size, they are one of the largest tribes of South Asia, and are to be found over a vast territory extending from Pakistan in the west through Rajasthan, Gujarat and Madhya Pradesh to western Maharashtra in the south. The Bhils, like the Van Vagris, catch, trap and shoot a variety of small game and birds. The technology they use for hunting, including the use of hunting dogs, is similar to that of the Van Vagris.

While the Van Vagris are totally nomadic, the government in special settlements away from peasant villages has now settled some of the Kal Beliya families. The Bhils, on the other hand, are a fully settled community. In the Aravalli hills they live in their exclusive villages, which consist of hamlets or *padas*, each *pada* consisting of a number of huts, which are perched individually on top of low hillocks. In the plains they live in mixed villages comprising many castes and are known as *gameti* or village dwellers. In these villages they have become a part of caste Hindus and are a good example of the transformation of tribes into castes. The Bhils practise primitive agriculture, keep livestock, work as labourers in the fields of village farmers and on public projects, besides indulging in the hunting of small game.

## Uttar Pradesh

### The Kanjars

The word Kanjar is believed to be derived from the Sanskrit word *kanan char*, meaning "one who wanders in the forest" or the forest dweller. The Kanjars are a major hunting-gathering community of South Asia and they are mainly found in Uttar Pradesh and northern India and roam across Punjab and Rajasthan in north to West Bengal and Assam in the east. Till the end of the nineteenth century they were almost entirely nomadic and were living in the forest, which, at that time, covered more than 50 per cent area of the land. However, now most of them have been settled in colonies away from regular village settlements; others have settled down in towns and cities but generally some distance away from the rest of the population. The government is providing them land for habitation and cultivation; and financial assistance for purchase of livestock, agricultural equipments and construction of houses.

Though some of them have adopted agriculture, but most of them have begun to practise animal husbandry. Some have also taken to petty trades. However, their main occupation is hunting and gathering. They subsist largely on wild animal foods and are essentially omnivorous in their diet. They kill and eat almost all kinds of terrestrial, aquatic and avian creatures. They hunt jackal, fox, wolf, porcupine, jungle cat, hedgehog, hare and monitor lizard. They trap and shoot squirrels and birds like pigeon, dove, partridge and quail. And they also snare or kill turtles, dig out snakes, mongooses, bandicoots, field rats, lizards and turtle eggs "or any other vermin that by chance may lob their way". Further they also scavenge carcasses of dead animals. Whatever a Kanjar kills, from a wolf to a reptile, he eats; and most of what he finds dead, he eats that too. The Kanjars also catch frogs both for their own consumption and also for sale to school and college biology laboratories for dissection. Besides, they also gather wild plant foods and extract juice from the palm tree which, when fermented, forms an intoxicating drink. In addition to animal flesh, the Kanjars consume milk, eggs, cereals, pulses, vegetables, etc.

### *Hunting Tools Used by Kanjars*

#### Khanta or Khanti

The principal tool and weapon of the Kanjars is *khanta* or *khanti.* The name is supposed to be derived from the Sanskrit root *khan,* meaning to dig or make a hole. The tool consists of a long (about 1.2 m) wooden staff and an iron blade (about 30 cm long) either rectangular in shape or sharpened into a curved point, something like the blade of a knife, and hafted at one end of the staff. The iron blade is procured from the local blacksmiths and the staff is made by the Kanjars themselves. According to J.C. Nesfield, the implement serves as a dagger or short spear for killing wolves and jackals; as a tool for carving a secret entrance through the mud wall of a villager's house, where burglary is contemplated; as a spade or hoe for digging out snakes, field rats, lizards, etc.; for digging edible roots and the roots of *khaskhas* grass; as a hatchet for chopping wood and as a tool for dragging out monitor lizards and other creatures from the hollows in trees. The *khanti* or short spear is not merely used in close combat, but is also thrown with an almost unerring effect while hunting wolves and jackals on the run.

#### Khabar

Another tool they use is *khabar* which is a large net used to snare wolves, jackals, foxes, porcupines, hares, etc. Woven from nylon string, the *khabar* is about 12 m long and 1.25 m broad. It is stretched along the edge of a field of sugarcane or other tall crop or bushes of *munj* (*Saccrum munja*) where the presence of animals has been identified beforehand. The *khabar* is supported at the base on a thick rope, and stretched vertically with sticks placed at intervals along its length. A group of Kanjars drives the animals from all sides of the field towards the net, thereby closing all escape points so that the animals get trapped in the net.

#### Ssuja

The *ssuja,* a long spear, is used to kill turtles as well as other animals.

### Khonch

The *khonch* is used to catch frogs from wells and ponds and consists of a cylindrical, open-mouthed cloth bag attached to a long bamboo pole.

According to J.C. Nesfield, the Kanjars display extraordinary skills in the use of their simple weapons. The weapon with which they kill little birds is nothing but a pole with a thin sharp spike of iron embedded at the pointed end. The man lies motionless on a patch of ground, which he has first sprinkled with grain, and as the birds come hopping around him to pick up the grain, he hypnotizes one of them by moving the pole in a serpent-like motion and then spikes the bird through its body. The Kanjars seldom use the bow and arrow, but they use a *gulel* or a pellet bow that requires much greater skill. The pellet is nothing but a little clay marble dried in the sun. With this they frequently shoot a sitting or flying bird. To trap a wolf in its lair, they place a net and a light at one end of the hole and commence digging at the other end. The wolf attracted by the light runs into the net and the Kanjar then batters its head with a club and kills it.

Their dogs are of great assistance to the Kanjars in their hunting activities and every family has two or more of them. The dogs are slim, supple and ferocious and are carefully trained to hunt. They are extremely efficient in catching fleeing animals like the jackal, fox, jungle cat and hare.

## CONCLUSION

For most of its history, the human species has lived by hunting animals and gathering wild plant foods. By drawing inference from the studies of peoples who even today live by such methods, it can be suggested that the relationship of hunter-gatherers with nature was relatively benign. The development of agriculture made hunting less important an activity to provide sole life support to man, but he still pursues it to protect crops, flocks, or herds as well as to procure food. The hunter's continual training with his implements and practice of tracking and stalking has a social value in maintaining group activity, earning prestige and preserving a vast amount of traditional knowledge.

# 4

# Ayurveda as *Praxis*

Ramashray Roy

## INTRODUCTION

The central question that I propose to address is the place of the Ayurveda in the Indian tradition of thinking that traces its roots to its *arche* source, that is, the Vedic world-view. In order to explore this question, it is necessary to make a sharp distinction between *techne* and *praxis*. This is so for several reasons. In the first place, *techne* or technology, as it is known today, has attained, in modern times, autonomy from the suzerainty of human purposes and now defines as well as prescribes what purposes men must pursue in order to be able to have a share in the good life of the modern conception. This state of affairs is symptomatic of the fact that what was considered previously to be of only instrumental importance has now assumed the status of the end, something which men must pursue; it is now dictating terms which must be accepted and allowed to mould and shape human existence itself. This world-view is in sharp contrast to that of the Vedic view. Hence in the following pages I shall not only try to emphasize on this contrast but also shall explain how Ayurveda is firmly rooted in the traditional world-view.

## DIFFERENCE IN THE WORLD-VIEW OF *TECHNE* AND *PRAXIS*

The Greek understanding of *techne* is based upon the instrumental role it plays in man's existence. The role it plays is conceived as something that assists men in producing goods and services necessary for realizing purposes. Determination of purposes is governed by certain philosophical considerations about who man is and what kind of life he must lead? Given the instrumental importance of *techne,* it is characterized by three important and distinctive features. First, it refers to subject-object divide and limits the role of *techne* to the world of objects alone, objects that are external to man. The second feature of *techne* refers to the fact that objects must not only be external to man, they should also be such that man can have a complete control over them in giving whatever particular shape he wants them to have. And, lastly, in addition to these two distinctive features, there must also pre-exist a model according to which the objects can be given particular shapes.

The question of the model one chooses to cast a particular object in, is inextricably linked with human purposes that are beyond the ken of *techne* itself. Once the question of purpose is brought to bear on the issue of the use of *techne,* it becomes necessary to subject the determination of life purposes to philosophical considerations about the spiritual needs of man and how they must be fulfilled. With a view of determining life pattern capable of fulfilling both material and spiritual needs of man, the traditional world-view, prevalent not only in Greece but also in India and other traditional societies, identified man's existence as defined by two types of life purposes. If one of these types of purposes involved the pursuit of higher life purposes, such as, self-realization self-knowledge or the life of good citizen, the other concerned the fulfilment of ordinary life needs involved in the process of production and reproduction. The latter referred to the need of acquiring wealth, power and prestige, the necessary elements in making life comfortable.

In the second place, what is also important to note in this connection is that the traditional world-view does not reject or condemn the claim of ordinary life needs. What it does consider as obnoxious, is to give exclusive importance to the fulfilment of ordinary life needs. To put it differently, the prominence in man's life of the pursuit of *kama* and *artha* paving the way for what *Chhandogya Upanishad* calls *kamachara* is what the traditional world-view considers as harmful to man and his world. It considers the pursuit of ordinary life needs to be necessary but only as infrastructural to the pursuit of higher life purposes. The subordination of the pursuit of ordinary life needs to the overlordship of the pursuit of higher life purposes also means the subordination of *techne* to *praxis,* that is, the primacy of higher life purposes in human existence.

This is reflected in the emphasis that the traditional thinking in India subordinates *kama* and *artha* to *dharma*. This raises the important question, what man substantively is? In modern times, man has been considered to be an entity that is biologically, psychologically and sociologically determined. In other words, he is considered to be a fully conditioned being by natural and social factors, a being who is determined by his biological nature and by the important inputs that his external environment, both society and nature, contribute to his making. It is these inputs that decide what man essentially becomes. In contrast to the modern view of man, the traditional view of man recognizes the importance of natural and social factors in the making of man but it also emphasizes that man's ultimate destiny is that of an unconditioned being. This means that the traditional world-view treats man to have a bivalent nature. As such, he has the possibility of rising above his conditioning and of emerging as an open entity, that is, as an ethico-religious entity. Man, as an ethico-religious being can, if he so chooses, overcome the limitations of his base nature and engage in the quest of certain higher values. If he follows the latter course, he, then, becomes an open entity, not fully conditioned by nature and society.

## BEARING OF TRADITIONAL WORLD-VIEW ON AYURVEDA

All traditional world-views treat man as an ethico-religious entity and expect him to engage in the act of self-transformation through self-knowledge. But to proceed on the quest of self-transformation man has to make a conscious endeavour to link his finite existence with the absolute source of truth, meaning and value. The significance of this linking is to attune one's soul to the divine. But the divine ground of being as the source of truth, meaning and value is not something that can be apprehended with the help of discursive reasoning. It can be experienced only by rare seers, mystics and philosophers whose "heart's eye" is opened by the momentary touch of the flash of eternity on their consciousness. The opening of the heart's eye can, however, give only a glimpse, a very fleeting glimpse at that, into the structure of order. This glimpse does not obtain a total blueprint of this structure but only a dim outline that, then, is elaborated in what Plato calls "a likely story" or the Brihaddevata calls *bhavavritta,* that is, *srishtividya* or cosmogony. It is this likely story that provides man with the clues about the structure of the world unseen and the mode of linking of the finite with the absolute. This linking becomes an established fact that forms the basis of a quatenarian primordial community of mortal and immortal and *prithivi* and *dyau* as the Vedic world-view suggests.

It is this linkage that constitutes the source of defining the vision of life that man must consciously try to realize and live. It is also this linkage that yields the essential principles determining not only the proper mode of living but also the mode of living together with other beings in this world. It is in keeping with this mode of living in communion (not only with immortals but also with other mortals) that allows us to participate in the exploration of a shareable commonality that forms the basis of community in the real sense of the term. It is this shareable commonality that yields the necessary consensus or what Gobinda Chandra Pandey calls *saman-chittata* (like-mindedness) underwriting both what ought to be the purposes of life as well as the ways and means of realizing these purposes. The understanding of both these dimensions of knowledge is designated, in the traditional Indian thinking, as *samskara* or *samyaka kriti*.

It is the idea of *samyaka kriti* that is the source of doing or *praxis* insofar as interaction between human beings is concerned. The idea of *praxis* abjures the notion of making human being as an instrument; that is, it rejects the notion that human beings should be treated as objects. If human beings cannot and must not be treated as objects, it follows that the application of *techne* must be completely ruled out and it must yield its place to *praxis*, that is, doing, regulating and disciplining elements in one's life. This raises the question of what is contemplated and how the result of that contemplation is made an integral part of living in the world.

Obviously, what needs to be contemplated is the cosmic order that constitutes the basis of order in the human world, both in the interior of man and his external world. It is the imitation of this cosmic order in life that provides the ground for the resolution of the ever-present problem of the possible conflict between the good of one individual and the good of all individuals. In order, therefore, to ensure the reconciliation of this conflict it is necessary not only to rise above the narrow concerns and interests of one's own existence and be attuned to the divine ground of being but also to live according to the principles derived from this knowledge. As we have already seen, it is possible to know these principles and to derive the impetus to live in accordance with these principles from the primordial insight into the structure of order. It is this primordial insight that yields, in concrete terms, the principles governing the determination of human purposes as well as the proper mode of realizing these purposes so that the above-mentioned conflict could be avoided.

It is against this background that we can appreciate the traditional insistence on deriving the concrete idea of the proper mode of life for man to live and, towards this, determine the life purposes man must seek to realize in his own life as well as the proper means of realizing these purposes. The traditional Indian world-view does not reject or condemn the pursuit of *kama* and *artha*; it only makes it necessary to pursue them under the suzerainty of *dharma* so that different desires do not become autotelic and become the ground of their own justification. In effect, the traditional Indian world-view insists on preventing the rise of what in modern times is described as the self-defining subject. This becomes possible only when certain trans-individual principles of the appropriate mode of living are accepted as binding, morally and pragmatically, in life. These trans-individual principles are symbolized by the term *dharma.*

The notion of *dharma* in India is drawn from and is grounded in the Vedic likely story of creation or, the transformation of the "one unknown" into many through the process of *yajna*. This *yajna* is described in the Vedic likely story as the *Sarvahuta Yajna* in which the *Purusha,* the "one unknown entity", sacrificed himself in the process of creation and appeared as the cosmos of which the phenomenal world or the *idam sarvam* is only a small part. It is this *Purusha* that stands in a homological relationship with man. This homological relation between the *Purusha* and the beings in the world underlines the organic nature of the cosmos conceived to be a great chain of being. To safeguard this great chain of being symbolizing the existence of the quatenarian primordial community of mortals, immortals, *prithivi* and *dyau,* it becomes necessary to contemplate and imitate the order inherent in the cosmos. It is this contemplation and imitation that is considered, in the traditional knowledge system, as *shastra*. The term *shastra* signifies both *shansanam* and *shasanam*. The former refers to the process of contemplation while the latter points to the need of embracing the principles of a better living in keeping with an ideal vision of life derived from the primordial insight into the structure of order. It is, therefore, not surprising that Ayurveda is called *shastra* in the true sense of the term because it contemplates who really man is and how the order inherent in man as a small replica of the Universal *Purusha* can be maintained.

The concept of order in the interior of man has been modelled on the cosmic order. It is this order underlying the being of man and reflected in his existence that is accepted as the subject-matter of Ayurveda. As such, Ayurveda deals with the central concern of what this order is, what are the factors that disturb this order and how this order can be restored or mended when it has been disturbed. It is this, which constitutes the central concerns of Ayurveda as *shastra*. Alternatively, Ayurveda is also considered to be a subsidiary Veda because the use of the noun Veda qualified by the adjective underlines the significance of Ayurveda as a system of specialized knowledge in two different but interrelated senses. The knowledge available in Ayurveda concerns itself, first, with the character of order that underlies and gives significance to the reality of man qua man as well as the possibility of his becoming what is inherent in his own nature. Insofar as the conception of order exemplifying man's existence is concerned, Ayurveda takes its inspiration from and is grounded in the world-view typical of the Vedic perspective on man and his world. It is not, therefore, surprising that Ayurveda accepts the notion of man as it has been delineated in the Vedic literature. It is a conception that posits the idea that man stands in a homologous relationship with *Purusha.*

In the Indian philosophical tradition, *Purusha* is the entity that is the real residence of *pura,* that is, all beings in the world. According to the Vedic theory of *anupravesha,* God created all the beings in the world and entered them. That is why *Chhandogya Upanishad* defines *Purusha* as the resident of *Brahmapur.* Or, as *Isopanishad* puts it, *isavasya idam sarvam,* that is, all that is spread before our eyes is the abode of the God. It is the Vedic cosmogony that describes the passage of the one unknown entity that is basically an Idea or form according to Plato into material form. The Vedic likely story of creation conceives of this passage from the non-material into the material in two stages, the first of which happens to be the non-material stage and the second relates to the transformation of the non-material entity into material forms. It is in the second stage that the one unknown entity enters gradually and in graded steps (symbolized as *Lokas*) into the realm of matter and assumes different *nama* and *rupa.* But unlike the creator god of Plato, the Vedic God creates the world and the beings in it and makes these beings as his abode. According to the *Purushsukta* of the *Rigveda, Purusha* manifests himself into *vak* symbolizing the five elements (*mahabhutas*) of matter that go into the constitution of every being in the world and enters into all these beings.

### Basis of Ayurvedic Treatement

In the process of passing from the state of being in a non-material state into material forms (that is, *enhylon eidos,* as Plato calls it), the *Purusha* becomes the resident of *Brahmapura* with eight different but interdependent attributes (or *purisha*). That is why Indian philosophy identifies the *Purusha* as the entity that resides in the eight *purisha.* These eight *purisha* are all five motor organs, five sense organs, the four parts of *antahkarana* and five *pranas* (live forces), five gross elements (*pancha mahbhuta*), *kama* (desire) and *avidya.* The *Brahmapura* is said to be constituted by these eight *purisha* that the *Purusha* makes his abode. This characterization of man invests human reality with a quality of transcendence with supra-physical and supra-mental nature. For, the *Purusha* is distinct and separate form, superior to, and beyond the eight kinds of substances including the mind, conscious or subconscious, though he himself is controlled by the Supreme. It is the reality of man thus constituted, that is, a combination of immortal and mortal elements that is the object of Ayurveda's study and subject of its treatment. It is, therefore, natural for Ayurveda to accept the *Purusha* as the source as well as the ground of its own specialized system of knowledge. And in its status as a specialized field of knowledge, the focus of its attention is *ayu* (life span of man). As such, it sets as its objective the knowledge that concerns itself with *sukha duhkhamayustasya hitahitam* (*Charaka Samhita,* to be referred to as CS, [1.39]), that is, the knowledge that has as its focus the well-being of *ayu*. However, CS (1.40) defines *ayu* as the conjunction of physical body, sense organs, mind and the soul. This conforms faithfully to the characterization of the reality of human beings as elaborated in the Vedic literature. Elaborating further, CS (1.44-45) observes that the combination of body, mind and the soul is identified in *Vaidyaka Shastra* as the *Purusha;* this *Purusha* is pure consciousness, the foundation of Ayurveda and the object of its focus.

Different sense organs (both motor and sensory) perform different functions. However, in performing their assigned functions with the help of the faculties endowed to them, the senses have to depend on the cooperation of mind and the soul. But mind and the soul are helpless without the cooperation of the senses. It is this interdependence and cooperation between sense organs constituted by *Panchamahabhuta* (the five-dimensional matter) and mind and the soul representing non-material elements that go into the making of the reality of human being and make him an organic entity. It is this reality as constituted by both material and non-material elements that is the subject matter of Ayurveda in terms of what is good for man and what is not. Though good or bad actions are determined by the mind yet it is influenced in its decision with the non-material element of his being, since mind itself is constituted, in part, by material elements (CS, 8.8).

As already pointed out, sense organs derive their attribute from five elements of matter (viz. *akasha, prithivi, agni, jal,* and *vayu*). But when different sense organs use their respective faculties in an improper way, disorder, insofar as health is concerned, results. That is, when these organs become prone to over-indulgence, under-indulgence, and improper indulgence, they suffer distortions. As a result, mind too becomes disordered and, therefore, does not function well. If, on the other hand, they function properly, mind functions well and the physical body retains its proper balance and, therefore, remains healthy. Sushruta (2.42), too, underlines the fact that the loci of diseases are physical body and mind. But they induce disease alone when they deviate from the right path of correct thinking and right conduct in conformity with the principles of *dharma* (righteousness). To follow proper rules of conduct is to act according to the tenets of *dharma*. To adhere to *dharma* is to remain healthy; to deviate from it is to contact disease.

It is in this sense that Ayurveda defines what is good or bad for *ayu*. Similar is the position adopted by *Charaka Samhita* when it underlines the fact that the proper combination of mind and intellect is the basis of health; when this combination goes awry, disease results (CS 8.13-14). It is, therefore, necessary to keep this combination in proper balance and order to maintain a good health and avoid contacting disease of any kind.

The maintenance of order in the human body is dependent, Sushruta points out, on the proper functioning of *vayu, kapha* and *pitta,* the three elements that constitute the necessary ingredients of the process of creation. *Vayu* is the surrogate of life force while *pitta* symbolizes *agni* and *kapha* represents *soma.* According to the Vedic story of creation, *agni* and *soma* represent two opposite but complementary elements whose combination, that is, *mithuna,* is necessary for the process of creation to begin and remain in progress. For the process of creation to begin and continue till *pralaya* (destruction of the cosmos) occurs, the one unknown has to undergo several processes of differentiation. One such differentiation pertains to the division of the one unknown into two elements, which is *agni* and *soma.* The other is its division into three different elements described in the Vedic literature as *trivittikarana,* that is, tripartite division of the one unknown into three different substances, viz. *manas* (intelligence), *prana* (life force), and *vak* (matter or *panchamahabhuta*). It is the interplay of *manas* and *prana* with *vak* that is the source of the creation of beings. It is these three elements that are necessary for constituting elements of human beings as an aggregate of consciousness, energy or life force and appetites or desires. A proper balance between them and their functioning in a balanced and proper way is the basis of good health.

As Sushruta points out, the human body is truly a machine composed of different parts, organs and faculties. But this machine is kept in working condition because of the different movements of the *pranic* energy, such as *prana, udana, saman, vyana and apana.* It is these movements of *vayu,* the surrogate of *prana* that regulate bodily movements (12.9). The element of *agni* manifests in the human body in the form of heat, that is *pitta,* and its assigned function is to control and regulate the fluctuations of heat and keep it in proper way (12.15). The function of *kapha* or *soma* is to determine the quality of certain attributes, such as, bravery/cowardice, fearlessness/fear, anger/attachment, the sense of happiness, etc. (12.16). All these three elements together constitute the reality of human person. It is this person constituted both by mortal and immortal elements that is the focus of Ayurveda. It is this person, again, that Ayurveda aims at the question of maintaining the order immanent in him; as such, it is concerned not only with the proper way of maintaining this order but also about how to go about restoring this order if it is disturbed for one reason or the other.

Similar to *Charaka Samhita,* Sushruta, too, refers to the same factors that are instrumental in causing disturbances in human body, intellect and psyche. According to Sushruta, there are basically three types of motivations operating in man's life and impelling to action (11.12). These motivations are: motivation to keep life in good order, to acquire wealth and to seek liberation (*moksha*). It is the combination of these three primary motivations that drive different sense organs to perform their assigned roles with a view to collecting appropriate information about the external world by directing their focus on and attaching themselves with external objects falling under their specific jurisdiction.

It is, however, the mind that organizes the obtained information into a systematic order and determines the type of action necessary for coping with a particular emergent situation. It also suggests the proper manner of going about realizing a particular purpose that mind has determined as desirable to realize. As such, the determination of purpose translates itself into action. But action takes place in a context characterized by different patterns of time-space continuum. The first set of conditioning factors affecting man's well-being, thus, refers to the possibilities and/or limitations involved with contextual variations caused by the pattern of time-space continuum. The second set of conditioning factors concerns the proper way of living one's life. These factors pertain to the need of living a righteous life, that is, a life lived in accordance with the tenets of *dharma*. To act according to the tenets of *dharma* is not only to install order in one's interior to accept the claim of the soul but also to install it as the ruler whose suzerainty must be accepted in determining the purposes for the individual in the sense of maintaining a proper balance and order in the physical, psychic and spiritual aspects of man's existence. It is also instrumental in maintaining order in the external world of society and nature.

Looking at the phenomenon of health from this perspective, Sushruta locates the causes of disease or health disorders in over-indulgence, under-indulgence and improper indulgence insofar as senses, action and time are concerned. Influenced by this perspective, Ayurveda does not only concern itself with the treatment of specific health disorders, whether caused by physical or mental factors. It also focuses its attention on what is proper conduct of man with a view to living a healthy and better life. Sushruta, therefore, underlines the need to avoid the enjoyment of all those things that are incompatible with righteous living (8.15). It also underlines the need of taking only those actions that are compatible with the claims of the soul. To be able to do so, the individual must follow the dictates of *dharma* and do things that conform to *dharma*. It is, therefore, not surprising that Sushruta discusses at length what these actions are and why these actions must be governed by the consideration of what is proper to do in any situational context – a context that is defined both by time-space continuum and the principles of righteousness.

## CONCLUSION

To put it briefly as well as sharply, the Ayurvedic concept of *swasthya* (health) is derived from the need to remain grounded in one's ethico-religious nature. That is to say, to remain so grounded, one needs to know what kind of ethico-religious entity he is and, then act in a manner that the needs of his being as an ethico-religious entity are fulfilled. That is why Ayurveda puts so much emphasis on remaining grounded in one's *swa,* that is, self not as *ahamkara,* but as something that has been touched by the momentary flash of eternity. It is this groundedness in one's soul that is the source of *sukha* (happiness). It is in this sense that Ayurveda proves itself to be a *shastra* or *praxis.*

# 5

# Water Resource Management Traditions in the Central-Western Himalayas

Ravi Chopra

## INTRODUCTION

India lies in the monsoon belt of the Earth. Rain and snow fall over a period of less than a third of the year. Over thousands of years, communities all across India learnt to collect rainwater, store it and husband it for a variety of purposes throughout the year. Thus, over centuries, a fantastic water-harvesting civilization took shape in India.

The Central-Western Himalayan region, comprising Uttaranchal and Himachal Pradesh, was no exception to the nation's water-harvesting traditions. A glorious profusion of *naulas, bawaris, nauns, dharas, chharedus, khals, chaals* and *khatris* stored rainwater that flowed down hillsides, percolated through rocks and emerged as springs in the mountain terrain; these water bodies were used for bathing, washing, drinking, worshipping, watering livestock, irrigating and village industries. Thousands of kilometres of hand-dug *kuhls* and *guhls* tapped mountain streams, carrying water for irrigation and powering thousands of *gharats* or watermills. Communities took pride in their water systems, as evidenced by the exquisite ornamentation and architecture of these structures.

An amazing aspect of these structures and systems is that many of them survive even today, hundreds of years after their construction. They function, even when the modern newly-built structures become dysfunctional.

The bases of these traditions lay in religious scriptures, cultural practices, jurisprudence and administrative systems. The faith and the enfranchisement of the local community have played a vital role in sustaining water management structures and systems. The sustenance of our present water management systems may well depend upon an acceptance of the wisdom embodied in the principles of traditional water management.

## WATER HARVESTING TRADITIONS IN UTTARANCHAL

There are several common features among the water harvesting traditions listed in Table 1. For example, the common traditional method of irrigation was based on diverting water from a mountain stream into a channel laid along a contour. The channel conveyed water to terraced fields. Traditionally, water for household use was obtained from springs, flowing mountain streams or rainwater harvesting structures built by people. Open water bodies, such as ponds, masonry tanks, *chappris, chaals* or *talaais* provided water for animals and for washing purposes. For human consumption, people preferred to harvest underground seepages in *bawaris, nauns* or *khatris* (Himachal Pradesh) and *naulas* (Uttaranchal). All these were usually common property resources. Until recently, the local communities looked after their maintenance and repair.

Table 1. Traditional Water Management Systems in the Central-Western Himalayas

| *Use (Uttaranchal)* | *Technology* | *Management Systems* |
|---|---|---|
| Animal consumption | Small earthen ponds called *chaals* are dug usually in the saddle part of a ridge. | No details available |
| Household consumption | *Naulas* are small stepped tanks/wells fed by underground seepages. | See text for details. |
| Drinking water | *Dharas* tap water from springs in the mountain slopes. The outlets are usually carved features in the form of an animal facemask. *Dharas* are of different types, depending upon their position above the ground and the kind of spout used. | No details available. |

Cont. Table 1

Table 1 Cont.

| *Use (Himachal Pradesh)* | *Technology* | *Management Systems* |
|---|---|---|
| Irrigation | *Hauzis* are small masonry tanks that harvest water from springs or rain for irrigating terraced fields. Depending on their size they may irrigate a series of fields one below the other. The outlet of a terrace can be blocked by a stone or boulder to flood it. | These are usually owned by individual farmers. |
| | *Guhls* are diversionary contour channels that convey water from a mountain stream to terraced fields. They are the most important irrigation systems in Uttaranchal (see text for details). | *Guhls* may be individually owned, community or state-owned. The management systems vary (see text for details). |
| Household consumption | *Chappris/talaais,* which are masonry tanks are used to harvest rainwater. *Chappris* are usually shallow dug ponds without any masonry work. *Talaais* are smaller ponds. Masonry tanks are usually open on one side to allow water from the catchments to enter the tank. Since these are open bodies, their water is often used by domestic animals. | These are community structures, but with the coming of piped water supplies their maintenance is neglected now. It is common to find a *peepal* or a banyan tree at the edge of these structures, indicating a once-sacred status. |
| | *Bawaris* and *nauns* are stepped wells that harvest water from underground springs and seepages. They are usually open masonry structures. Sometimes *bawaris* may have a roof. *Nauns* are usually larger than *bawaris*. *Bawaris* are a source of drinking water in Himachal even today, particularly | Though they are community resources, their maintenance usually suffers negligence. There are no well-defined rules of usage as in the case of irrigation systems. |

Cont. Table 1

Table 1 Cont.

| *Use (Uttaranchal)* | *Technology* | *Management Systems* |
|---|---|---|
| | when piped water supplies fail. *Nauns* are more often used for bathing and washing clothes. | |
| | *Khatris* are sub-surface structures carved out of hard sandstone in various parts. They harvest water that seeps through fractures in the rock. Being underground, evaporation losses can be avoided. Steps lead down a *khatri* to the water. | *Khatris* are often family owned. |
| Irrigation | Diversionary channels, known as *kuhls,* provide water to most of the irrigated areas. They are similar in construction to the *guhls* of Uttaranchal. | Most of the *kuhls* are community or state-owned. The distribution of water in community-owned *kuhls* is done by a *kohli,* acting on behalf of the water users' community. Repair and maintenance of a community *kuhl* is organized by the *kohli* with the support of the water users. Refusal to participate in these activities can lead to denial of water or a fine. The management rules are codified in documents called *Riwaz-i-abpashi* maintained in the village (Coward 1990). |
| | In Lahaul-Spiti *kuhls* tap glaciers. Glaciers tend to melt during the day and the flow builds up by the evening, when farming is suspended. Hence the water is collected in a circular tank late in the day. It is emptied the following day through an exit channel. This cycle is repeated every day. | Large landowners called *badaghars* own water rights. Other farmers may purchase water from the *badaghars.* Water shares are adjusted seasonally according to need, but they cannot be sold in perpetuity. Usually, the family that contributes the most to the construction of a *kuhl,* gets the larger share. The water rights thus established are hereditary. Repair and maintenance is usually a community exercise, organized by the *badaghars* (Agrawal and Narain 1997). |

Traditional water harvesting systems in Uttaranchal include a variety of community-managed systems. Their diversity arose from variations in the local conditions. Many of these systems were originally constructed by local rulers, feudal lords or by well-to-do families in the community. They displayed a diversity of technologies and minimal state intervention in water rights or management. Sometimes these systems failed to ensure social justice in water use (Upadhyay and Bisht 2001), but their flexibility, diversity, use of local materials, skills and designs made them compatible and relevant to the patterns of water use of hill communities over centuries. Many of these technologies are still in use, and meet a significant proportion of the water needs of communities in this region.

### *Chaals, Khals, Talaais, Chuptyaulas* and *Simars*

A variety of natural formations or depressions in the mountainous areas of Uttaranchal are used for rainwater harvesting. The most common are *chaals* or *khals*. These depressions are usually found along mountain ridge tops or in the saddle between two adjacent crests. They were formed in the past by the glacial action of snowmelt, resulting in the formation of small lakes or ponds with a relatively thick soil bed.

The larger *khals* (lakes) can store several thousand cubic metres of water. The water caters to the needs of people and their livestock. It also seeps through porous spaces, fissures and fractures in the underlying rock to recharge springs at lower elevations. In Pauri Garhwal district alone, 70 well-known *khals* have been enumerated (Sharma *et al.* 1996). Smaller, dug ponds are known as *talaais* in the mountains.

Other natural rainwater harvesting structures include *chuptyaulas* and *simars*. The former are rudimentary structures, found in the high-altitude areas of Uttaranchal, which collect water from springs or where it oozes out of the earth. These are normally used as watering holes for animals and occasionally for human use. Wild animals and birds depend on these structures as well. *Simars*, on the other hand, are natural features – a sort of quicksand that is found in agricultural fields in this region. High quality crops like *basmati* rice are sometimes grown in *simars*. Some medicinal plants and herbs are also grown in them.

### *Naulas* and *Bawaris*

*Naulas*, sometimes also called *bawaris*, are stepped wells. *Naulas* are found mostly on the slopes of middle-Himalayan villages of Uttaranchal, particularly in Kumaon. They are designed to collect water from subterranean seepages or springs. The flow of these subterranean springs is fairly sensitive and can be disrupted by seismic activity, deforestation and alterations to the structure, design of the well or other human disturbances.

Most *naulas* have a similar basic design; they consist of a tank that is closed on three sides and covered on the top. The fourth side has steps that lead down into the structure. The source of water may be at the base of the well or a short distance away and conveyed into the well by a channel. The drainage is usually designed so that the source is not contaminated by any of the well's uses. Animals are prevented from entering the tank area.

The structure of *naulas* and *bawaris* can vary considerably. Some *naulas* are massive and intricately ornamented structures with rooms and platforms for bathing and washing clothes. Elaborate drainage systems keep the source water clean. Other structures might be just basic step wells, surrounded by trees and made of locally available materials. Usually, wells in the villages are of the latter type, while those in towns or built by the local rulers are of the former type. In his *Gazetteer*, Atkinson (1984) mentions that *naulas* "in most of the region are covered reservoirs only. Some have been built by ex-rulers and exhibit architectural features. There is a pillared veranda around them. Sculptures have been engraved for the interior decoration. Because the construction of *bawaris* is considered honourable, therefore, these kinds of structures can be found in the neighbourhood of almost all villages and along the side of main highways".

*Naulas* were distinctly community property. There were no detailed rules of management. Villagers traditionally revered their *naulas* and the rituals observed in constructing them were similar to those of a temple's construction (Upadhayay and Bisht 2001). The water was sacred and basic rules of sanitation and hygiene were observed. Tree species considered sacred, like the *peepal* and the banyan, were planted near a *naula* to signify its sanctity and to protect and shade it. The *naula* water was often treated with medicinal plants such as *amla* and *neem* (Agrawal and Narain 1997).

### Current Status

Today, thousands of *naulas* in Uttaranchal lie forgotten and decaying. Their degraded condition reflects a decline in community water management, ecology, culture and traditions that supported these systems over the centuries. Ecological disruptions like deforestation, landslides, earthquakes, changing land-use patterns, increased population pressure and other factors disrupt the subterranean flows that sustain *naulas*. Where alternative sources of water have been provided, the cleanliness of *naulas* becomes the biggest casualty. Most significantly, the skill in locating sources, building and designing these structures has been forgotten (Upadhayay and Bisht 2001).

A vast majority of *naulas* in Uttaranchal are perishing under the onslaught of modern development. In Champawat district, the ancient *tapnaula* was buried during the construction of the Lohaghat-Barakot motor road. Similarly, the *nagnaula* of Dungra village in Champawat, *bhannaula*, the *naulas* of

Gangolihat block in Pithoragarh district and the *naulas* of Almora city are neglected, silted up or paved over and lost. A wide-scale revival of community management and traditions of using these structures is crucial for their preservation. In some cases, revival efforts have been made. *Tharkot ka naula* and the *naula* of *Hat-borgaon* are examples of local efforts to preserve these structures.

DHARAS/MUNGURUS (This section is largely based on Upadhyay and Bisht 2001)

A common source of drinking water in Uttaranchal is the *dhara* or *munguru*. It is essentially a drinking water fountain. Water from a spring or a subterranean source is channelled out through a carved outlet. The latter are often in the shape of either simple pipe, figures of women with water pitchers or animal facemasks. The shape of the outlet is such that even with low water pressure, water can be easily drunk. The degree of detail and ornamentation of a *dhara* varies according to the status of the builder. *Dharas* often bear inscriptions paying tributes to the rulers.

### THE HISTORIC NAULAS OF KUMAON

In Uttaranchal *naulas* are more commonly found in Kumaon than in Garhwal, and are characteristic of regions that face chronic water shortages. In Kumaon, historic *naulas* are found near old towns and settlements, like Champawat, which was the capital of the erstwhile Kumaon state, and in Sor, Sirakot, Gangoli, Almora, Dwarahat area and Katyur valley.

Many of these *naulas* still serve the populations of these towns and cities during times of drought. They are also exceptional works of art and architecture. The *Ekhathia* and *Baleshwar naulas* of Champawat and the *Syunarakot naula* of Almora district were built 500-700 years ago. These *naulas* are elaborate structures, built by rulers of Kumaon and other states and were not only sources of water, but places for social gathering and cultural exchange, much like temples. In fact, the art and sculpture found in *naulas* is among the finer examples of the art and architectural heritage of these regions. The *Nagnaula* of Dungra village in Champawat has sculptures of *Vishnu*; *Patan-ka-naula* in Champawat has an idol of *Ganesha* and several other deities. Other historic *naulas* exist in Jakhpuran and Tharkot areas near Pithoragarh city. *Bhannaula,* a very large and elaborate structure, with finely carved rocks and a seven-terraced tank lies on the Rameshwar-Pithoragarh track road. Investments made in these structures by local rulers reflect the importance of water management in statecraft. Although most of these historic *naulas* are dysfunctional and decaying, there are some that are still used and managed today by local government and villages. The *naula* of Hat-Borgaon near Balakot still fulfils the needs of the village, although it is not clean. In Meldungari village, a historic *naula* was renovated in 1958 and is still used.

Historic *naulas* give us clues about the intentions of their builders, the society and the state at the time, and the importance of water in the context of this system. For

> example, the Jahnvi *naula* near the Kali temple of Gangolihat was built for the use of devotees visiting the temple, and this *naula* is still heavily used today. Rulers also built *naulas* along major pilgrimage routes, like Kedarnath and Badrinath for travellers to rest and have freshwater. The Chand kings built over 360 *naulas* in Almora city, their capital, which provided for the entire population's needs.
>
> The number and scale of Kumaon's *naulas* reflect a vision of water management among rulers and communities, and a strong commitment to provide and sustain water management systems that worked well to enhance their well-being (Translated and extracted from Upadhayay and Bisht 2001).

There are three types of *dharas*, depending on their height above the ground. If one can drink from a *dhara* while standing straight, it is called a *sirpatia dhara*. These *dharas* are sometimes decorated with facemasks of animals like cows, lions, elephants, snakes or crocodiles. If one has to bend over to drink from one's hand or to fill a container to drink from the *dhara*, then it is called a *mudpatia dhara*. These *dharas* also have animal facemasks or simple pipe structures. The third type of *dhara* is a seasonal one. During the monsoon season, wooden spouts or broad leaves are stuck in the path of a flowing spring or seepage to create them. They are called *patvinyan dharas*. Often one has to sit on the ground to drink water from them.

*Dharas* are evenly distributed in Uttaranchal, from mountain crests to the valleys. They are also found in old towns and cities. The main road of district Pauri Garhwal is called *Dhara Bazaar*, after an ancient *dhara* there, which has now dried up. It used to be a major source of water for the town and fed a system of *guhls* and canals. Water flowing from *dharas* is usually fit for human consumption and other household uses since the source is either spring or subterranean seepages. They are also used for other purposes. In the villages with predominantly Bhotia (a local tribe) population, special *dharas* were made for cleaning wool. Sometimes their water is stored in tanks for human and livestock use. *Dharas* with large flows are used for irrigation.

## Current Status

Many urban and rural settlements still depend on *dharas* for a secure supply of water. Two *dharas*, *parda* and *sipahi*, supply water to a large population in Nainital. In Gopeshwar, a perennial *dhara* near a Shiva temple supplies water to the city. Ghunsera, Nakuleshwar (Panchdhara), Berinag, Devalthal, Chopta, Thal, Harinanda, Kantheshwar Mahadev of Pithoragarh district and Naini, Jainti and Trinetreshwar of Almora are all places with ancient *dharas*. Tharkot village, near Pithoragarh district, has several old *dharas*, which still provide the village with water. These *dharas* are beautifully carved and ornamented. As an example of this ornamentation at one place, there are several idols of deities; along with that there is an idol of a woman who is carrying an urn and the water emerges from it.

*Dharas,* however, are very sensitive to environmental disturbances and geological activity. In the Garhkot watershed of Tehri Garhwal district, an old perennial *dhara* called *amni-ka-dhara* dried up after the 1991 Uttarkashi earthquake. Deforestation and the associated reductions in groundwater storage and water retention capacities also affect *dharas*. The loss of this resource can have a severe impact on the local community. Pauri, having lost its ancient *dhara,* is now a water-starved town.

### *Guhls*

Cultivation in the Himalayan region is largely done on terraced fields. The problem of irrigating them has been historically resolved by diverting water from nearby mountain streams through channels, called *guhls* in Uttaranchal, that are dug along the contours of a slope. *Guhls* are perhaps the best example of water resource management in the Indian Himalayas. The technology has evolved locally. The systems may be individual, community or state-owned. The community managed *guhl* systems strive to be equitable, despite the complexities.

Typically, a *guhl* will irrigate a few hectares, serving from one to many farmers. Some *guhls* are several kilometres long and provide water to fields in more than one village. The system usually consists of a diversion point from a mountain stream or *gäd*. The diversion wall simply consists of large river boulders. It builds up a small head of water behind the diversion. Distribution is done by a canal, which has a trapezoidal cross-section and varies in size according to the flow capacity required. Along the length of the *guhl* are outlets that at times lead to smaller, secondary canals that take water to the fields. Flow to the fields is controlled by a boulder placed at the outlet. Usually there is an outlet at the lower end of every field, which allows excess water to pass on to the lower terraces. The excess water drains back into the *guhl* at the lowest point, and usually ends downstream in the *gäd*.

The construction of a *guhl* mostly requires rocks and boulders from local streams and human labour. The diversion wall is meant to be a temporary structure. It often gets washed away during the monsoons but can be easily reconstructed when water is required in the system. Canals can be simple hand dug, lined with rocks or plastered with cement. The more permanent cement-lined ones reduce seepage losses. The construction of the head wall and the canals varies according to local conditions, local requirements and the skills of the community. The selection of a site for the head wall, the layout of the *guhl*, maximization of the irrigation area and reduction of leakages require lots of skill.

### The Legend of Maletha's *Guhl*

This legendary *guhl* was built in Maletha, a chronically dry village, by Madho Singh in the reign of Tehri's king Mahipat Shah (1625-1642). Madho Singh had to dig through hard rock to bring the waters of Chandrabhaga river across the hill to Maletha. Legend has it that Madho Singh had a dream in which he was anointed by a goddess to undertake this task. He picked up a shovel and began digging. Inspired by his courage the community joined him. It was a truly courageous and skilful effort. Today, 350 years after its creation, Maletha's *guhl* still brings water to the village. With its broad irrigated terraces, this village is a symbol of prosperity.

*Guhls* have been constructed for several centuries in Uttaranchal. They are the principal form of irrigation in the state, accounting for a major fraction of the total irrigated area in 1999. They exist in almost all the villages with irrigation. Since most *guhls* irrigate the fields of a number of farmers and sometimes stretch across several villages, a variety of innovative methods of managing the water have been devised.

There are two challenges of equity in most *guhl* systems – how to achieve an equitable distribution of water among the users of the *guhl*, and how to balance the use of water between different *guhls* that draw water from the same stream. Upstream users and those who are close to the head of a *guhl* are generally likely to receive a greater flow than users at the tail end of the system. Seepage losses can be significant along the length of a *guhl*.

The water users manage most *guhls*. Sometimes a local farmer is designated to act as water tender. He is given the responsibility to distribute the water and organize the repair and maintenance of the system. For this each farmer pays him a portion of the harvest. All the villagers respect his decisions.

### Managing Guhl Irrigation

One of the well-known community managed irrigation systems in Uttaranchal is that of Ladyura *gram sabha* in Almora district. It has a very well-developed irrigation management organization. Organization constitutes of *sinchai samiti* or irrigation council and the *sabhapati* (chairperson) who is usually a Thakur, an upper caste landowner. Most farmers are either Rajputs or Harijans.

To ensure an equitable distribution of water along the length of the *guhl*, the diversions to individual fields along the *guhl* are blocked by rocks which get successively smaller along the *guhl*. Members of the *gram sabha* are concurrently members of the 10-person *sinchai samiti*, which makes decisions on water distribution and enforces correct allocation. Major decisions are made at meetings which are open to the villagers. Decisions about allocations of water are made before the cropping season begins, and the *sabha* serves as a conflict resolution body too. In Ladyura, there is an annual or biennial reversal of the order in which farmers receive water, in order to ensure equity of distribution. The *sinchai samiti* makes decisions on these rotations and their decision is generally respected.

The *sinchai samiti* has a *chowkidar* who is responsible for preventing water thefts, ensuring the correct supply of water to each farmer and preventing cattle from damaging fields. If the *chowkidar* notices any farmer interfering with the system, he will publicly inform the offender at a general meeting. And if the meeting fails to address this complaint, then a *nyaya panchayat* penalizes the offender. The *chowkidar* is paid about 2 kg of grain for his services by each irrigator. If the crop fails, the *chowkidar* is paid less than his due, and similarly, if the crop is damaged by cattle, the *chowkidar* must pay part of the fine for the damage. This system of incentives and disincentives ensures that the *chowkidar* discharges his duties sincerely and honestly. The fines collected are used to maintain the *guhl*'s infrastructure and the villagers also volunteer their time to help maintain the system. Usually, villagers help clean and repair the *guhl*, and those who cannot personally contribute, hire labourers to fill in for them (Extracted from Pande 1997).

### Hara System

A contractual irrigation system, known as the *hara* system, exists in the Saryu valley near Sheraghat, on the boundary of Almora and Pithoragarh districts (Pande 1991). The *guhls* were mostly created in the early 1920s, though the first contractual system was established around 1896. Contour channels were constructed and maintained by contractors who entered into 30-year contracts with farmers for the supply of irrigation water. The payment for these services was in kind, and initially farmers paid as much as a third of their produce at the beginning of a contract, when the contractor invested a large sum of money to build the *guhl*. Currently the rate is about one-tenth to one-eighteenth of the produce, mainly for maintenance and repair of the canal. Usually, the contractor and the irrigator sign a legal document. The contractor can cut off irrigation water for farmers who default on their payments. In this system the community is less involved, and sometimes this results in delays due to disputes amongst farmers. A single system irrigates 15-50 hectares. These systems still exist and are used in Uttaranchal.

### Multiple Irrigation Systems

Thirty irrigation systems take off from the 12 km long *Mansari gadhera* (stream) in Almora district (Pande 1991). The systems use diversion and *bunds* or river boulders, which often get washed away during the monsoons, but are quickly repaired by the beneficiaries acting together. The narrow channels ensure that only a limited amount of water can pass through any one system. There are no major water sharing conflicts between the upstream and downstream villages. The systems collectively irrigate about 350 ha. The state's irrigation department does not operate in this valley.

## THE BASES OF WATER MANAGEMENT TRADITION

Traditional water management systems have been sustained over time by religious teachings and a highly evolved system of cultural practices, property rights and administration. They were largely governed by local customs. Their rules were defined through well-established social relations and divisions, and they allowed for private as well as communal property rights.

### Religious Precepts

Several religious scriptures declare that water is sacred. In the *Srimad Bhagvatgita,* Lord Krishna says that water is his home, implying that it is sacred.

> From time immemorial, I have myself named water as Naar.
> Since (my) home (*aayan*) is in this Naar, I am named Narayan.

Reverence of rivers is clear from Bhishma's evocation in the *Mahabharata* (Mishra 2002):

> O, King! All rivers are mothers of the world; they yield great benefits.
> I am not aware of any one else capable of bestowing such benefits.

Personal rules of water use, codified in the *Manusmriti,* led to sustaining the purity of water bodies:

> Polluting substances like excreta, urine, spit or blood should never be released in water.

The *Brihatsamhita* on the other hand offers advice on how to clean polluted water:

> If water becomes polluted, bitter or salty, it should be cleaned by mixing a powder of collyrium (*kohl*), the grass *anaropogon nuricatum, amla,* etc.

To minimize the miseries of floods, the *Naradiya Purana* defined practical rules on how far settlements had to be from riverbanks.

> The bank of a river stretches 150 hand measures (roughly 70m) from the river-bed. The area lying within one *yojana* (about 14.5 km) from the bank is the river's regime.

The *Naradiya Purana* forbade dwelling in the river-bed zone or on the riverbanks, permitting it only in the river plain (Mishra 2002). The modern flood plain zoning which defines a prohibited zone, a restricted zone and a warning zone is only a new version of this ancient wisdom.

The *Agni Purana* recommended the construction of water bodies as an act of worship:

> Along with the worship of *Vishnu* and *Varun*, water reservoirs should be constructed.

### Customary Practices

The religious precepts were observed and became part of the local cultural practices and customs. The sanctity of water was symbolized by the presence of sacred trees like *peepal* and banyan, at the edge of a water body. Even today, a new Kumaoni bride on her first arrival at her husband's home offers a ritual prayer at the village *naula*.

Rivers symbolize divine life-giving forces, and ritual bathing for purification and the use of water in religious ceremonies has been a part of Hindu culture for millennia. The construction of public water facilities like tanks or lakes was considered a very praiseworthy deed, and was encouraged by rulers with incentives like tax rebates.

Islam also recognized the importance of water, and said that free water for all was a birthright.

Recognition of ecological principles as a basis for water resource development was enunciated in ancient texts like Kautilya's *Arthashastra* and Kashyapa's treatise on agriculture. The *Manusmriti*, and several *sutras* and *shastras* contain recommendations on water management policies, the enforcement of rights and duties pertaining to water and descriptions of water management practices.

In the scriptures, five basic principles of water resource development have been summarized (Paranjpye 1994):

1. Water resources should be developed at the source or *udgamsthana* of a river. These sources are sacred and temples should be constructed at the source to protect it. In the Central Himalayan region, this is true for the sources of many rivers and streams.
2. There should be minimal obstruction (*nyunatam gati-avarodh*) to the natural flow of water. There was an understanding of the importance of the hydrological cycle.
3. The principle of *suvarna madhya* or golden mean refers to the relationship between the development of water harvesting and management structures and the economic, social and organizational

competence of the water users. In essence, this principle recommended optimal rather than maximal development of water resources, balancing the needs and abilities of the users.

4. While managing water resources, their ecology should be understood. Kashyapa refers to the interdependence of water, forests, land and biota. In accordance with this principle, sacred groves were established at the headwaters, confluence points and mid-regions of a watershed. The development of small-scale water harvesting structures interspersed with these groves was essential to the maintenance of ecological balance and the sustainability of the water source. The "zabo" system of cultivation that is practised by the Chakhesang tribals of Nagaland is a living example of this principle (Agrawal and Narain 1997).
5. *Sahabhag*, *swabhava* and *sanskara* that is participation and self-determination are also important elements of water resources development. Different social groups played essential and different roles. The king was responsible for commissioning and financing water projects, fixing water rates and collecting user fees. The brahmins were responsible for supervision and advising the king on projects. The construction and maintenance of systems as well as the allocation of rights and responsibilities to specific groups and water users was to be done by village communities collectively.

## Laws and Administration

India's traditional legal administration was a set of parallel systems instead of a hierarchical one, with different levels enjoying autonomy. Local laws were not overruled by other higher institutions or political bodies. Systems at different levels constantly interacted and affected each other.

Traditional Indian law was derived from *dharma*, royal order and custom, as opposed to statute, precedent and doctrine, which underlie the modern legal system (Vani undated). In the legal context, *dharma* could be defined as "a code of conduct supported by the general conscience of the people"(Radhakrishanan 1936). The rule of *dharma* became law only after it entered into the realm of behaviour and was accepted by the general population as a customary rule (Basham 1998). Thus, custom represented a special body of laws and rules which regulated the behaviour of different social and economic groups. It evolved as a holistic approach from relationships between individuals, society, the state, nature, religion and many other elements of human existence in the world. The role of a ruler was to maintain social order and promote peace, security and prosperity for the subjects.

*Dharma* was thus the supreme authority and the final word in the legal system, and judges were called *dharmastas* or "upholders of *dharma*". Custom was sustained by *dharma* and the king. Though a king had the power to pass royal orders, *dharma* and custom were usually inviolable. The ruler could intervene in the domains of *dharma* and custom only to prevent discontent and disorder. Under Islamic law, there was a pluralistic judiciary, with a hierarchical organization of courts, but there was little interference in the functioning of lower courts, and Hindu law was preserved and applied by Muslim rulers (Vani undated).

Within the context of this traditional law, administrative and political framework, natural resource use was largely managed by local communities through a dynamic system of norms, institutions and cultural traditions referred to as custom or traditional law. But the system also had severe inequities built into it. A common negative feature to all types of resource use was that social structure, caste, lineage and clan networks were major determinants of resource use. Inter-caste relations and customs maintained the interdependence and cohesion of social hierarchy and shaped rights and duties of different groups with respect to natural resources. In the remote area of Lahaul-Spiti, the role of the social hierarchy is still distinctly preserved by the dominance of the *badaghars* (Agrawal and Narain 1997). In the Central Himalayas there are still cases of certain water bodies or sources where access is denied to the scheduled castes (Upadhyay and Bisht 2001). As mentioned earlier, religion also played a role in defining rules for resource use and management.

The State had little regulatory power over natural resources. Villages and communities were granted a large degree of autonomy. In the absence of the State intervention, villages and rural society were primarily governed by custom and tradition. Very limited taxes were imposed on agriculture and resource use, and the State largely recognized the rights of local communities to independently manage, allocate and use their agricultural land, forests and water (Vani undated).

In the realm of law enforcement, there were penalties and punishments for the misuse or pollution of water. The *Dharmasutra* of Apastamba, a treatise on civil and criminal law, the *Manusmriti* and the *Vishnu sutras*, all refer to punishments for stealing water, the destruction of embankments, tanks, ponds, lakes or rivers and the pollution of any water body (Vani undated). The *Vishnu sutras* even recommend capital punishment for the destruction of embankments and heavy fines for the misuse of public tanks. Kautilya's *Arthashastra* mentions a detailed system of penalties for failure to maintain waterworks.

## EMERGENT ISSUES

### Loss of Tradition of Methods of Water Resource Management

The primary purpose of British colonial rule in the Indian subcontinent was to maximize the extraction of wealth. Water laws drafted by the colonial governments sub-served this overarching purpose. To ensure a stable legal regime for maximizing revenue from water resources, they gradually established the State's monopoly over all water resources. Though most of the laws were related to irrigation, some affected other commercial uses, like water mills in the Himalayan region.

The British government legally acquired a range of powers – taxation, collection, distribution and jurisdiction over all water resources – amongst others. It thereby almost totally transformed the traditional method of ownership, use and management systems. In many areas, however, some of these rights continue to be recognized in the interest of maintaining law and order.

The colonial rule made territorial laws which included various acts related to natural resource management, common to all. At the same time, however, it left personal laws under the purview of the various religious communities, untouched (Vani undated). The effect was to separate natural resource use and management practices from customary social behaviour and religious or ethical values. Natural resource management administration was not only centralized but it was separated into different departments, thus breaking the traditional Indian interlinkages of land, forests and water. Nowhere was the impact of this de-linking as critical as in the Himalayan region, where deforestation and monocultures enhanced surface runoff, reduced recharge of springs and increased slope instability. Finally, the linkage between rights over resource use and duties towards their preservation was also gradually eroded. Colonial natural resource management laws gave precedence to private and State property rights over common property rights and related management practices (Vani undated).

A distinctive feature of all the colonial regulations regarding water use and management in Uttaranchal was that they did not apply to drinking water resources. As a result, village communities continued to look after their *naulas, bawaris, dharas* and other water harvesting structures without any sense of alienation.

The basic approach of the Indian State towards the colonial legal and administrative framework was to adopt it, expand it or in some cases amend it. The colonial laws were rarely repealed or bureaucracies abolished. The most dramatic changes were made during the Emergency period (June 1975-March 1977) when several States passed legislations affirming the State's total ownership of water resources. Ownership, use, jurisdiction and management rights were transferred from individuals and communities to the state governments. The Himalayan region did not remain unaffected by these changes; consequently, here even drinking water became a State responsibility. The overall impact of all the changes during the colonial and post-colonial periods has been a steady decline in the functioning and maintenance of the traditional water management structures and systems in the Central-Western Himalayan region.

### People's Faith in the Traditional Water System

Having withstood the greed and mismanagement under colonial rule and the vagaries of time, the traditional water resources enjoy a status of loyal friend in the hearts of the people. That is why, the local people still consider their functioning resources to be more reliable than the systems newly installed by the government departments. Despite their weakened condition, the sources that still exist are used by the local communities when the government's water supply systems fail. *Guhls* in Uttaranchal and *kuhls* in Himachal Pradesh irrigate a majority of the irrigated area.

### Traditional Wisdom Holds Promise

Perhaps the most amazing aspect of traditional water management systems is their longevity. Many *naulas, bawaris, chharedus* and *kuhls* in use today are hundreds of years old. Clearly the traditional water management systems showed a high degree of sustainability.

In today's world there is a lot of concern about the sustainability of natural resources. It is hardly possible now to revive the traditional systems and many, like the *Dalits,* would not even want to just ensure sustainability without equity. But it may be less difficult to build a new system by distilling the wisdom embodied in the past experience.

Three basic principles that helped ensure sustainability in the past stand out and should be the point of reference for any new endeavour. These are:

- Water was revered as sacred. Since the water bodies were considered to be sacred, they were well-maintained.
- The local communities had the right of ownership and first use over the local natural resources. The State recognized this right. As this right eroded over the last century or so, the traditional structures started to fall into disrepair and disuse.
- The principle of golden mean gave the insight of tampering development (or wants) in order to ensure the sustainability of the natural resources.

## CONCLUSION

But how likely is the modern world or culture to accept these principles? Accepting the principle of golden mean would amount to inventing a new culture. Today's consumer culture emphasizes the maximum over the optimum– a value that is the anti-thesis of sustainability. Can today's culture believe in intangibles? Can it dare to believe that water is sacred – when nothing other than money appears to be sacred?

On the other hand, do we really have a choice?

## BIBLIOGRAPHY

Agrawal, A. and S. Narain (eds.), 1997. *Dying Wisdom.* New Delhi: Centre for Science & Environment.

Atkinson, E.T. 1984. *The Himalayan Districts of North Western Provinces.* Allahabad.

Basham, A.L. 1998. *The Wonder That was India.* New Delhi: Rupa & Co.

Coward, E.W. Jr. 1990. 'Property Rights and Network Order: The Case of Irrigation Works in the Western Himalayas', *Human Organization* 49 (1): 78-88.

Mishra, D.K. 2002. *Living with the Politics of Floods: The Mystery of Flood Control.* Dehra Dun: People's Science Institute.

Pande, U.C. 1991. *State and Farmer Managed Irrigation Systems in District Almora in UP Hills.* New Delhi: Water & Land Management Institute.

——. 1997. 'Stream Sharing' in *Dying Wisdom,* A. Agrawal and S. Narain (eds.). New Delhi: Centre for Science & Environment.

Paranjpye, V. 1994. 'Preliminary Look at ARUN III in the Light of Tehri Experience', *Water Nepal* 4 (1).

Radhakrishnan, S. 1936. *The Heart of Hindustan.* Madras.

Sharma, B. *et al.* 1997. *Rainwater Harvesting Structures – A Solution for Water Crisis in the Himalayas: A Case from Ir Gad Microwatershed in Pauri District, Garhwal Himalaya.* Paper presented at a workshop on Futuristic Model Habitat, Pauri.

Upadhayay, A. and P. Bisht. 2001. *Uttaranchal Mein Jal Prabandhan: Ek Sinhavlokan.* Nainital: PAHAD.

Vani, M.S. (undated). *Law and Custom in Water Resource Administration: A Case Study of U.P. Himalayas,* Part 1. New Delhi: Development Centre for Alternative Policies.

# 6

# Standing Firm: Traditional Aseismic Architecture in the Western-Central Himalayas

Rishi Das

## INTRODUCTION

The Himalayan mountain range is one of the world's most active seismic regions. According to Plate Tectonics theory, the seismic activity in this region is caused by the collision of the Indian subcontinental and the Eurasian plates. The relatively rapid northeasterly movement of the Indian subcontinental plate at the rate of 5 cm/year causes the lifting of the Indian plate, with its consequent deformation in the wide arc, which is the Himalayan mountain range (Le Pinchon 1968; Fitch 1970). A tremendous amount of strain accumulates along this convergence zone, which is highly inelastic. This means that instead of deforming the rock landmass, the potential of the rock to slip equals the rate of convergence. Out of 10 equally spaced regions of the Himalayas, there are six regions with a slip potential estimated at about four meters, and in some places it may exceed six metre (Bilham *et al.* 2001). The 1950 Assam earthquake, the most powerful of all intra-continental earthquakes ever recorded, released about four metre of strain (Bilham *et al.* 2001). Several research studies have warned of the probability of several great earthquakes in this region and according to some of these studies the estimates of casualties range to hundreds of thousands and some even estimate casualties in the millions in more densely populated regions (Bilham *et al.* 2001; Arya 1990). The geological activity in this region has always been a menace to human settlements which are virtually at constant risk of earthquakes, landslides and numerous other hazards.

A defining feature of indigenous rural houses around the world is that they are non-engineered structures, constructed by native artisans who primarily use locally available materials like mud, stone and wood. These indigenous and traditional construction practices evolved in the context of local culture, environmental constraints and empirical knowledge. Over several centuries of human settlement in the Himalayas, indigenous housing throughout the region has a variety of adaptations and reinforcements, which help in resisting damage during earthquakes. The western-central Himalayas have several indigenous types of construction, which have earthquake-resistant or aseismic features. In Himachal Pradesh timber, slate, stone, mud and bamboo are used in traditional architecture. The *kath-ki-kuni* style of housing in central Himachal Pradesh makes highly effective use of timber beams as binding elements and the *pherols* of Garhwal's Uttarkashi region have similar architecture. Another type of construction found in Kashmir and Himachal Pradesh is *Dhajji-diwari*, or structures with diagonal wooden bracing in the walls, which are effective in helping the building resist shear and tension during earthquakes.

However, the western-central Himalaya's native heritage of aseismic construction techniques are being rapidly lost, replaced by reinforced cement concrete (RCC) construction. This decline is due to a variety of factors, including changing cultural values, demographic and economic transitions and rural development programmes. While RCC construction can be highly earthquake-resistant, the manner in which this new technology has proliferated in the western-central Himalayas has created vulnerability to earthquake disasters and poses many questions of the sustainability and appropriate use of newer technologies. Indigenous construction techniques still have much to offer in terms of their inherent sustainability and appropriateness. The Peoples' Science Institute (an NGO based in Dehradun) has studied and documented the aseismic aspects of indigenous and traditional construction techniques. This paper presents prominent examples of such architecture in Himachal Pradesh and Garhwal, a discussion of their aseismic qualities and some observations on the aspects of sustainability and appropriate technology.

## ASEISMIC ARCHITECTURE AND CHALLENGES IN RURAL HOUSING

The impact of an earthquake on a building depends on a complex interaction of factors during an earthquake. These include the depth of the epicentre, magnitude, frequency, intensity and duration of shaking, conditions of soil and the quality of construction (ISET 1989). One of the most common fallacies of post-earthquake assessments of damage to buildings is the assumption that buildings left standing or relatively undamaged are assumed to be earthquake-resistant. It is important to understand how different forces generated during a quake affect a building, behaviour of building materials and interactions between different structural elements of the building.

Ground movement is the primary cause of damage to buildings because it causes the base of the building to move while the inertia of the superstructure (a function of its mass) causes it to resist motion. This results in the deformation of the superstructure. The action of three types of forces is equivalent to a horizontal seismic force or load acting on the building. The inertial seismic load is a function of the mass and location of the centre of gravity. Thus lower mass and lower centres of gravity make a building less likely to topple over during an earthquake (Chopra *et al.* 1993). In structural engineering terms, most rural houses are "load-bearing" structures, which means that the weight of the roof and upper storeys rest upon the walls of the structure. Under normal conditions, the structure bears vertical or compressive loads. During an earthquake, the combination of compression, tension and shear forces act in complex and differential ways on the structure and its constituent elements, causing complex deformations and the constituent elements to behave differently and independently of each other. The risk of critical failure of the overall structure increases. Weaker elements may fail and lead to a domino effect, causing the failure of other elements. Thus it is also essential to interconnect the structural elements using tie bands and bracing so that as far as possible the structure behaves as a single unit and does not disintegrate. The stress on component elements also tends to accumulate at corners and openings in a building, and so it is important to reinforce the corners and keep openings small and properly spaced in order to minimize the risk of failure due to the accumulation of stress. It is important to have strong bonding with mortar. There has been some discussion on the importance of rigidity in the overall structure. One of the most touted aspects of RCC construction is its rigidity and high compressive strength. However, the goal of aseismic architecture is not to design buildings that do not fail, rather it is to allow controlled failure in order to allow the dissipation of the tremendous stresses experienced during an earthquake. One of the problems of using cement in rural construction is that if the strength of the cement mortar exceeds the strength of mud bricks, the latter may shatter, while the former resists the force (Langenbach 1986). The behaviour of different materials is also important to consider. Very often, the un-thought combination of traditional and modern construction materials can lead to disastrous consequences. The primary principles and features to be included for the resistance of earthquake in non-engineered structures are summarized in Table 1.

Table 1. Basic Principles and Construction Features for Earthquake-Resistance (from Chopra *et al.* 1993)

| *Principle* | *Effect in an Earthquake* | *Construction Features* |
|---|---|---|
| Structural stability | Avoids overturning and collapse | Subsoil bears loads<br>Adequate tying elements<br>Proper ratios<br>Geometric regularity<br>Uniform rigidity distribution<br>Masonry courses planned |
| Minimize inertia | Lessens moments of overturning | Light building materials<br>Thin walls |
| Strong and well-tied frame | Transfers inertial forces to the ground | Tie bands<br>Triangulation of the frame<br>Corner reinforcement |
| In-plane stiffness in both directions | Resistant to the inertial forces of earthquake | A fewer openings, proper spacing<br>Cross-walls and buttressing |
| Low centre of gravity | Lessens possibility of overturning | Low heights of the storey<br>Light building materials |
| Shear centre close to centre of gravity | Reduces local stress and initiation of collapse | Symmetrical and regular building forms<br>Maintain ratios of length and breadth<br>Simple designs (minimum projections/openings/cut-outs) |
| Increase ductility of structure | Absorbs inertial forces | Use ductile materials at points of structure tensile stress, e.g., steel/bamboo reinforcement at corner joints |
| Damage is preferable to collapse or destruction | -do- | Increase redundancy<br>Provide several supports for key structural elements.<br>Multiple columns support for long portions of the building |

The tremendous destructive force that can be potentially generated by earthquakes and practical constraints make it impossible to build an "earthquake-proof" structure. In a rural context, where there are sustainability issues, limits on the availability of construction materials and inadequate knowledge about the appropriate use of newer technologies, indigenous construction techniques offer many features that help in ensuring the earthquake-resistance of housing. Many of the materials that are available in rural areas also have good qualities for aseismic architecture. Wood and bamboo have high tensile strengths and are effective in tying the structure together. Stone and mud bricks when prepared correctly can be highly effective in bearing compressive and shear forces. Slate has high compressive strength.

## TRADITIONS OF ASEISMIC ARCHITECTURE IN THE WESTERN-CENTRAL HIMALAYAS

### *KATH-KI-KUNI*

*Kath-ki-kuni* literally means "timber-cornered". This type of architecture is found predominantly in central Himachal Pradesh in Kullu and Mandi districts, and parts of Shimla and Solan districts. Several of the buildings are about 100 years old and some of the more massive structures, like temples or palaces, are several centuries old. This style of architecture was noticed by officers, from the Geological Survey of India after the 1905 Kangra earthquake, who were impressed by the remarkable lack of damage to these buildings. They commented,

> The long gentle slope from the Beas river up to the pass, a total ascent of about 4,000 feet, was not remarkable for much damage to the village and hamlets situated thereon. This at first sight appeared unnatural on account of the apparently rather top-heavy construction of the houses – all of the hill type – until one came to realise the natural resisting power of their timber-bonded walls…which, whether intentional or not, seems a suitable form of hill architecture for earthquake countries (Middlemiss 1910).

As the account mentions, these buildings are particularly noticeable for their top-heavy appearance, which is especially accentuated by the external balconies on upper storey and the use of the upper storey as granaries. As the name of the architectural style suggests, the extensive use of timber, as a bonding element in the structure is the signature style of these houses. A variety of structures fall within this architectural style – ranging from the ornate palace of the Maharaja of Kullu to some of the massive towering temples of Mandi district, to simpler houses in old Manali. This style bears close resemblance to the *pherols* of Uttarkashi. The geographical proximity and similar nature of the terrain and environments of these regions would suggest a large number of indigenous artisans in the region who used common principles and techniques in constructing houses, granaries, livestock shelters, temples, palaces and other buildings.

### Aseismic Features of *Kath-ki-kuni* Style

The prominent features of earthquake resistance of this type of construction are as follows:

#### *Timber Tie-bands*

A pair of parallel wooden beams traverses the entire length of the walls at regular intervals. The pairs of wooden beams alternate in direction; the alternating pairs are placed perpendicular to each other. The space between the beams in the pair is usually filled with dry stone masonry, although there are variations depending upon locally available materials. These also serve to course the stone masonry in the walls. These beams act as tie bands and connect the superstructure, helping the building resist tension and lateral forces.

#### *Interconnection and Corner Reinforcement*

The pair of timber beams are interconnected at regular intervals along the length of the wall with wooden pegs, and at the corners the perpendicular pairs of beams are interconnected vertically at four points. This provides vertical as well as lateral tying of the structural elements in the building. This helps in the strengthening of the corners and distributing the load vertically and also in preventing the wall from splitting under high compressive force. The joinery reflects the skilled craftsmanship of indigenous masons.

#### *Well-dressed Stone Masonry*

Although the composition of the walls varies by location, usually they are composed of dry stone masonry and the stones used are long and flat. These stones are well laid in order to evenly distribute compressive strain vertically and prevent outward movement of stones in the wall. Many of the older *kath-ki-kuni* buildings have massive, almost monolithic, stone blocks, which have been well-dressed. The massive construction stands testament to the technological capacity of the indigenous masons. The walls range in thickness from 40 cm to over 100 cm in some cases, and the thickness of the walls gives much needed insulation from the cold and also distributes compression in these load-bearing structures.

### *Small Openings and Low Storey*

Doors and windows are kept small and have heavy wooden reinforced frames, which help bear the accumulated stress on the openings during an earthquake. The placement of openings is staggered so as to avoid vertical alignment of the openings which otherwise could weaken the wall. The frames and doors have diagonal bracing elements, which are exquisitely carved. The heights of the storeys are also kept low that keeps the centre of gravity low.

### *Stable Geometry*

The floor plans of *kath-ki-kuni* houses reveal that structures are very nearly square and the ratio of the sides usually lies within a proportion of 3:2. This geometry reduces excessive strain on longer walls and maintains a shear centre close to the centre of gravity. Taller structures have wide bases and a tapering construction to reduce moments of overturning. Thus even massive structures like the temples of Jungi village in Mandi district are very stable.

### *Roofs*

The roof frames in *kath-ki-kuni* houses are most commonly made of bamboo, which is generally available in this region. In some areas the construction is of wood or of both materials. Bamboo is an excellent material for roof frames since it is flexible and has high tensile strength. These are essential qualities to negotiate the compression and tension of vibrations in the roof during earthquakes. The roof tiles in *kath-ki-kuni* architecture are thick slabs of slate, which are very heavy. A very sturdy roof frame is used to support the weight of the roof.

## Other Features of *Kath-ki-kuni* Style

Apart from the aseismic qualities of *kath-ki-kuni* architecture, this type of construction shows great adaptation to traditional livelihoods, environmental conditions and cultural norms. These features are as below:

- Use of Material: In terms of materials, the use of stone, slate, wood, mud and bamboo reflected primary use of local resources and an intimate knowledge of the qualities and manner of using these materials with each other.
- Plan of House: The typical plan of a *kath-ki-kuni* house provides space for livestock on the bottom storey, a granary on the first storey and the living quarters on the uppermost storey. There is usually an attic above the living space. The living space usually has an external

verandah, which adds floor space without making the structure top-heavy. This general layout is adapted to the agrarian lifestyle of the region. The placement of the living quarters on the upper storey makes this space warmer, both by allowing in more sunlight and capturing the body heat of the livestock rising from below. There was also some danger of wild animals entering houses, so the grain and people stayed on the upper storey and the access to these spaces was from the top instead of the ground. The heavy slate roofs and thick walls are adaptations to the extreme cold in these regions. Sloping, thick roofs were needed to bear the weight of heavy snowfall, and the thick walls provided good insulation against the cold.

- Layout of the House: Clustered layout of kath-ki-kuni houses reflects a communitarian style of living. This layout facilitated the families to live together and share storage space or livestock. "Technology is as much a product of a society's culture as its knowledge or resource base" (Chopra *et al.* 1993).
- Encouragement to the Finer Arts and the Traditions: Amongst the cultural aspects of this type of construction, the ornamentation of the heavy door frames usually includes a carving of the household or ancestral deity. As one woman in old Manali explained, "My grandfather used to tell us that in the old days, men knew respect for the gods and so every time you entered their houses you had to bow your head to enter (because of the small openings) and show reverence for the household deity".

### *Dhajji-diwari*

The distinguishing feature of this type of architecture is the presence of diagonal wooden bracing in the walls. In Himachal Pradesh this type of architecture is found in different regions and shows a great deal of variability in form and application. Two regions where *dhajji-diwari* was observed in the present study are Dharamsala and Karsog areas of Mandi district. The buildings found here are mostly government buildings, which were built after the 1905 Kangra earthquake (Arya 1990). It is unlikely that the colonial administration used local artisans and masons' technologies for this construction since it is not seen elsewhere in the region. Thus, this example is not indigenous to the region but similar architecture is found in other parts of Himachal, like Mandi district and also further north and in Kashmir (Langenbach 1986). Therefore the general principles of using wooden diagonal bracing must have been encountered by the British.

### Prominent Features of *Dhajji-diwari* Style

The examples in Dharamsala show very sturdy bracing and other design elements, which make these buildings resistant to earthquakes. These features are as follows:

#### *Diagonal Bracing*

The use of wooden diagonal bracing in the walls adds a high degree of resistance to shear forces, which cause great damage to longer walls and the corners of openings. By using diagonal bracing, triangular stability is added to the walls, which means that deforming forces of compression, tension and shear are distributed and dissipated by the frame. At the intersection of the bracing, triangular blocks of wood are used to stabilize the brace and iron pins are used to tie these elements and to add further tensile strength.

#### *Light Structure*

The roofs of these buildings are made of corrugated iron sheets or wooden frames with tiles, which reduce the mass of the structure and lower the centre of gravity. The walls are also generally thinner since they do not have to bear the weight of a heavy roof.

The *dhajji-diwari* encountered in Mandi district bears some interesting parallels to the *dhajji-diwari* of Kashmir described by Langenbach (1986). The aseismic quality of this type of *dhajji-diwari* is different from that of the Dharamsala examples. Here, the diagonal bracing is achieved by using a different pattern of bracing with smaller pieces of wood and loosely coursed masonry. While the basic principle of diagonal bracing is the same, the frame does not have the same bracing as the Dharamsala examples. As in the Kashmir examples, this type of construction has the added advantage of flexibility in the structure and the weak masonry absorbs much of the stress and may shatter during an earthquake but the structure will not fall. These houses in Mandi district are about 60-70 years old.

### *Pherols*

After the 1991 Uttarkashi earthquake, some engineers with the representatives from the Peoples' Science Institute visited the affected regions and conducted a study of how the countryside housing stock had fared in the earthquake. They noticed that Uttarkashi's *pherols*, some of which were over a century old, had survived (yet another) earthquake. Overwhelmed by this fact, the team conducted a detailed study on how these remarkable structures were resistant to earthquakes. According to the findings of this study, *pherols* bear strong resemblance to *kath-ki-kuni* architecture in Himachal Pradesh, especially in the use of heavy slate roofs, thick walls, wooden tie-bands, corner bracing, multi-storeyed construction and the geometry and functions of different parts of the building. As mentioned above, the parallels suggest that these indigenous construction techniques were closely tied to the cultural and social conditions of these regions and they also have in common the use of locally available materials (for details see Chopra *et al.* 1993).

## TECHNOLOGICAL TRANSITIONS AND SUSTAINABILITY

The aseismic construction techniques described above are all in a state of decline in the western-central Himalayas. With the advent of new economies, social and demographic changes and perhaps most importantly, cultural changes, the people of this region are increasingly moving away from traditional architecture. The common perception of old rural houses of stone, wood and mud construction as *kuccha* and the new RCC as *pucca* or stronger is ubiquitous among villagers in the region. In Kullu and Manali old *kath-ki-kuni* houses are surrounded by new multi-storeyed RCC, fuelled by the tourism industry and immigrants from Delhi, Punjab and other parts of the country. In villages all over the region, people want houses with concrete slab roofs; and cement and steel continue to penetrate deeper into the heart of the hills, backed by aggressive advertising by cement companies, government programmes and even voluntary organizations. The advertising of cement with images of once backward villages beginning to prosper and develop with the use of cement presents a commentary on the perception of old versus new. The woman in Manali who related her grandfather's story about showing reverence while entering traditional houses explained that in modern times men do not want to bow their heads to anyone, and so their houses also have high door frames which show this change in attitude.

It may not be so far-fetched to draw a parallel between this arrogance and the transition to cement construction. One of the highly-touted values of cement construction is its high compressive strength and the rigidity it adds to a structure (Langenbach 1986). While the correct use of cement with the correct complement of materials and building architecture do make for a strong, earthquake-resistant structure, the very same qualities in rural, non-engineered structures may lead to increased damage to the structure instead. For example, in the *dhajji-diwari* construction where weak mud bricks are used in the walls, the compressive strength of cement exceeds that of the bricks and during an earthquake these bricks may shatter first instead of the cement mortar; as a result, the wall may even collapse. As opposed to the rigidity of engineered cement and concrete structures, the strength of rural aseismic housing is its flexibility and capacity to yield and release strain while reducing the risk of critical failure. While the use of new materials is warranted and beneficial in many ways, it is important to remember the context of their use. These are new materials that indigenous masons do not have any experience working with, and this leads either to inappropriate techniques of use or reliance on outside masons, who do not have much sensitivity to the particular needs of hill architecture.

The maligning and systematic abandonment of traditional and indigenous construction techniques is a great loss. In a conversation with a mason of the Thavin caste, whose traditional craft was constructing *kath-ki-kuni* houses, we learned that a major reason this knowledge is being lost is the lack of access to local resources, which are essential for such construction. Timber and slate are particularly difficult to procure due to government restrictions and no effort is made to keep these construction practices alive and evolve them with newer technology.

But there have been some efforts to revive and adapt these traditional construction practices and aesthetics. Didi Contractor, an architect in Sidhbari village near Dharamsala has been working to preserve and adapt many of the principles of traditional construction in some 18 houses and a clinic that she has designed and built in the village. She has trained local masons in these construction techniques by combining their knowledge and working to improve upon several techniques of construction. For example, in the roofs and storey of some of these houses, she has combined bamboo and ferro cement. She has also worked on techniques to improve the durability of this construction. She is using new materials like epoxy resins with old ones (like cow-dung and mud) in the plastering and also she has introduced the new methods of treating bamboo to increase its life in the construction. These houses offer many more wonderful innovations such as the use of passive solar elements, solar heaters, aseismic elements using bamboo, wood and steel in reinforcements. Her work with local materials and artisans means that the local economy and society capture over 80 per cent of the economic activity in the construction. This is in contrast with RCC where the majority of economic activity is captured by external agents. Ms. Contractor's work in Sidhbari is an inspiring example of how traditional practices still have so much to offer for modern housing and its inherent nature of adaptability offers a promise of new life.

## CONCLUSION

In an environment fraught with constant threats of earthquakes, landslides and extreme climatic conditions, indigenous and traditional construction technologies remain valuable even today. The myth of the infallibility of RCC has been shattered with earthquakes all over the world showing that these buildings suffer as much damage as the old ones and can also fail. At the same time, local materials and local knowledge can be developed to incorporate new materials and adapt to new social, economic and cultural conditions. Losing the rich traditions of indigenous architecture would not just be an unfortunate loss but a potentially devastating mistake.

## ACKNOWLEDGEMENTS

I would like to thank Randall Sanderson for his assistance in the documentation for and preparation of this paper. I am also deeply grateful for the valuable time and guidance offered by Didi Contractor and Ajit Kumar of the Dhauladhar Public Education Society. Their assistance in identifying sites for visit and in giving information about the structures made this study possible. I would also like to thank P.P. Raina and the staff of the Kullu-Manali Town & Country Planning Department and Keval Ram Sironta of LKAVM, Karsog for assistance.

## BIBLIOGRAPHY

Arya, A.S. 1990. 'Damage Scenario of a Hypothetical 8.0 Magnitude Earthquake in Kangra Region of Himachal Pradesh', *Bull. Ind. Soc. Earthq. Tech.* 297, 27 (3): 121-32.

Bilham, R. *et al.* 2001. 'Himalayan Seismic Hazard', *Science* 293: 1442-44.

Middlemiss, C.S. 1910. 'The Kangra Earthquake of 4th April, 1905', *Memoirs of the Geological Survey of India,* 37.

Chopra, R. *et al.* 1993. *Earthquake-Resistant Traditional Architecture in Uttarkashi*. Dehradun: People's Science Institute.

Fitch, T.J. 1970. 'Earthquake Mechanisms in the Himalayan, Burmese, and Andaman Regions and Continental Tectonics', *Central Asia Jour. Geophys. Res.* 75: 2699-2709.

Indian Society of Earthquake Technology (ISET). 1989. *A Manual of Earthquake Resistant Non-Engineered Construction.* Roorkee.

Langenbach, R. 1986. *The Uses of Masonry in Earthquake Zones: A Perspective on Traditional and Contemporary Construction Practices Utilizing Un-reinforced Masonry.* Berkeley: University of California.

Le-Pinchon, X. 1968. 'Sea Floor Spreading and Continental Drift', *Jour. Geophys. Res.* 73: 3661-97.

7

# Traditional Indian Iron Technology

## Problems and Prospects

Vibha Tripathi

### INTRODUCTION

Iron technology in India has a glorious tradition dating back to the second millennium BC. One can trace almost an uninterrupted history of metallurgical excellence, especially in iron, working right up to the British times. India produced the best iron and steel in the ancient world carving out a niche for itself in the annals of history of metallurgy. As early as fifth century BC, the Greek ambassador to India was presented with steel swords that were recorded with appreciation by contemporary historians. Alexander, in the next century, also received gifts of iron ingots and swords along with items like gold dust and other precious items as a tribute. The wootz steel that was marketed in the ancient world as Damascus steel originated in India. Some of the more important examples of ancient metallurgical skills still surviving today are the Delhi iron pillar, the Konark and the Dhar beams of extraordinary weight and length. The ancient Indian iron technologists thus earned a name for themselves due to the excellent iron metallurgical skills they possessed.

One wonders whether the technology disappeared without leaving a legacy behind. The metallurgical processes known to the artisans hold the key to understanding of this question. The intricacies of this craft need to be fully understood and recorded. This may be achieved with the help of those societies that could manage to preserve and protect the technique for centuries. This they have done against great odds. To locate them and to see whether they still have the technical know-how is a difficult if not an impossible task. A study of iron working technique of the traditional societies is being attempted here with a view to underline the metallurgical specification of their working, environment, mode of resource management and methods adopted by them to ensure a regular and uninterrupted supply of these resources through customs or inbuilt socio-cultural norms. The techno-cultural and economic viability of iron working by these societies under the present circumstances may be worked out in the end. It may be apt to take a quick look at the iron working as practised by the Agarias of Sarguja, Chhattisgarh and Rourkela districts and those of Netarhat plateau of Bihar as a backdrop of our inquiry. However, the tenacity of the people engaged in this craft helped in its survival in some remote areas. Though it is almost dead today but a close survey of those regions where it flourished in the past, one may still find some groups vaguely familiar with their ancestral craft. The present discussion is focused around them.

## AN OVERVIEW OF TRADITIONAL IRON TECHNOLOGY

The British period records, time and again mention the thriving industry of iron making in different parts of India right up to eighteenth-nineteenth century. The sword of Tipu Sultan made news recently. The British engineers tried to examine and analyse the indigenously produced iron and steel to test its quality. To cite a few examples, Captain Presgrieve of Sagar mint tested the iron being produced at Tendukhera near Hoshangabad. He reported, "...bar iron of most excellent quality, possessing all the desirable properties of malleability, ductility at different temperatures and of tenacity for all of which I think, it cannot be surpassed by the best Swedish iron; the Agaria piece ...when brought to bend, it showed itself possessing the power of elongating ...and stood bend better than the general run of English iron purchased in the bazaar...." Similarly, McWilliams tested the iron produced at Mirjati in 1918 at Tata Steel, Jamshedpur and also in the laboratory at Sheffield. He too arrived at a similar conclusion. He classified the Agaria iron as mild steel possessing varying degrees of carbon such as 0.26, 0.3-0.68 and 0.78 per cent in various objects. His comments in this context are significant indeed, "It appears that in his simple bloomery the Agaria smelter could get various grades of iron by controlling the process".

But this technical skill, which the contemporary British or Swedish artisan could not match, almost vanished because of the variety of impediments that were created in the way of production of iron by framing unfavourable laws.

Due to a variety of constraints, the ironworkers have either discontinued working or moved to interior and inaccessible terrains to live and continue iron production. This could partially be attributed to the British who came heavily on such groups. Their finished goods were confiscated; the weapons they produced were destroyed, albeit with great difficulty. The final blow to the traditional iron technology was dealt with firstly, by framing hostile laws and secondly, by flooding the Indian market with cheap imported British pig iron.

Though iron working has survived in certain other parts of the country like the hills of Kumaon and Garhwal but to the best of my knowledge, only smithy is being carried out with scrap metal in these parts of India. It may be stated at the outset that the basic technique of smelting remains the same but for minor variations in most of the areas where it has survived.

## TRADITIONAL IRON WORKING

Before we sit on judgment on this ancient craft, debating its merits and demerits, it may be proper to examine the iron working and the precise nature of traditional technology.

The first step of iron working of pre-industrial smelting, naturally, is locating the right kind of ore and its procurement. Generally, the Agaria community resides in close proximity to ore deposits. It perhaps saves time and energy. It is well known that iron deposits are profusely distributed in India, therefore, not much deep digging is required. Nodules are picked up from the surface by the Agarias who have a very good understanding of the types. The surface exposed by the rain gullies or *nullahs* are favourite spots for ore collection. Each trip to such areas covering about 15-20 sq. km ensures enough ore for 4-5 days of smelting. Incidentally, most of these groups including Agarias of Wadruffnagar and Sarguja prefer low-grade ores like limonite and goethite. The Chhattisgarh Agarias, however, prefer hematite. Those living in Pratappur block of Wardruffnagar prefer magnetic river-sand. As raw material, they feel it is much superior and purer being free from gangue and yield what is locally called *charka loha* or "white metal" of high quality. The most significant point about the mining activity of such groups is that it is usually shallow. This fact is in contrast with the modern mining that vitiates the environment as it results into the fines. During the rainy season, the dust gets washed down to the rivers and pollutes the water too. In contrast, the traditional way of handpicking is eco-friendly and least damaging to ecology and surface form.

Crushing, cleaning, winnowing and roasting painstakingly, they prepare the ore thus procured. Sanctity pervades the Agaria workshop. The process of smelting is preceded by ritualistic offering to *Lohasur, Agayasur, Koelasur,* etc. with a prayer for a successful conclusion of smelting. The traditional steel working is a three-tier process, viz. smelting, forging and smithy. The smelting takes place in small clay furnaces raising temperatures up to 1200°-1300°C lasting approximately 4-5 hours. The temperature however is merely distributed through the furnace. It is up to 1500° in tuyere zone and temperature is lower on the upper section of furnace. It yields a red-hot bloom, a spongy mass with plenty of slag inclusions in the matrix of iron. This bloom is worked again in open hearths by building the temperature up to 750°-780°C. A repeated heating and hammering imparts the ingot homogeneity and compactness. The wrought iron also imbibes some carbon due to its prolonged contact with charcoal adding to its quality and strength. Further contact with charcoal fire in course of smithy raises the carbon content, especially on the working edges adding to its quality. The objects prepared thus are very much in demand in the local market because of its durability, ductility and capacity to provide better and longer lasting working edges.

A comparison of the indigenous iron with the one produced by the British or Swedish companies engaged in the work, as pointed above, proved the superiority of the former type. It is meaningless to elaborate on the high quality of the indigenous iron in view of above observations. We may only add a couple of points here to reinstate the superiority of the traditional iron product over industrially produced iron. For instance, the indigenously manufactured iron takes care of two basic irritants of modern steel, i.e. sulphur and phosphorus. It is attributed to use of charcoal for low sulphur and to lower temperature for manganese content, according to the report published by the Indian Institute of Technology (IIT). If Delhi iron pillar could be a guide, it has a greater corrosion resistance. Till date wherever iron working is surviving as a cottage industry, it is in greater demand for traditional tools in preference to factory-produced implements. This speaks for itself so far as the quality of the steel is concerned. This possibly is the cause why the traditional iron making could survive against all odds in some remote areas.

The issue, which deserve a serious consideration, here is whether it is technologically feasible, ecologically balanced and economically viable in the present day context. I will examine these points first before discussing the issue of revival of the technology to the level of profitability and productivity of the commodity.

## Technical Feasibility

We have just now examined the nature of traditional iron working as it survives in certain remote parts of the country. We have also noted the superior nature of the product coming out of the small furnaces operated by these workers. Yet there appears to be a need to take a fresh look at the technological feasibility of this product because of the changing politico-cultural and socio-ecological constraints.

It has been alleged that the traditional iron making is wasteful both from the point of view of raw material, i.e. ore as well as consumption of charcoal which entails destruction and depletion of forest reserves, a precious resource today.

In view of these facts we have to re-examine the traditional working for its alleged shortcomings. There is, however, a need to take a fresh look at the problem in view of the changing circumstances. We need to weigh afresh the pros and cons of our policies and the outcome thereof after 50-55 years. In this context the alleged wastefulness of the resource needs to be reviewed.

However, responding to the first of above two allegations we have to remember that our calculation, however, ignores the fact that first, these ethnic societies are tapping those ores, which are many a time rated low grade and not considered worth smelting by modern steel mills. Second, significantly, they also locate and exploit those mail pockets of ore deposits, which have not even been recorded in geological texts while listing economically viable mining zones. In our considered opinion it is maximization of resource utilization. We have already described the gentle way of ore picking by these groups. Third, as pointed above, mining by these groups does not result into fines, which are a source of pollution caused by the steel plants. Fourth, it may be emphasized in this context that they also make use of magnetic sand from rivers. Thus they utilize a discarded material, which would otherwise be washed away and wasted. Can there be a better example of human enterprise in the modern world?

Thus by no standards this working may be called extravagant, so far as the utilization of ores is concerned. We may return to this a little later.

The second allegation relates to the heavy exploitation of forest for charcoal. What has been ignored in our calculations however is that there are taboos, sanctions, socio-religious prohibitions against indiscriminate cutting of trees. Mostly charcoal is made with dead trees lying in the forests. The trees in the jungle are conceived to be the abode of deities or ancestor spirits bestowing welfare upon the people. Inviting their wrath pronounces doom. If a fire breaks out in the forest, around Dhenkanal in Orissa every family has to participate in putting out the fire or else face social sanctions, inform Fernandes *et al.* (1988). On the basis of their study in specific context of Orissa, they further reiterate the economic measures taken by such groups in use of forest resources. The Agaria families of Chhattisgarh and Chhotanagpur that visit the jungle for coal burning collect, pile and burn the wood and bring back "Sal" leaves to use as plates for meals. But the number of leaves a family can bring is rationed. Even leaves cannot be plucked indiscriminately or carelessly, what to speak of trees? They have a sanctity, honour and respect for the trees in general. It is this kind of fully internalized respect for nature, especially trees that helped the survival of both the traditional industries as well as forests. Maximum threat to the forest has been posed by indiscriminate felling and scavenging of trees in recent years when the tribes were dispossessed and displaced from their age-old habitat. Both the jungle and the man have suffered due to this so-called modernization or "acculturation" process.

In this light one can say that our view of traditional technology appears to be superfluous. The technology, however, has suffered first at the hands of the British and subsequently by the planners of the independent India. If the traditional art of steel making has survived albeit on a small scale, there must be some reasons for it. We need to look into them. The other reason that is perhaps more urgent is that our planning in this direction has not yielded desirable results and reconsideration of earlier policies becomes essential for survival of the human race. We cannot retrace our steps altogether but we can positively modify and accommodate what we had discarded as of little significance. Some calculations may, however, be made here in support of our contention.

Though charcoal is the most difficult commodity in today's context yet this can be resolved by giving 20-25 hectare land between 10 and 12 villages for survival and revival of an ancient industry. This will ensure a decent living, job opportunity, stability and the revival of a high quality product of immense techno-cultural value to India. It can help in the preservation of cultural ecology in an otherwise endangered social set-up involving a fairly large population. Besides this, in the longer run this may also help in revival of forests and its products (which are now vanishing fast). Thus it will ensure a more stable ecosystem or ecological balance – both natural and cultural. The same sort of argument is also put forward by a group of metallurgical engineers of IIT Bombay who worked on the problem of revival of indigenous iron and steel technologies of India (Ballal *et al.* 1993).

## Ecological Viability

On the basis of the aforesaid, it may be reiterated that in the present time of ecological crisis, the traditional craft in general can play a crucial role in saving the environment and making it pollution free. In an attempt to evaluate the traditional technology and its suitability, it may be apt to weigh the cost of these crafts against the ecological cost of modern steel plants. There are several conspicuous factors, and some of these are being enumerated below.

The traditional iron working is in the nature of small-scale household industries distributed over a wide area. Resource exploitation of these workings therefore is shallow, expanding over an extensive area. Thus both the ore and fuel used by these industries are not damaging in true sense. We have talked above in greater details about the ore deposits. The charcoal as the source of energy is far less a pollutant in comparison to fossil fuel burnt in modern steel plants. Coal or fossil fuel produces carcinogenic by-products. The acute polluting effects have resulted in the ban-on installations of new ovens in the developed countries. Charcoal (having low sulphur content), on the other hand is not a pollutant. Besides, the small furnaces are less damaging to the atmosphere. We have also shown above that the cost of wood can be met by systematic regeneration of the fuel by plantation on waste lands which will also act as catalyst for promotion of better ecological conditions in the surrounding regions. We need not enumerate the advantages of forest, which are self-evident to all.

Taking the clue from the traditional iron working, modern metallurgists (like Gupta 1997) are engaged in experiments to produce steel with biomass as a residue and presented such facts and figures, which indicate the hazardous results of modern steel plants classified as heavy industry. Thus even the modern metallurgists are taking inspiration from the traditional workers in using renewable resources because of its advantages.

## Economic Viability and Revival of Technology

We have considered the status of the resource management and the ecological advantages of the traditional iron working. In a general way, the data presented above leads us to construe that the traditional craft of iron making has an economic viability in the present context. If we compare the small-scale industries with the mechanized mass productions, this is incommensurable. The native techno-systems are prone to wilt and wither under the aggressive onslaught of mass production of modern technology. Could there be a comparison between the hand spinning and weaving of looms and cloth mills? Yet the weaving is protected, facilitated and subsidized. This kind of sympathetic attitude towards a few selected handicrafts is discriminatory. Is this favour primarily due to the sizeable population and their politically volatile nature? There is scope for several other traditional crafts to be brought under the purview of similar consideration.

There are many angles to the issue of promotion of traditional iron technology. The tribals are a politically disempowered community. They have been rendered homeless from their familiar surroundings on the pretext of being exploitative of forest and its products. This premise is basically wrong. One can go on quoting statistics that the felling of forest trees for the industrial uses is many times more exploitative and reckless than that of the original forest dwellers and their lifestyle. The latter have a deep respect for nature and if at all they need to cut, care is generally taken to leave behind the roots and shoots to ensure regrowth. They have had a symbiotic relationship with nature and have also been guardians of forests for generations. If this fact is realized and the tribals are left alone or if need be helped, they would ensure regeneration of a precious resource while earning their livelihood too.

Today when we have to move from the phrase of big is beautiful to "small is beautiful" as stated by Schumacher (1973), the small furnaces of the traditional smelters are not only eco-friendly but with a bit of incentive and assistance may become economically viable.

The value of the pure iron is far more in comparison to standard factory produced pig iron. The rust free 90-98 per cent pure iron that is low in sulphur and other corrosive ingredients may be used in several vital areas including defence. Instead of importing such iron, it may be produced indigenously by those adept in this art with a little incentive.

## CONCLUSION

So far there has been one view of technological development: adoption of western, energy intensive and highly centralized mega technologies on the basis of their techno-economic advantages. They have been earning profit for individuals or organizations. However, the problems created by them have been collective and global. This phenomenon is now well recognized as the "tragedy of the commons". Last few decades have seen a growth of alternative philosophies for industrial production in movements like "appropriate technology" and "small is beautiful".

We need to review our industrial policy after over 50 years of independence. The native techno-systems that have withered away under the aggressive onslaught of mass production have to be given their chance. The politically and culturally disempowered communities of specialized craftsmen have to be given a sympathetic treatment as well as government encouragement, incentive and patronage. This has already been done for certain communities like weavers. Several other craft groups need similar consideration. Iron worker's community is one of the important groups awaiting their turn.

These communities have been dispossessed of their habitat and thrown into an alien world without being equipped to face the harsh new world. They have been deprived of their traditional means of livelihood. Since we are now realizing the potential of their craft and viability of their technological skills, this has to be given a new lease of life. The western world is refusing the setting up of new steel industries because of the carcinogenic fumes emanating from the furnace. In view of this, these smaller furnaces distributed over a larger area may be an asset as less polluting industry. It may not be capable of replacing modern blast furnaces but can indeed supplement and complement it. Besides, it will open job avenues to a deprived community.

There is a fair possibility of applying advanced scientific and technological research tools in improving the traditional ways of metalworking. It may be possible to "engraft" such changes without interference in the acceptable socio-technical system of the traditional societies. It is never too late to rethink and review our policies for social, cultural and ecological well-being of all. It will be a multi-pronged policy-benefiting the people who have been deprived of their means of livelihood, a techno-cultural recognition of their expertize and economic independence to these communities in their familiar surroundings. At the same time it is bound to benefit the cultural and physical ecology. Simultaneously, it will help reinvent our cultural heritage with a glorious past.

## BIBLIOGRAPHY

Ballal, *et al.* 1993. *Draft Report on Indigenous Iron and Steel Technology of India*. Bombay: IIT.

Deo, S.B. and A.P. Jamkhedkar. 1982. *Excavations at Naikund*. Nagpur University.

Elwin, V. 1942. *The* Agaria. London.

Fernandes, W. and G. Menon. 1988. 'Forest, Environment and Tribal Economy', *Tribes of India Series*: 168.

Franklin, J. 1829. *The Mode of Manufacturing Iron in Central India: Indian Science and Technology in 18th Century*. Hyderabad: Academy of Gandhian Studies.

Gupta, R.C. 1997. *Eco-friendly Metal Smelting Technology Over the Centuries*. Paper presented in the conference on Ecological History and Tradition, Centre for Science and Environment, New Delhi.

Hegde, K.T.M. 1991. 'An Introduction to Ancient Indian Metallurgy', *Geological Society of India*: 40-50.

McWilliam. 1920. 'Indian Iron Making at Mirjati, Chhotanagpur', *Journal of Iron and Steel*.

Prakash, B. and V. Tripathi. 1986. 'Iron Technology in Ancient India', *Metals and Materials, Historical Metallurgy*, London.

Sharma, G.R. 1960-61. *Excavations at Kaushambi*, Allahabad.

Tiwari, R. 1998. 'In Quest of Early Iron Age Sites in Karamnasa Valley', *Pragdhara* 8: 57-67.

Tripathi, V. 1990. 'Origin and Development of Iron in India and its Economic Implications' in *History of Science and Technology*, G. Kuppuram and K. Kumudmani (eds.). New Delhi: Sandeep Prakashan.

——. 1993. 'Prachin Bharat Mein Lauh Yug', in *Vishwadriti* (Vols. I &V), Venkatachalan (ed.). Sampurnanand Comm. Vol., Varanasi.

——. 2002. 'The Age of Iron in India – A Reappraisal', *Indian Archaeology in Retrospect, Prehistory Archaeology of South Asia*, Vol. I: 287-312.

Tripathi, V. and A. Tripathi. 1994. 'Iron Working in Ancient India: An Ethno-archaeological Study', *Wisconsim Archaeological Report*, 3: 241-51.

# 8

# *Lokavidya*: Conceptualizing People's Housing in India

## A Case Study of the Koch-Rajbansis of North Bengal

Smriti Kumar Sarkar

### INTRODUCTION

Housing represents a basic requirement of human society since the early period of its transition. An index of one's material attainments, the housing was an important means of achieving status, hence a matrix of studying the mobility process of different social groups in a historical perspective. At the same time, it has a conceptual structure too; hence a history of its own. As in other fields, however, the housing in India has been studied mostly with reference to the structure of archaeological and architectural importance – the building and palace built with durable materials by emperors, kings and the elite. The important question as to what were the types of houses used by the common people that were most often built with less durable and locally available materials; why has this largely escaped the earlier research attention?

Does it mean that these houses were built without conceptualizing their utility, long-term stability and adaptability to the local ecological conditions whatsoever? Yet the majority of Indian population lived in these houses. This is an attempt to explore the people's technique of house building and understand its rationale in a relatively backward region of our country. The source materials necessary for a study of this nature being extremely fragmentary, hence what follows here is, largely explorative in character, based on a methodology only infrequently used so far in the field of historical research. The people's housing is an important aspect of traditional knowledge available at the lower levels of society described here as the *lokavidya*.

## CONCEPT OF *LOKAVIDYA*

*Lokavidya* denotes the knowledge, which was invoked, preserved and used by people for their everyday use. It can also be described as the working knowledge of the individuals without formal education, hence quite distinct from the institutional knowledge or the *pratisthanik vidya*. The term *loka* is often used to mean *loukik* or the material world as opposed to the *paraloukik* that is the world beyond. In that sense, the *lokavidya* seems to suggest the knowledge, which primarily deals with materialism as opposed to spiritualism or the higher strata of human knowledge. Hence, the term "*lokayata* had been used to mean not only the philosophy of the people but also the philosophy of this-worldliness or materialism" (Chattopadhyay 1978: 3).

The *lokavidya,* therefore, refers to the collective wisdom inherited and applied by people in understanding the material world and in formulating their actions accordingly. The *pratisthanik vidya,* based on the systems developed over a long period of time, was mostly distinguished by an uninterrupted continuity, while the *lokavidya* systems mostly passed on unrecorded. In the true Indian tradition of *parampara,* the *lokavidya* was inherited by people, sometimes lost in the process and was invoked again, may be in an altogether different form, from their experience of everyday life and empirical observations unlike the institutional knowledge. Such *vidya* widely differed from region to region. Hence, it was much more adaptable to the local conditions and had a very wide support base. In reality, the *lokavidya* actually suggests both the extent and continuity of our material tradition at the lower levels of society in particular.

Traditionally, there existed a process of adjustment between the institutional knowledge and the widely varied structures of what we call the *lokavidya* today. The introduction of the western system of education in India during the colonial period struck at the root of the systems of *lokavidya* tradition, interrupting the process of adjustment between knowledge evolved at the upper and the lower levels. In some cases, colonial rule had imposed upon people such systems of knowledge which were often alien to the local conditions. The notion of filtration, that is knowledge introduced at the top would interact and percolate down to lower levels benefiting all sections of society in the long run, did not work. There was hardly any attempt to make it acceptable to people at the bottom of society, or to understand the structure of their traditional knowledge base.

## METHODOLOGY

The feasibility of a study of this nature within the parameters of the existing historical research is often questioned on the plea of non-availability of data. Yet much of the ethno-historical evidence left by European observers of the early colonial period could help us in reconstructing this knowledge base. Without these enterprising, dedicated and pioneering observers, our present-day knowledge of India's pre-colonial past would have been immeasurably poor. Nevertheless, on a close scrutiny it appears, European evidence concealed more than it actually revealed. Many things stood in their way-the foreign observer's power and position, his upbringing as well as his cultural background. The method of their compilation also partly accounted for their limitations. For, the information must have been either first hand or received from their interpreters. In case of the first hand information, relevant cultural–ecological barriers had in most cases forced European observer to look from a "distance", while the interpreter's own conjectures and notions used to prejudice the alternative source of information.

Compared to European evidence, a different perspective of traditional knowledge is available in the indigenous literature arising out of the inquiries into India's past. This indigenous literature had been encouraged firstly by the growth of a consciousness of nationalism in India and then by the emergence of caste/community-based solidarity movements since the early nineteenth century. However, the indigenous literature is also not without its limitations, which has been widely discussed in the recent years with regard to nationalist historiography. Similarly, the data found in caste literature often does not corroborate with the empirical evidence. Notwithstanding these limitations, what is unique of such literature is its extremely rich collection of local usage retrieved largely from contemporary oral traditions. Available in the different parts of India, this extremely useful vernacular evidence has only been infrequently used so far in historical studies in general.

Exploring the domain of the common man's knowledge simply by depending on evidence mostly used in historical research is difficult because it is difficult to know as to what were his notions of the problems he encountered or how did he solve them? There may be two ways of looking at his mind, the rationale between his means and action. Usually, an individual at the bottom of society is projected primarily as a receiver of the knowledge evolved at the higher level in an otherwise integrated structure. He has, therefore, only a passive role in either evolving or improving the quantum of knowledge that descends, his relative position thus being dependent on the nature of social mobility.

The other way is to explore the knowledge at the popular level from the viewpoint of their actual users. Under this scheme, it is believed that the individual working at the lower level not only understands his problem but also has a preconceived notion of executing his work. All these involved a good deal of calculations and measurements mostly made in the actual user's working language and gestures, handed down to generations in the *parampara* (tradition). Analyzing the common man's perception of his work in the light of oral history, myths and legends, supported by fieldwork among the still-surviving backward social clusters in different parts of India, could go a long way in reconstructing traditional knowledge. This is a highly neglected field of work, which requires urgent attention of scholars looking for an alternative approach to the present-day dominant research tradition. It is a difficult task by any measure, since thinking of an "alternative" might sound ethnic in these days of universal model.

It is this methodology that has been used here to analyse the relatively unknown area of the people's housing with reference to the Koch-Rajbansi people. Dalton (1872) found them extremely "numerous" in the ancient Kamrupa region comprising the lower Assam, northern-most parts of Bengal, Rangpur, Purnea and extending west as far as the boundary of the ancient Mithila with their nucleus in the kingdom of Kuch Bihar (Dalton 1872: 89).

## PEOPLE'S HOUSING IN INDIA: AN OUTLINE

The traditional pattern of people's housing in India can be divided into three broad categories – rectangular ground plan with horizontal roof, rectangular ground plan with inclined roof and circular ground plan with conical roof. Houses with horizontal roof were found mainly in the low rainfall regions–south-western Kashmir, most of the Punjab, most of Rajasthan (excluding the eastern districts), parts of Uttar Pradesh, Madhya Pradesh and Maharashtra. In south India, horizontal roof-top houses were limited only to some parts of the present day Andhra Pradesh and Karnataka. Houses with horizontal roof could be further subdivided into the northern and southern types in conformity with their layout, i.e. the existence or non-existence of courtyard and its location. The way the roof was made and the materials used in them also varied from region to region.

The rectangular ground plan with inclined roof represents the most common type of people's housing in India. Found in the high to medium rainfall regions, these houses can be distinguished into some major groups according to the shape and slope of their roof, their layout and the materials used in constructing them. Primarily people at a very low level of social development used the houses with circular ground plan and conical roof. These houses were more of a temporary nature, which could easily be removed and relocated to a new site, often at short notice. In the late nineteenth century, nomadic groups like the Birhors of Chhotanagpur and Orissa, the Chenchus of Andhra Pradesh, the Mer, Wagri, and Rabbri of Saurashtra and Kutch; and Kauras of Tamil Nadu lived in these type of houses.

Looking at an all-India perspective, therefore, the average Koch-Rajbansi house thus conforms to the predominant Indian pattern of rectangular ground plan with inclined roof. Within this large group again, the Koch-Rajbansi house subscribes to the convex roof type of the Bengal cottage. In Bengal, the ridge pole and the whole surface of the slopes are convex, so that the ends of the eaves come close to the ground and entrance can be had at the centre where it is high. This particular kind of curved roof has a beauty of its own and was widely copied in stone and brick balconies of the Mughal and Rajput buildings. Hence, this roof style was known in north India as *Bangali chhatri* or the Bengali roof (Biswas and Behura 1961).

Thus, while the rectangular ground plan with inclined roof suggests a continuity of the broad Indian tradition in the Koch-Rajbansi housing, the convex roof style indicates its uniformity with the predominant type of eastern India. Nevertheless, the way the walls were constructed and the material used in them, distinguished the Koch-Rajbansi housing from the houses widely found in Bengal. Three broad influences contributed to making of the Koch-Rajbansi culture. Most important of them came from the north-east, far beyond the Brahmaputra, Barak, and even the Manipur basins. There was also the influence of the trans-Himalayan region and the influence of the Indian heartland areas. These influences could clearly be distinguished in the ethnic composition of the Koch-Rajbansi population, their culture and folk traditions in the main society.

## HISTORICAL PERSPECTIVE OF KOCH-RAJBANSI HOUSING

The historical background to development of the Koch-Rajbansi concept of housing was a two-way transition of indigenous society. For the groups existing at the lower levels of this society, this transition characterized a straightaway jump from the pastoral nomadic to the village-based settled agricultural life. But for most others, this was a transition from the earlier form of shifting agriculture with rudimentary tools to the plough-based wetland cultivation of rice.

It has been broadly agreed upon that Koch-Rajbansi society's transition from the hoe to plough-based agriculture took place sometime in the sixteenth century. A transition to settled village life and an increasing shift to the cultivation of wet rice had accompanied this. The result was the emergence of a cluster of local leaders based on land control.

### Early Phase

The historical pattern of the development of Koch-Rajbansi housing concept can hardly be determined with any amount of certainty. Nevertheless, certain broad patterns could be distinguished in order to understand the transition of this technique from its early phase to the later development by easy stages.

As in the case of similar other primitive tribes, houses used by people in the early stage of their pastoral nomadic life must have been built with an eye to meet their immediate needs. Mostly made of readily available materials of less durable nature, these were generally mono-room structures with broad opening on the one side to facilitate herding of domestic animals. Using separate enclosure for domestic animals was a later development. The limitation of their tool technique must have discouraged them to use timber necessary for constructing the truss capable of bearing heavy load of the roof made either of stone or tree planks.

This explains as to why people at this stage used small houses mostly with circular or semicircular ground plan having low height roof. If the nineteenth century literature on nomadic tribal clusters found in other regions of India, north-east in particular, could be used as evidence, the structure of their house at this stage varied from hemispherical to conical hut. The latter were usually of two types – low houses with low walls and those with relatively high walls and the exact variety depended on the climatic conditions and the materials available in the region. These houses were characterized by their predominant uniformity in circular ground plan.

With this theoretical construction, let us try to suggest the type of houses used by primitive groups, somewhere in a process of transition from pastoral nomadic life to the shifting agriculture.

The important point, which deserves attention here, is the existence of some Koch-Rajbansi sub-castes distinguished by the type of houses they lived in. In the early twentieth century accounts of the Koch-Rajbansi people, we come across groups like the Khoprias, Gobrias and the Tongias. Since this type of sub-caste formation has a direct relevance to the theme of the present discussion, a little elaboration of the point would be useful at this stage (Risley 1891).

The Khoprias built small huts with conical or hemispherical roofs, mostly with a circular ground plan. The term Khopria has a phonetic resonance with the word *Khupri* meaning a small room of eastern Indian origin. This is clearly indicative of an influence of the house building technique coming from that region. However, one thing is certain that the people living in this type of houses were in a process of transition from the earlier methods of shifting cultivation to a relatively more settled form of agriculture. On the other hand, the Gobrias (derived from the term Go meaning cattle) were identified on the basis that they shared their houses with their animals, an indication of their pastoral status. These houses were found mainly in northern part of the Koch-Rajbansi territory, and probably built under the influence of similar other nomadic tribes living in the lower Himalayan region.

The Tongias lived in houses built on a horizontal platform set upon poles driven into the ground. From the observer's point of view, therefore, their houses were constructed on *Tong*, which in the local language suggests an artificially raised height. The term *Tong* is neither Sanskrit nor a proto-Bengali word, hence must have been of an origin external to this region. This is supported by anthropological observation regarding the absence of similar houses in other parts of India, and their occurrence among tribal population of north-eastern India. An origin in Southeast Asia, however, could be a good guess. The Koch-Rajbansi term Tongia has, therefore, closer phonetic similarity with the Myanmar word *Taungya* meaning the traditional form of shifting cultivation practised in the thickly wooded hilly areas with a very high rainfall (Hwa 1968). The compulsions of limited resources and the uneven hilly ground must have forced them to build their houses on poles. The burning down of forest for land clearing at regular intervals gave them ample supplies of good timber for the purpose.

The technique had travelled into north-eastern India through cultural contacts, favoured by its topography and climatic conditions. The nineteenth century evidence on this region frequently refers to the Tongia-type house on poles, of which the Garo house perhaps remains the best example. Similarly, the Miris in the Brahmaputra basin lived in the house, locally known as *chang garh*, or the house built usually on the banks of the river with raised floors and space underneath for the pigs, poultry, etc. The bottom plan of these houses was usually rectangular with inclined rooftop. Their construction suggests an improvement in the tool technique, compared to the house used by pastoral nomadic groups (Dalton 1872).

However, the existence of a number of Koch-Rajbansi sub-castes named after the type of their houses suggests that these were exceptions to the type of houses more usually found in this region. In the eyes of the local people, therefore, social groups like the Khoprias, Gobrias and the Tongias actually marked a departure from the predominant practice of the land. This is largely true even if we accept it as an account by an external observer. Finally, from the point of view of the development of Koch-Rajbansi housing concept, types of houses used by the Khoprias, Gobrias, and the Tongias seem to suggest a process of systematic development of the house building technique in this region, encouraged, among other things, by the upward mobility of social groups.

### Later Phase

For the later development of the Koch-Rajbansi housing we have more definite information. Buchanan (1833) in the early nineteenth century had described the homestead of a well-to-do man of this region generally consisting of eight or nine small huts within an enclosure and that of the husbandman of six or seven huts. Each of these huts was usually of the size of 15 to 20 feet long and about 7½ to 13 feet broad. Many of the well-to-do cultivators had more substantial dwellings with verandahs, etc., usually facing their courtyards (Hunter 1876). This description of the Koch-Rajbansi houses is indicative of their rectangular ground plan with inclined roof, in an overall conformity with the people's houses found in other medium to high rainfall regions of India.

Apparently, the general pattern of Koch-Rajbansi house does not look much different from similar houses found in other parts of India. And if we compare Buchanan's (1833) statement made in the early years of nineteenth century with what had been recorded in the late 1950s, the pattern does not seem to have changed much over the period. From the point of view of the construction technique also, houses built by the Nagas, Garos and other people of north-eastern India were relatively well-built structure with massive use of timber and tree-trunk, hence more durable than the average Koch-Rajbansi house. Thus if we go by the evidence of Mr. Scotts, the first Commissioner of Assam, while the average Koch-Rajbansi hut measured about 15-20 feet long by 10 feet broad, the Garos could build "large gloomy mansion about 260 feet in length and 42 in breadth" (Dalton 1872). Evidently, therefore, the Garos, Nagas and similar other north-eastern tribes had better iron tools than the Koch-Rajbansi people could possibly use.

## WHAT'S AND WHY'S OF KOCH-RAJBANSI HOUSING

What is then special of the Koch-Rajbansi house to have drawn our research attention? The question could be answered only by exploring their contexts. Formed by the successive deposits by numerous rivers with their origin in the mountains on the north, Kuch Bihar, the hub of Koch-Rajbansi culture, is a plain land characterized by its absolute dead level. The soil condition before the post-colonial construction of river embankments was "singularly uniform in character throughout, consisting of from ½ to 2 or 3 feet of light friable loam, superimposed on a deep bed of pure sand". Its active rivers, flooding and frequently changing their course almost at a regular interval, characterize the entire tract. Yet another important consequence of this river action, Captain Lewin writes, is that "the country possesses little or no timber, for before a fine tree could grow to respectable dimensions, it would probably be swept away by some swerving yellow river flood." With an average rainfall of 124 inches, recorded between 1872 and 1875, Kuch Bihar was also known for its moist, malarious climate (Hunter 1876). All these must have discouraged the growth of a relatively stable human settlement in this extremely fertile tract.

These factors had accounted for the continuation of a form of shifting agriculture in this region till the early sixteenth century; and in some parts even as late as the early nineteenth century. In this system, paddy was broadcast over uncultivated land immediately after floodwater had receded. This traditional Koch-Rajbansi much less labour intensive technique of paddy cultivation did not necessitated the settlement of village close to their rice fields which kept on changing almost every year with river actions and the successive deposits of fertile silt over land. By the sixteenth century, however, Kuch Bihar began to shift slowly to the plough-based wetland system of paddy cultivation. Associated with this agricultural change were the Brahmins, who had been moving into this region in small groups following the Muslim occupation of south Bengal since the early thirteenth century. The migrant Brahmins had brought with them the new technique of wetland cultivation and tribal labour force as their followers, the Santhals in particular, from south-western Bengal.

A by-product of these changes was the evolution of a new technique of house building, which was in reality a fusion of the *Tong* or *Chang* type houses, indigenous of the north-eastern India, with the cottage of Bengal proper, distinguished by its convex roof style, and the Santhal reed craft. The development of this composite technique had solved the long-standing problem of a relatively stable human settlement in this region. The houses traditionally built by north-eastern tribes, the Khasis, the Garos and the Nagas involved massive use of timber logs and planks. The Koch-Rajbansi housing, described as the composite technique hereafter, was on the other hand almost entirely built with bamboo. The use of bamboo in house building was a major invention for the local people. More so, because it was available in plenty in the Koch-Rajbansi territory, where timber was scarce and the soil unfit for raising the mud wall, as it was done by people in most other parts of eastern India.

Lewin, Commissioner of Kuch Bihar, thus remarked, "Bamboos grow extensively all over the country, and form the fuel supply of the people, besides being used largely in the building of their houses. Trees as a rule are scarce" (Lewin 1876: 383; Bandyopadhyay). The bamboo was not only very cheap but some of the varieties (such as *Makla*) were immune to worms and moisture. This explains why even the royal families traditionally lived in "mat-huts" built inside the brick built barricades (Hunter 1876).

The average Koch-Rajbansi house was a constellation of a number of separate huts of the modest size determined by traditional methods of calculations. For instance, if the length of a room is 16 cubits, the length of the top (*tuhi*) of the roof should be 17 cubits. The length of the rafter (*ua*) that is each side of the roof should be 16÷3 cubits. The width of the inside floor should be 16÷3+1/3(16÷3) cubits. The length of the floor inside the room should be 14 cubits. However, all these were related to the type of the roof preferred. In case of a flat-roofed hut (*dhepa ghar*), therefore, if the length of the room is 16 cubits, the width of the floor should be 16÷3+1/3 (16÷3) +1 cubits.

The construction of a four-roofed hut (*cowari ghar*), however, involved altogether different calculations. If the length of the room is 16 cubits, the length of the front roof at the eaves should be 16+2 cubits. The top of the roof should be 16×1/3 cubits. The length of the side roof at the eaves should be 16×2/3 cubits. The rafter should be 16×2/3 cubits and the width of the floor 16×2/3 cubits. The length and width of the floor inside the room should be usually 2 cubits less than the entire covered area of the room. The most important part of the Koch-Rajbansi house is called *dari ghar*, which often combined the guest/drawing and business room into one. The size and the roof style (two or four-roofed) of this hut often varied with social position of its owner. Bamboo matting usually made the walls; poorer people sometimes did it with a long type of grass (*nol* or *bena*). The covers of both the door (*mokha dzhap*) and window were all made of bamboo.

All measurements were made with the simple aides of various types of bamboo poles and string made either of jute or reed. The construction site was first divided and then subdivided into a number of small spaces, each earmarked either for a specific hut or open. The huts big or small were thatched with grass called *kusa poa* or with paddy straw fastened to a bamboo casing. The roof trellis on each slope was first made on the ground and then raised and fixed on the ridge poles and stringers. The work of thatching started from the eaves, arranging bundle of grass lengthwise in ascending order and carried to the top of the roof, which got thickest cover of grass, nearly 18", slowly declining to 6" at the eaves (Sanyal 1965). The acute slanting of the roof made it perfectly water resistant at least for three years when thatching had to be renewed. As stated above, the region had more than 100" rainfall a year. The roof truss was so constructed as to allow an open space between the wall end and the roof. A ceiling of bamboo matting often separated the roof and the room inside, a technique also followed by the Santhals of south-western Bengal. Thatched roof had air gaps inside, which had a cooling effect inside the room during the daytime and an opposite impact in the night.

This description, based on data recorded in the late 1950s, suggests the importance of bamboo in the construction of the Koch-Rajbansi house. The ritual followed in every Rajbansi house, worshipping a piece of bamboo as the household deity (*bastu thakur*), perhaps remains the other important evidence of the contribution of bamboo in solving their housing problem. *Bastu-ghar* (dwelling of the deity) was located on the north-eastern side of the house; besides the worshipping purposes it was also used for storage of seed paddy and the stock for their daily consumption.

The general layout of the Rajbansi housing also exhibits an awareness of their ecological conditions. The oft-repeated Rajbansi adage epitomizing the whole concept of the general plan of their house building is, *uttare gua, dakhine dhua; pube has, pochime bas* (areca nut on the north, keeping the south open, duck in the east, and bamboo clamp on the west). Located just below the lower Himalayan range, the cold wind flows in Kuch Bihar from the north often accompanied by storms. The Rajbansi, therefore, place several rows of areca nut trees on northern side of their house as barriers to the cold wind. The refreshing wind blows from the south, which they always keep open. The pond that serves as the source of water supply to the family is invariably dug out in the east so that it gets ample sunshine. The western setting sun is widely believed to be harmful for the health. Hence, a bamboo grove is placed on that side; also by way of obstructing storms that most often visit this region from the north-western corner between March and May every year (Sanyal 1965).

## CONCLUSION

Let me conclude by emphasizing three important points. Firstly, the technique of constructing bamboo houses had solved the problem of a relatively stable human settlement in this flood-prone but extremely fertile tract. This is a technique local people were quite unaware of before the coming of the Santhals from south-western Bengal, although they made other uses of bamboo. The fusion of the Santhal technique of house building with that of the north-eastern India is reflected in the rituals associated with the Koch-Rajbansi house construction. A detailed analysis of the same had to be avoided here for want of space. The bamboo worship is primarily an extension of the Santhal veneration for the *Sal* and similar other useful trees (Roy 1912), while the rituals relating to fixing the *muli poi* (main pole) on the first day of their house construction reminds us of the practices widely followed in north-eastern India (Gourdon 1907). The development of this composite technique was closely related to the extension of paddy cultivation into this region based on wetland farming.

Secondly, the general layout of the Koch-Rajbansi house, briefly referred to above, and their arrangement of huts around a rectangular courtyard suggests their acquaintance with some of the basic principles of traditional Indian concept of *vastu*. It has been held that houses constructed according to *vastu* tradition not only lasted long but also enabled their inmates to enjoy charm and spiritual bliss (Sabharathnam 1995). It may not be a just coincidence, therefore, that the Koch-Rajbansi built *dari ghar* and granary, the most important part of their house on the east, which in the *vastu* tradition belongs to the Lord of Happiness and Prosperity (Indra). The reverence for north, the sphere of God of Wealth (Kubera), is suggested by their locating *bastu ghar* to the north-east of their house – the corner, where lies the head of the *vastu purusha mandal.* Following the popular eastern Indian usage of throwing ash to the Yama's face, they used to have their kitchen on the south, of which the Lord of Death (Yama) is the *Dikpati* (Lord of the Side). However, during the rainy season, the Koch-Rajbansi shifted their ovens to another hut specially built for the purpose in the south-east corner of their house, traditionally known as sphere of the Lord of Fire (Agni). Afraid of incessant rains and regular floods, the Koch-Rajbansi maintained bamboo clamp by the way of raising artificial barriers on the west, the sphere of god of Rains (Varuna), according to the *vastu* tradition of India.

In brief, broad features of the Koch-Rajbansi houses suggest that the people, who had masterminded their general layout, were conscious of the basic principles of traditional Indian structural science. Known as the *vastu vijnana,* this tradition ascertains the details of house building based on the five gross elements – earth, water, fire, air and space.

Thirdly, the visible influence of the *vastu vijnana* on the Koch-Rajbansi notions of house building indicates the existence of an invisible link between institutionalized knowledge or *pratisthanik vidya* and the *lokavidya* tradition, widely followed by people. A process of vertical integration was very much active, although it seems quite contrary to the conventional notion of pre-colonial Indian society. The physical extent of the diffusion of this knowledge base is, however, very difficult to ascertain. It is interesting to note here that the Angami Nagas of north-eastern India shared a similar notion of the good and evil sides. Like the Koch-Rajbansi, therefore, they considered west *kistasa* or the backyard. All these tend to suggest the vision of an altogether different pattern of socio-cultural mobility that has yet to be recorded in the history textbooks on pre-colonial India.

## BIBLIOGRAPHY

Bandyopadhyay, B. *Kochbiharer Itihas,* Kuch Bihar.

Bhadra, G. 1983. 'Two Frontier Uprisings in Mughal India' in *Subaltern Studies II,* R. Guha (ed.). Delhi: Oxford University Press.

Biswas, S.K. and N.K. Behura. 1961. 'Types of Cottages' in *Peasant Life in India: A Study in Indian Unity and Diversity,* N.K. Bose (ed.). Calcutta: Anthropological Survey of India.

Buchanan, F. 1833. *Geographical, Statistical, and Historical Description of the District or Zila of Dinajpur in Province or Subah of Bengal*. Calcutta.

Chattopadhyay, D. 1978. *Lokayata*. Delhi: People's Publishing House.

Chaudhury, H.N. 1903. *The Kuch Bihar State and its Land Revenue Settlement*. Kuch Bihar: Government Press.

Dalton, E.T. 1872. *Descriptive Ethnology of Bengal*. Calcutta: Government Press.

Eaton, R.M. 1994. *The Rise of Islam and the Bengal Frontier 1204-1760*. Delhi: Oxford University Press.

Hunter, W.W. 1876. *A Statistical Account of Bengal*. London: Trubner & Co.

Hutton, J.H. *The Angami Nagas*. London.

Hwa, S.C. 1968. *The Rice Industry of Burma 1852-1940*. Singapore: University of Malaya Press.

Karve, I. 1977. *Hindu Soceity – An Interpretation*. Pune: Deshmukh Prakashan.

Lewin, T.H. 1876. *An Account of the Coochbehar State*. Kuch Bihar: Government Press.

Majumdar, B. 1996. 'Toto Janajatir Artha Samajik Itihas', *Lokasruti* 12. Folk and Tribal Culture Centre, Government of West Bengal.

Risley, H.H. 1891. *Tribes and Castes of Bengal*. Calcutta: Government Press.

Roy, M. 1902. 'Some Notes on the Rajvansi Caste', *Journal of the Asiatic Society of Bengal* LXXI (3): 50-61.

Roy, S.C. 1912. *The Mundas and Their Country*. Calcutta.

Sabharathnam, S.P. 1995. *Temple of Space Science*. Madras: Vastu Vedic Research Foundation.

Sanyal, C.C. 1965. *The Rajbansis of North Bengal*. Calcutta: The Asiatic Society.

Taniguchi, S. 1998. 'Uttarbanga and Asamer Rajabanshi Sampradaya and Bhumibyabsthar Paribartanshil Kathamo' in *Jati, Barna O Bangali Samaj*, S. Bandyopadhyay and A. Dasgupta (eds.). Delhi: International Centre for Bengal Studies.

9

# Rice Cultivation: Associated Rituals and Festivals with Special Reference to Central Himalayas

J.S. Kharakwal and A. Yano

## INTRODUCTION

This paper attempts a brief survey of rituals and festivals associated with rice in South Asia, particularly in Central Himalaya. Recent evidence has shown that rice is the earliest cereal that was cultivated by man in the valleys of the middle Yangtze river in China, around 14000 years BP (Yasuda 1999). Subsequently other regions of Asia and the world might have learnt rice cultivation technology. A particular type of pottery known as Cord Impressed Ware is associated with the early rice growing regions (e.g. Ganga Valley, North-Eastern India, South-Eastern China, Thailand, Japan) indicating some interlinks among these regions (Chang 1970; Gorman 1970; Pal 1986; Kuzmin and Orlova 2000). There are large number of rituals and festivals associated with rice in these early rice growing regions and several among them are common or analogous. Rice is held in high esteem in these societies, hence it plays a very important role in the cultural life of Central Himalayas as well as rest of South Asia. This paper is an attempt to understand the meaning of those diverse rituals/festivals that are associated with rice.

## RICE CULTIVATION

Rice (*Oryza sativa*) is perhaps the most versatile crop as it grows at more than 3000 m elevation in the Himalayas and at sea level in the deltas of the great rivers of Asia. Its production all over the world was over 468.275 million tons in recent years (Bajaj 1991). Rice is a very important cereal as it is the staple food of two-thirds of the world's population (including Latin America, parts of Africa and the Middle East) and about 90 per cent of the world's rice is grown and consumed in Asia. Brown rice has more calories per 100 gm (447) than wheat (436) (Bajaj 1991). Rice is the first crop to have its genome sequenced (John Whitfield 2002).

The *japonica* and *indica* types of rice, predominant in Asia, are supposed to have been developed from the wild *Oryza rufipogon,* which has both perennial and annual types. It is pan-tropical in distribution. The molecular, genetic and archaeological studies have shown that *japonica* variety was developed out of perennial type whereas origin of *indica* type is unknown (Sato 1996). The *japonica* variety specifically carries isozyme and neucleo and cyto alleles at high frequency. *Indica* and *japonica* differentiated before domestication (Sato 1996). Some experts believe that *indica* was developed out of intermediary type of *rufipogon*. Sato suggests that perhaps the introduction of *japonica* genome might have been responsible for the domestication of *indica* variety of rice in the tropical regions.

Following are the vernacular names of the some of the major varieties of rice grown in the Central Himalayas. In dry land regions the varieties grown are *nandhyan, chudkuli, lalu, dud* and *bakul*; and in the wetland *thapchani, nandhani/nandhan, gadant, lali, daubadav, rajmati* and *siwaie* varieties are grown.

## FESTIVALS AND RITUALS RELATED TO RICE

### In Central Himalayas

In the Central Himalayan region rice is associated with various festivals, rituals and agricultural rites. A few among them are as follows:

#### Ropai

*Ropai* or the transplantation of rice is done in Kumaon-Garhwal (Central Himalayan) region in the month of *Asad* (mid-June to mid-July) when the hills receive the maximum rainfall. Either a small make-shift kind of shrine is made or women offer vermillion and intact grains of rice to the bunch of rice plants that are to be transplanted. This kind of ritual is also common in the Ganga valley and many other regions of India. Among Santhals besides rice grains and vermillion, rice beer, mustard and *urad* cereals are also offered. In fact, this is a symbolic worship of the rice deity/goddess.

#### Hiljatra

*Hil* means mud or sticky soil and *jatra* means travel or walking. It is purely an agricultural festival as it is the mimicry of transplantation of paddy. This festival is celebrated every year in the month of August/September in eastern Kumaon particularly in Pithoragarh and Askot. This festival certainly demonstrates agriculture as the main occupation and subsistence of life and possibly points out the antiquity of rice. Even goat is also sacrificed during the festival. According to a local legend, Kuru, a Chand king, once went to Sorar (Nepal) where he killed a buffalo for sacrifice. The people of Nepal gifted him masks of *lakhiabhoot, halwaha,* two bullocks and an implement (perhaps an iron hoe). He eventually introduced this festival in Kumaon. It is believed that this festival was introduced in western Nepal from Tibet (Hideo Tabata, personal communication). We do not know if this indicates the introduction of rice in Kumaon-Garhwal and Himachal region from the eastern corridors of Himalayas.

### Haang Ropan

On the auspicious day of *harela sankranti* in the month of July, a small branch of *mehal* is planted in the fields where *ropai* has been done perhaps to cure the plants from certain pests and to ensure the growth of plants. This is also common in the Ganga Valley and among the Mundas, where *soso* is used instead of *mehal.* It is known among the Santhals as *batauli puja.*

### Chyura

*Chyura* (roasted and pounded rice) festival is celebrated after harvesting the crop. Among the Santhals of Bihar, *chyura* festival is known as *navakhani.* This festival is also celebrated in the north-eastern parts of India, Indonesia and Japan. In Japan it is known as *yakiyome.* In some regions, e.g., among Santhals of Bihar *chyura* is prepared only from dry cultivated rice (*goda dhaan*). Moreover, this variety of rice can be eaten only after the festival is observed. Could this be pointing out the antiquity of dry rice compared to wet cultivation or respect for indigenous variety? In some areas the rice plants along with grains are worshipped after harvesting and cow dung is placed on the heap of rice so that the soul of rice will not go away. What is common to all these regions is that this festival is celebrated to worship the rice deity after harvesting, as *chyura* is sent to every member of the family as blessings.

### Mana Hatyali

*Mana hatyali* is a curing festival both for people and animals and it is celebrated on Diwali. In the Central Himalayas rice paste (liquid form) is applied by making palm impressions on the back of people as well as animals wishing a good health throughout the year. However, among the Santhals and other early rice growing communities, e.g. in Indonesia, the paste is applied on the face. Intact grains of rice are used by *jagarias* or *dangarias* (shamans) to drive away evil sprits, identical to South-East Asia, to find out lost persons, to narrate the past and future events, etc.

### Fooldyo

*Fooldyo* festival is celebrated on the first day of the new year of the Hindu calendar, by offering rice grains and flowers to each house by chanting or singing the following lines. The lines are sung by children in order to wish that the grain storage remains full and the house may remain prosperous throughout the year:

*Phool dei chhamma dei*
*Daino dwar bhariye raijo bhakar*
*Teri dei sau sau namaskar*

### Rice cooking

Rice is held in high esteem in the Himalayan society as it can be either cooked by those men who wear the sacred thread (*yajnopavita*) or only by those women who have undergone certain *Brahmanic samskaras* (ritual). Barring kids, no one else eats rice if it is not cooked by either of these authorized people. Each house has a special place, slightly elevated with U'-shaped hearths to cook rice. It cannot be cooked by everybody in the village.

## Other Regions

### Orissa

According to a legend popular among Gadaba and Bonda tribals of Orissa, Mahaprabhu drilled a hole on the back of a tortoise and a girl was born. When she grew up, the tortoise told her that Mahaprabhu is her father. Mahaprabhu refused, but permitted her to stay with him. Once the girl caught hold of Mahaprabhu and accused him of having sex with her. Mahaprabhu became furious and killed her with a knife. From her blood, the earth was formed. From her right eye emerged the sun and from the left the moon. Her bones formed the hills. Her hair turned into all kinds of flora and vegetable available on the earth. Rice was also part of this vegetation which grew on the earth. When her belly was cut open by Mahaprabhu, a boy and a girl came out. As a result of their cohabitation, human society developed. This legend is identical to South-East Asian myth of origin of rice (Tiziana and Baldizzone undated).

### Assam and South India

*Bihu* and *Pongal* are very important festivals celebrated on a large scale in South Asia. The *Bihu* (*kati, magh, rangoli*) of Assam is purely an agricultural festival. The *rangoli* or *baishakh bihu* (in April) is celebrated at plantation time; the *kati* or *kangali bihu* (September-October) is celebrated at the harvest time; and *bhogali* or *magh bihu* marks the collection of rice grain. It is said that perhaps the *Pongal* of south India is the parallel of *bhogali* or *magh bihu*. Various dishes of rice are cooked to celebrate these festivals. In south India the *Pongal* is celebrated in mid-January and rice dishes are predominantly cooked. The place of worship is smeared with cow-dung and *kolams* (ground patterns). These patterns are generally drawn with rice flour and it is believed that the insects would feed on it and bless the household.

## VALUE OF RICE IN THESE SOCIETIES

### INDIA

In India intact (*akshat*) rice grains are applied on the forehead with vermilion as blessings in order to live a successful day and achieve complete success in the *karma*. Similar theme also reflects in religious and ritualistic animal sacrifice as it is maintained that any animal which is ill or whose legs, horn or any part of the body is broken cannot be sacrificed. It is believed that sacrificing complete and healthy (*akshat*) animal only gives completeness to the aim. Rice is believed to be the best (*sarvasrestha*) among seven main staple grains. According to Hindu mythology, the intact grain on the forehead symbolizes the supremacy of rice on all other grains/cereals, well-being of a person and completeness of life. In South Asia gods and deities are only offered rice and not any other grain. Rice is believed to have a soul and is invariably worshipped as deity. Rice flour is used in almost all the festivals and ceremonies to smear the ground to make it pious or to worship deities, etc. Rice plays a very important role in various regional and national festivals, e.g., *Diwali, Pongal, Bihu*. It symbolizes beauty, prosperity and fertility.

*Khil* (processed rice) is thrown behind by the Hindu girl while marrying her husband. This symbolizes that though she was born and brought up at her natal place she would bloom, flourish and achieve everything in her life at her husband's place. When she enters her inlaws/husband's house, in certain regions, for the first time, she hits a utensil full of rice at the entrance or dips her hands in the rice paste and makes hand-prints on the entrance. Both these customs symbolize that she is to bring prosperity to the family or home. In some parts of the Ganga Valley she carries away rice to her husband's place, which also symbolizes wealth (V.N. Misra, personal communication).

Bray (1994:18) writes that,

> The glutinous characteristic is one that has been much valued by Asian rice farmers. Glutinous rice is highly valued as a ceremonial food and as the chief ingredient in rice wines or beers. Cakes made of glutinous rice are exchanged

at weddings and religious festivals all over Asia. In Malaya a large cake of glutinous rice, coloured brilliant red, yellow or purple and decorated with eggs and flowers, is offered to the bride as a symbol of fertility. In south China cakes of glutinous rice, wrapped in broad bamboo leaves and steamed, are exchanged on the day of the Dragon Boat Festival.

### South-East Asia

In South-East Asia the rice cultivation by and large is done by shifting type of agricultural method. Various myths of rice goddess particularly about the origin of rice connect this region to South Asia (Knappert 1985). The Mnong Ghar people of Central Vietnam perform rice rituals and buffaloes are sacrificed as the most valuable offering. The sacrificial buffaloes and beer are offered to the spirits for harvest rituals. The blood of sacrificial chicken is poured into the jars of beer and then the buffaloes are anointed with the mixture of beer and blood.

In several regions of South-East Asia, e.g. Indonesia, Java, Sumatra, etc., similar rituals are connected with rice cultivation. de Jong and Josselin (1965) have given an excellent account of various annals, myths, legends and rituals which vary from region to region and are connected with respective geographical features and centre round the cultivation of rice. They write,

> The Sudanese and Javanese myths state that rice originated out of the body of a woman who was buried. The Javanese myth adds that before the rice came forth, a nimbus of light was seen on her grave. The Malay annals maintain the story of appearance of three young men on the earth who were born and brought up at the bottom of the ocean. They also cause a mysterious light to shine over a field, and this announces the appearance of a supernatural rice-harvest. The sub-aquatic youths are associated with a wonder working cow, which vomits a man. A Chinese source recounts an 'ancient tradition' from the very same area that cattle came out of the earth. And finally, modern Malay agricultural rituals involve burying a goat in the rice field before planting begins, and an implement called a goat's hoof makes the holes in the ground which are to take the rice seeds. In fact, all over Indonesia the goat is accepted as the substitute of buffalo for sacrifice and whoever cannot afford buffalo may offer a goat. Finally, we have the medicine man that vomits out the rice as an augury of a plentiful harvest (de Jong and Josselin 1965:287).

de Jong (1965) also points out considerable Hindu and Buddhist influence in South-East Asian myths and legends. After harvesting, the soul of rice is led ritually from rice field to home and the medicine man again chants to various spirits. Some such ritual is also prevalent in South Asia. In fact, the similarity in rituals, particularly connected with rice or performed by rice, is not merely confined to rice cultivation but also can be visualized in daily life. For example, in Malay society the shamans practise various rituals to cure the patients. Rice plays a very important role in most of the rituals as often popped-rice is used for rituals or rice paste is applied on the forehead of the sick person to protect him from the airy heat of the spirits. Sometimes various human as well as animal figurines (both living on the land and sea) and miniature pots are made of rice flour and water to offer them to the spirits (Laderman 1991). We have also noted above that rice is used by shamans for similar purposes in Central Himalaya and other regions of South Asia.

### JAPAN

It seems that rice played very important role in Japanese life for millennia as during seventh-eighth century AD various regions were well known for rice cultivation when power was centred at Nara. Itse, a Sinto shrine, is connected with rice rituals, plantation and agricultural rites. Osada (2000) equates the rite of deer sacrifice of Japan with that of buffalo in Indonesia to obtain better crop. In Okinawa (Japan) pork blood was used to perform the rite and grains are smeared in blood too. Osada (2000) quotes various legends of Japan which reveal rituals and rites related to rice cultivation. In Shizukoka prefecture *shishi* or *tanetori* or *obisha* festival is celebrated by symbolic hunting of a deer. This kind of ritual hunting also characterizes the agricultural rite, which was performed before planting or seeding grains in order to have better crop. Sasaki (1971) suggests that the ritual hunting was introduced even prior to the beginning of rice cultivation in Jomon period by those who were practising slash-and-burn kind of farming. This kind of ritual certainly reminds of ancient tradition of soaking the rice grains in deer blood. Depending upon its availability the animal has chosen. Ohnuki-Tierney (1993) has visualised important features of rice, e.g. role of rice in ancient rituals, rice as staple food, as wealth, power and aesthetics, symbolism, etc., in Japanese society.

## ARCHAEOLOGICAL EVIDENCE FOR RICE CULTIVATION

### CHINA

Though Watabe, a well known scholar of rice, had proposed that rice cultivation originated in Assam-Yunnan region, but now in recent years the earliest domestication of rice (*japonica*) has been found in the middle reaches of the Yangtze, China. These sites are Hemudu, Pentoushan (9000 years BP), Bashidang (10000 BP), Yuchanyan (14000 BP) and Xianrendong (14000 BP) (Higham and Lu 1998; Yasuda 1999).

MacNeish *et al.* (1997) have reported the oldest evidence of rice grain from Jiangxi province dating back to 16000 years BP. Sato (in press) writes that all these early dates and sites are lacking the evidence of cultivated rice; however cultivated rice has been dated well beyond 10000 years BC (Wenming 2000; Yasuda in press). Moreover, study of plant opals (phytolith) recovered from soil layers and pottery from several sites in the middle Yangtze have indicated that *japonica* was cultivated as early as 11000 years BP, which subsequently reached other parts of Asia (Sato in press). Most of the Japanese scholars agree that rice cultivation was introduced in Japan (Kyushu region) during the Yayoyi period around the middle of first millennium BC by the immigrants (Kim 1982).

### South-East Asia

Though Xom Trai cave near Hanoi and some other sites yielded evidence of rice dating back to 17000 to 19000 BP but they are believed to be wild varieties. In 1970s fifth millennium BC dates were proposed for the beginning of rice cultivation in Thailand particularly at Ban Chiang (Korat plateau) and Non Nok Tha (Bayard 1971; Gorman and Charoenwongsa 1976); however recent AMS dates have placed this beginning around the last quarter of third millennium BC. At Ban Chiang and Khok Phanom De in Thailand, the early rice growing people were also using Cord Impressed Ware (Gorman and Charoenwongsa 1976). The Cord Impressed Ware has been found from all the early rice growing regions of Asia. In mainland South-East Asia rice, *taro* and *yam* are believed to be sister domestication, and rice did not become very popular in several islands until middle and late third millennium (Glover and Higham 1996).

### South Asia

There are a large number of archaeological sites across India which have yielded evidence of rice cultivation. A brief list of such important sites is given in Table 1. The Ganga Valley and Vindhyas, dotted with Mesolithic-Neolithic sites, have yielded solid evidence of early domestication of animals and plants (Thomas and Joglekar 1994); for example, at Chopani Mando, Koldihwa (24°, 54', 30" N, longitude 82°, 2' E), Mahagara and few other sites (see Table 2) (Sharma *et al.* 1980). At some of these sites, e.g., Koldihwa wild rice (*oryza sativa*) as well as domesticated one was discovered. The earliest evidence of cultivated rice comes from Chopani-Mando, a proto-Neolithic site located in the valley of the river Belan in Uttar Pradesh, which has been assigned to eighth-seventh millennium BC (Sharma *et al.* 1980). Ghalegay period (2600 BC) has yielded evidence of rice (Meadow 1996). Besides these, we have good evidence of domesticated rice at various sites in late Harappan context, at Pirak (around 1800 BC) (Possehl 1999) and at Khairadih 2600 BC (Glover and Higham 1996). The radiocarbon determinations for several Ganga Valley sites also place them in early and middle of second millennium BC, which appears to be concordant with these sites. However, Sharma *et al.* (1980) have assigned, according to some, the beginning of rice cultivation to ninth-sixth millennium

BC in the Ganga Valley, though such early beginning has not been widely accepted by other scholars. On the other hand, recent researches have inferred that *japonica* was domesticated as early as 11000 BP in the middle Yangtze Valley, China, whereas we do not know where and when exactly *indica* was domesticated. It is quite likely that its beginning in South Asia may also be much older than what is known to us.

Table 1. Early Occurrences of Rice in South Asia
(After Possehl 1999 and references therein)

| | | |
|---|---|---|
| **Neolithic** | | |
| Baraunha | Eastern Neolithic | IAR 1982-83:149 |
| Manigara | Eastern Neolithic | IAR 1983-84:178 |
| Chpoani Mando | Vindhyan Neolithic | Sharma *et al.* 1980:23, 69. |
| Mahagara | Vindhyan Neolithic | IAR 1981-82:106; 1982-83:149 |
| Koldihwa | Vindhyan Neolithic | IAR 1975-76:80, 88 |
| Gufkral | Northern Neolithic | Kumar 1988: 79 |
| Semthan | Northern Neolithic | Buth *et al.* 1982 |
| **Mature Harappan** | | |
| Lothal | Lothal A | Ramesh *et al.* 1985 |
| Rangpur | Period II A | Ghosh and Lal 1963. |
| **Late/Post-Harappan** | | |
| Pirak | Period I | Costantini 1979 |
| Hulas | Late Harappan | IAR 1979-80:114; 1982-83:149-50 |
| Un | Late Harappan | IAR 1979-80:114; 1982-83:150 |
| Atranjikhera | OCP and B-&-R | Chowdhury 1983 (PGW ? NBP) |
| **Chalcolithic** | | |
| Ahar | Chalcolithic | Vishnu-Mittre 1969:230 |
| Koldihwa | Chalcolithic | IAR 1974-75:80 |
| Mahisdal | Late Chalcolithic | IAR 1982-83:150; Vishnu-Mittre 1974:17 (B-&-R) |
| Chirand | Chalcolithic | Vishnu-Mittre 1971:20 |
| **Chalcolithic** | | |
| Navdatoli | Malwa Phase | Vishnu-Mittre and Gulati 1961:18-9, 43-44, 51-52 |
| Inamgaon | Malwa-Jorwe | Kajale 1988:735, 783 |
| Oriup | B-&-R ? | Kumar 1988:61 |

Cont. Table 1

Table 1 Cont.

| | | |
|---|---|---|
| Pandu Rajar Dhibi | Neolithic-Chalcolithic | Kumar 1988:68 |
| Barudih | B-&-R | Kumar 1988:61 |
| Baidipur | B-&-R | Kumar 1988:61 |
| Sonpur | Chalcolithic | Vishnu-Mittre 1974:17; IAR 1970-71:5-6 |
| Balathal | Chalcolithic | Kajale (Evidence presented July 2002 in a seminar "Mewar through the Ages", Rajasthan Vidyapeeth, Udaipur.) |
| **Late Bronze Age and Early Iron Age Sites** | | |
| Pirak | Period I & III | Costantini 1979 |
| Hastinapur | PGW | Chowdhury and Ghosh 1954-55:120-24 |
| Noh | B-&-R and PGW | Vishnu-Mittre 1974:17; Vishnu-Mittre and Savitri 1974 |
| Hallur | Neolithic | Vishnu-Mittre 1971 |
| Narhan | Pre-NBP to E. Hist. | IAR 1984-85:162; 1984-85:163 |
| Sringaverpura | Pd. I&II 1050-700 BC | IAR 1982-83:149; 1983-84:178; 1984-85:161 |

Table 2. Rice Growing sites of Gangetic Doab
(Early Agriculture – Gangetic Doab and Eastern India)

All BP ages are based on 5568 yr half-life of radiocarbon. Calibrated ages are given in BC\AD (after Possehl 1993).

| *Site* | *Sample No.* | *5568 Yrs. BP* | *Calib. Dates* | *Culture* | *Material* |
|---|---|---|---|---|---|
| Chirand | TF-1032 | 3600±150 BP | 1961 cal. BC | Period I, Neolithic | Charcoal |
| Chirand | TF-446 | 1930±105 BP | 72 cal. AD | NBP | Charcoal |
| Chirand | TF-1035 | 3125±100 BP | 1418 cal. BC | Period I, Neolithic | Charcoal |
| Chirand | TF-1031 | 3525±135 BP | 1884 cal. BC | Period I, Neolithic | Charcoal |

Cont. Table 2

Table 2 Cont.

| *Site* | *Sample No.* | *5568 Yrs.* BP | *Calib. Dates* | *Culture* | *Material* |
|---|---|---|---|---|---|
| Chirand | TF-1126 | 2290±120 BP | 391 cal. BC | Period I, Neolithic | Charcoal |
| Chirand | TF-1125 | 3365±150 BP | 1679 cal. BC | Period I, Neolithic | Charcoal |
| Chirand | TF-1127 | 3230±95 BP | 1516 cal. BC | Period I, Neolithic | Charcoal |
| Chirand | TF-1034 | 3420±110 BP | 1740 cal. BC | Period I, Neolithic | Charcoal |
| Chirand | TF-1036 | 2485±120 BP | 761,681,659 596,633,577, 561 cal. BC | Period I, Neolithic | Charcoal |
| Chirand | TF-1033 | 3390±110 BP | 1730,1729, 1689 cal. BC | Period I, Neolithic | Charcoal |
| Chirand | TF-334 | 2715±120 BP | 890,845, cal. BC | Period I, Neolithic | Charcoal |
| Chopani Mando | BS-129 | 4540±110 BP | 3338,3213, 3203 cal. BC | Period III, Vindhyan Neolithic | Charcoal |
| Koldihawa | PRL-224 | 8280±210 BP | None | Neolithic ? | Charcoal |
| Koldihawa | PRL-56 | 820±100 BP | 1225 cal. AD | Chalcolithic | Charcoal |
| Koldihawa | PRL-227 | 2050±110 BP | 92 cal. BC | Chalcolithic | Charcoal |
| Koldihawa | PRL-101 | 6295±180 BP | 5240 cal. BC | Neolithic ? | Charcoal |
| Koldihawa | PRL-100 | 7180±230 BP | 6075,6059, 6043, 6018, 6001 cal. BC | Neolithic | Charcoal |
| Koldihawa | PRL-102 | 2380±105 BP | 405 cal. BC | Chalcolithic ? | Charcoal |
| Koldihawa | PRL-99 | 2900±150 BP | 1092 cal. BC | Chalcolithic | Charcoal |
| Koldihawa | PRL-223 | 3300±120 BP | 1607,1554, 1544 cal. BC | Neolithic | Charcoal |
| Kunjhun River | BETA-6414 | 4010±110 BP | 2569,2538, 2503 cal. BC | Vindhyan Neolithic | Unknown |
| Kunjhun River | BETA-6415 | 4600±80 BP | 3360 cal. BC | Vindhyan Neolithic | Unknown |
| Kunjhun River | BETA-4879 | 3120±70 BP | 1414 cal. BC | Vindhyan Neolithic | Unknown |
| Mahagara | PRL-409 | 3260±150 BP | 1523 cal. BC | Neolithic | Charcoal |
| Mahagara | BS-128 | 3330±100 BP | 1628 cal. BC | Neolithic | Charcoal |
| Mahagara | PRL-407 | 3300±100 BP | 1607,1554, 1544 cal. BC | Neolithic | Charcoal |

In the valley of Kali in high Himalayan area of Nepal, there is evidence of rice (*Oryza sativa*) cultivation dating back to middle of first millennium BC (Knorzer 2000) along with a variety of millets. It may even date much earlier in the Central Himalaya as the archaeological record is better studied and varied rituals are prevalent. In fact, it is highly probable that the technology of rice cultivation reached Central Himalaya and then on to the Ganga Valley from South China. Sato (in press) writes that the starch in rice seeds is responsible for difference between glutinous, sticky or sweet and non-sticky or ordinary rice, an important feature in identifying the origin. There are several types of rice cereals in the Central Himalayan area which are sticky and sweet like *japonica*. This can be confirmed through a multi-disciplinary study. Experts believe that dry rice can only be grown in shifting cultivation (Bajaj 1991); however this is not correct as dry rice is grown throughout the Himalayan region along with wet rice.

## LINGUISTIC DATA

Linguists (like Blust 1996; Reid 1988; Bayard 1996) and others generally agree that the Yangtze River and the eastern Himalayan foothills (covering the valleys of Salween, Mekong) are the homeland of the Austric people. One of their rice cultivating groups, known as Proto Austro-Asiatic, began to move down the valleys of Salween, Mekong (Proto-MonKhmer) with pre-Munda speakers moving westward down the Brahmaputra around sixth millennium BC (for detail, see Agrawal and Kharakwal 2002). Zide and Zide (1976) illustrated strong relationship between MonKhmer (Munda) languages and rice cultivation. White (1997) also argues for a sixth millennium BC beginning of agriculture and supports Blust's argument for the expansion of the MonKhmer family of languages. Munda and MonKhmer language groups are two branches of the Austro-Asiatic family. Bayard (1996) visualizes the westward expansion, under the stimulus of agriculture, of Austro-Asiatic language from Nanhailand through Vietnam, Laos, Cambodia and Thailand to Burma and ultimately to eastern India. Linguists have now reconstructed a number of terms related to agriculture in Munda, e.g., *baba* (paddy), *gele* (ear of paddy), *tuku* (pestle), *seel* (mortar), *sii* (plough), *jan* (grain seed), *loyon* (wet paddy field) and some of these go back to Proto-Munda and Austro-Asiatic (Osada 1995). Hence it can be stated that the rice cultivation spread from east to west with Proto-Munda expansion. Therefore it is now important to examine the archaeological evidence to understand the relationship among different regions. Osada (1995) concludes that the rice cultivation in the Yangtze belongs to the Austronesian group whereas in Assam-Yunnan and South Asia it belongs to Austro-Asiatic people.

There are many Austro-Asiatic aboriginal languages still spoken in Thailand (Bayard 1996). Munda and MonKhmer language groups are two branches of the Austro-Asiatic family. Grierson (1967 and 1968) in his linguistic survey of the Himalayas had identified some residue of MonKhmer words in the Kumaoni dialects. In Kumaon, the Doms are supposed to be Kols, speakers of Munda dialects (Sharma 1988). Elsewhere we have discussed (Agrawal and Kharakwal 1998) that the Kols are said to be the first ethnic people of Kumaon, who had descended from the Munda speaking group related to the Austro-Asiatic sub-group. They represent the aborigines of Kumaon, occupy the lowest rung in the hierarchical status in Kumaoni society and are the traditional blacksmiths. It is, therefore, possible that the Munda speaking people introduced rice cultivation as well as metallurgy in the Central Himalaya.

While discussing the relationship between Austro-Asiatic and Austronesian languages and their implications for archaeology, Higham (1996:115) describes the South-East Asian rivers as spokes in a wheel, "with the hub in the eastern foothills of the Himalayas.... In a westward direction, ancestors of the Munda moved, perhaps down the Brahmaputra into eastern India". Obviously, the movement did not stop there but went further westward to the Central Himalayas. This type of movement to south-east and westward probably explains the expansion first of the rice cultivation and second of metallurgy.

## DISCUSSION

There is conjectural evidence that early agriculture spread from China to South-East Asia and to Brahmaputra Valley, as also along the Himalayan corridors. We will not be surprised if the antiquity of rice goes back to thousands of years in these regions. Linguistic evidence, which has been discussed in the forgoing pages, also supports the notion of diffusion of agriculture. Like Southern China and South-East Asia, the Cord Impressed Ware is also found from the early rice cultivation area of the Ganga Valley, Vindhya and north-eastern India (Pal 1986). Various agricultural rites and rituals are prevalent in the rice growing regions, e.g. Yunnan (China), Japan, Taiwan, Thailand, Vietnam and Indonesia and many of them share common agricultural rites, myth of origin of rice and so on. For example, Osada (2000a) finds that several features of Munda (Indian) rice agricultural rites are quite similar to Japanese ones. He illustrates the example of flattened rice (*chyura* in Hindi, *taben* in Mundari, *yakigome* in Japanese, a festival celebrated after harvesting the crop), which was perhaps derived from the time of origin of rice cultivation somewhere in eastern Asia (Osada 2000a).

On the other hand, rice has been associated with rituals and festivals in South Asia for millennia. The Vedic texts and epics of South Asia refer to a large number of rituals that are performed only with rice, e.g. to achieve success, to regain the kingdom/village, to get rid of disease/misfortune; animal sacrifice to worship gods and goddesses, to cure people and so on (Kumar 1988). In fact, the agricultural rites are prevalent particularly in the Himalayan region and among the tribal groups in the Ganga Valley and in the north-east e.g. the Oraons, the Mundas, the Santhals, the Gonds, the Porojas and the Mikirs, Dimasa Kachgaris and Zeoni Nagas. In some of these tribes such as Mundas and Oraons, rice cereal plays important role in birth, marriage and funeral ceremonies (Nita Mathur, personal communication). Hence the archaeological evidence, agricultural rites, rituals and festivals connected with rice and deep respect for rice in all point to an early domestication of rice in South Asia. Could this be *indica* variety. Moreover, what is interesting is that the Central Himalayan rice is also sticky unlike rest of the Indian varieties. The *indica* variety of course has some sticky types but we do not know if the Central Himalayan brown rice belongs to *indica* or *japonica*. This can be confirmed only after DNA analysis (Azusa Yano, Japan, is analysing some samples of Central Himalayan rice varieties). Though there is considerable controversy about the early dates in the Ganga Valley, yet we think that the domestication might have started much earlier than second millennium BC as the dates would suggest.

It is interesting that almost all the early rice growing regions of monsoonal Asia have yielded the Cord Impressed Wares, though they vary in decorative patterns, shapes and sometime in surface treatment but they are generally associated with the Neolithic cultures. As the pottery shapes also reflect the food habit and economy, a close examination of this ware, particularly cooking pots, would be quite useful to understand the expansion of *japonica* or *indica* type.

## CONCLUSION

The early evidence of domestication of *Oryza sativa* has certainly emerged from the Yangtze where it has been dated well beyond 10000 BP (*japonica* type). However, in South-East Asia (5000 BP) and Japan (3000 BP), the cultivation technique arrived much later. Though the Ganga Valley has yielded some early dates ranging from 9000 to 6000 BC, but they have not been appreciated widely. Therefore, the beginning of the cultivated *indica* type is still a mystery. Chang (1985) and Sato (in press) suggest that perhaps the introduction of *japonica* genome might have been responsible for the domestication of *indica* variety of rice in the tropical regions. In South Asia the radiocarbon dates of Pirak, the Ganga Valley and north-eastern region have suggested the beginning of cultivation around 4000 BP if not earlier.

A large number of rituals and festivals are associated with rice in Central Himalayas, the Ganga Valley and elsewhere. Rice is believed to have soul, invariably worshipped as deity, believed to be a symbol of prosperity, beauty, fertility, well-being and so on. It is applied on the forehead of the deities as well as human beings with vermilion every day in South Asia. The shamans use intact grains to ward off evil spirits, to cure patients, to locate missing person, to narrate past and future events, etc. It is a highly valued cereal across the monsoonal zone of Asia. In the Central Himalayas, only the authorized people can cook rice in special hearths that made in each house. It is interesting to note here that the Central Himalayan rice is sweet and sticky like *japonica*.

Hence, no other cereal has such incredible respect in the society, perhaps because it was the first cereal people cultivated in different regions of South Asia. Though, the early dates for domestication of rice in South Asia have yet to be fully accepted, all these rituals and festivals which are part of our traditional knowledge system, clearly indicate that rice (*indica* type) cultivation has a great antiquity than what is generally accepted today.

## ACKNOWLEDGEMENTS

We are indeed grateful to Prof. D.P. Agrawal, as he not only suggested to work on this issue but also offered constant support. We express our gratitude to Sri Mundaji (Jharkhand), Profs. Y. Yasuda, H. Tabata, O. Toshiki and Madhu Purti (Kyoto) for giving us information about rituals and agricultural rites of Japan, Nepal and the Munda tribe respectively. We sincerely thank Prof. V.N. Misra (Pune), Smt. Bachuli Devi, Sri Keshar S. Rana, Dr. Diwa Bhatt (all from Uttaranchal), Smt. Lila Kharakwal (Bareilly), Smt. Mamta Dev (Bhopal), Ms. Nirmla (Kyoto), Dr. Pramod Dobal (Kanpur), Prof. M.L. Sharma (Kotputali) and Dr. Nita Mathur (Delhi) for informing us about a variety of rituals and agricultural rites and discussions.

## BIBLIOGRAPHY

Agrawal, D.P. and J.S. Kharakwal. 2002. *South Asian Prehistory*. Delhi: Aryan Books International.

Bajaj, Y.P.S. 1991. 'Biotechnology in Rice Improvement' in *Biotechnology in Agriculture and Forestry*, Y.P.S. Bajaj (ed.). Springer-Verlag.

Bayard, D.T. 1971. *Non Nok Tha – The 1968 Excavation*. University Monographs in Prehistoric Anthropology 4. University of Otago.

——. 1996. 'Linguistic, Archaeologist and Austronesian Origins: Comparative and Socio-Linguistic Aspects of the Meacham-Bellwood Debate', *Bulletin of Indo-Pacific Prehistory Association* 15(2): 71-86.

Blust, R. 1996. 'Beyond the Austronesian Homeland: The Austric Hypothesis and its Implications for Archaeology' in *Prehistoric Settlement of the Pacific*, W. Goodenough. (ed.). Philadelphia: Transactions of the American Philosophical Society.

Bray, F. 1994. *The Rice Economies, Technology and Development in Asian Societies.* London: University of California Press.

Chang, K.C. 1970. 'The Beginning of Agriculture in the Far East', *Antiquity* XLIV: 175-85.

——. 1981. 'In Search of China's Beginnings: New Light on an Old Civilization', *American Scientist* 69: 148-60.

Chang, T.T. 1985. 'Crop History and Genetic Conservation: Rice – A Case Study', *Iowa State J. Res.* 59 (4): 425-55.

——. 1987. 'The Impact of Rice on Human Civilization and Population Expansion', *Interdisciplinary Science Review* 12 (1): 63-69.

Choe, Chong-Pil. 1982. 'The Diffusion Route and Chronology of Korean Plant Domestication', *The Journal of Asian Studies* XLI(3): 19-29.

De Jong, and P.E. Josselin. 1965. 'An Interpretation of Agricultural Rites in South-East Asia, with a Demonstration of Use of Data from Both Continental and Insular Areas', *The Journal of Asian Studies* 24(2): 283-90.

Glover, I.C. and C.F.W. Higham. 1996. 'New Evidence for Early Rice Cultivation in South, Southeast and East Asia' in *The Origins and Spread of Agriculture and Pastoralism in Eurasia,* D.R. Harris (ed.). London: University College.

Gorman, C. 1970. 'Excavation at Spirit Cave, North Thailand', *Asian Perspectives* 13: 97-107.

Gorman, C. and P. Charoenwongsa. 1976. 'Ban Chiang: A Mosaic of Impressions from the First Two Years', *Expedition* 18(4): 15-26.

Grierson, G.A. 1967-68. *The Linguistic Survey of India,* Vol. 1(1) and Vol. 9(4). Calcutta: Central Publication Branch. Govt. of India.

Higham, C. and L.-D. Lu Tracey. 1998. 'The Origin and Dispersal of Rice Cultivation', *Antiquity* 72: 867-77.

Higham, C.F.W. 1996. 'Archaeology and Linguistics in Southeast Asia: Implications of the Austric Hypothesis', *Bulletin of Indo-Pacific Prehistory Association* 14 (1): 71-86.

Kim, Won-Yong. 1982. 'The Origin of Rice Agriculture in Korea', *The Journal of Asian Studies* XLI (3):513-18.

Knappert, J. 1985. 'The Myth of the Rice Goddess in Java', *Orientalia Lovaniensia Periodical* 16: 245-71.

Knorzer, Karl-Heinz. 2000. '3000 Years of Agriculture in a Valley of High Himalayas', *Vegetation History and Archaeobotany* 9: 219-22.

Kumar, T.T. 1988. *History of Rice in India: Mythology, Culture and Agriculture*. Delhi: Gian Publishing House.

Kuzmin, V.Y and L.A. Orlova. 2000. 'The Neolithisation of Siberia and the Russian Far East: Radiocarbon Evidence', *Antiquity* 74(284): 356-64.

Laderman, C. 1991. *Taming the Wind of Desire: Psychology, Medicine, and Aesthetics in Malay Shamanistic Performance*. Berkeley: University of California Press.

MacNeish, R.S. *et al.* 1998. *Second Annual Report of the Sino-American Jiangxi, Origin of Rice Project*. Andover: Andover Foundation Publication.

Meadow, R.H. 1996. 'Agriculture and Pastoralism in North-western South Asia' in *The Origin and Spread of Agriculture and Pastoralism in Eurasia*, D.R. Harris (ed.). London: University College.

Nelson, S.M. 1982. 'The Effects of Rice Agriculture on Prehistoric Korea', *The Journal of Asian Studies* XLI (3): 531-43.

Ohnuki,T.E. 1995. 'Structure, Event and Historical Metaphor: Rice and Identities in Japanese History', *The Journal of the Royal Anthropological Institute* 1 (2): 227-54.

Osada, T. 1995. 'The Rice and Food Culture of Munda in Eastern India: An Ethno Linguistic Study', *Bulletin of International Research Center for Japanese Studies* 21: 65-94.

——. 2000a. 'The Agricultural Rites of Mundas in Eastern India: A Comparative Study of Asian Rice Culture', *Bulletin of International Research Center for Japanese Studies.*

——. 2000b. 'Agricultural Rites and Animal Sacrifice Notes on the Description and Citation of Harimakokuhudoki (1)', *Bulletin of International Research Center for Japanese Studies* 20: 81-123.

Pal, J.N. 1986. *Archaeology of Southern Uttar Pradesh*. Allahabad: Swabha Prakashan.

Possehl, G.L. 1999. *Indus Age – The Beginnings*. New Delhi: Oxford University Press.

Reid, L.A. 1988. 'Benedict's Austro-Tai Hypothesis: An Evaluation', *Asian Perspective* 26(1): 19-34.

Sato, Yo-Ichiro. 1996. 'Origin and Dissemination of Cultivated Rice in the Eastern Asia' in *Interdisciplinary Perspectives on the Origins of the Japanese*, O. Keiichi (ed.). Kyoto: International Research Centre for Japanese Studies.

——. (in press). 'Origin of Rice and Rice Cultivation in the Yangtze River Civilization' in *Monsoon and Civilization*, Y. Yasuda *et al.* (eds). Delhi: Roli Books.

Sharma, D.D. 1988. 'Kumaoni Language and Dialects' in *Kumaon Land and People*, K.S. Valdiya (ed.). Nainital: Gyanodaya Prakashan.

Sharma, G.R., *et al.* 1980. *Beginning of Agriculture.* Allahabad: Avinash Prakashan.

Singh, O.K. 1998-99. 'Cord-Marked Pottery Making Tradition in Manipur', *Puratatava* 29: 60-67

Thomas, P.K. and P.P. Joglekar. 1996. 'Faunal Remains from Balathal, Rajasthan: A Preliminary Analysis', *Man and Environment* 21(1): 91-97.

Tiziana and G. Baldizzone (undated). *Tribes of India.* India: Bookwise.

Wenming, Y. 2000. 'The Origins of Rice Agriculture, Pottery and Cities' in *The Origins of Rice Agriculture, Pottery and Cities,* Y. Wenming and Y. Yasuda (eds). Beijing: Cultural Relics Publishing House.

White, J.C. 1997. 'A Brief Note on New Dates for the Ban Chiang Cultural Tradition', *Bulletin of the Indo-Pacific Prehistory Association* 16: 103-6.

Whitefield, J. 2002. 'Rice Genome Unveiled', *Nature News,* 5th April, 2002.

Yasuda, Y. 1999. 'The Forest Dwellers Started Rice Cultivation in China', *ECGP Newsletter.*

——. 2000. 'The Oldest Remains of a Chinese Circular Walled Fortification with a Ritual Earth Mound Related to Rice Cultivation', *YRCP Newsletter* 3(1): 1-4.

Zide, A.R.K. and N.H. Zide. 1976. 'Proto-Munda Cultural Vocabulary: Evidence for Early Agriculture' in *Austro-Asiatic Studies*, P.N. Jenner *et al.* (eds). Honolulu: Oceanic Linguistics Special Publication 13.

# 10

# Folklore Biomedicine for Some Veterinary Diseases and Disorders in Western Part of Almora District

Rohita Shah, P.C. Pande and Lalit Tiwari

## INTRODUCTION

The western part of Almora district in the state of Uttaranchal is endowed with rich and diverse plant wealth. Chamoli borders the study area in north, Pauri Garhwal in the west and Nainital district in the south. It lies between 79° 5′ to 79° 56′ E longitude and 29° 7′ to 29° 40′ N latitude. A large section of population living in the rural areas practises agriculture. Most of the people largely depend on plants' resources growing in their surroundings to meet their requirements including ethno-veterinary herbal medicines. Survey of literature (Issar 1981; Gaur *et al.* 1992; Pande *et al.* 1992; Khanna *et al.* 1993; Tewari *et al.* 1998; Pande and Joshi 1999, 2001; Mathpal and Pande 2000; Pande and Mamgai 2001; Pande and Chandra 2001; Pande and Pandey 2002) shows that very little attention has been paid to ethno-veterinary aspects of plants in Uttaranchal.

Keeping this in view, the present paper is an attempt to compile the ethno-veterinary medicines of western part of Almora district of Uttaranchal Himalaya. In all, 62 plant species are used by the natives of the study area for the treatment of 25 diseases of domestic animals (cow, buffalo, ox and goat). Most of the uses were found to be new compared with those in published literature (Jain 1999) on ethno-veterinary science.

## MATERIAL AND METHODS

Remote villages of west Almora district of Uttaranchal were surveyed by one of us, Rohita Shah, during the year 2000-2001 and ethno-veterinary information was collected through interviewing local medicine men and experienced people. The information was further verified by cross-checking with other knowledgeable persons of the study area. Voucher plant specimen were identified with the help of floras and deposited in the herbarium of Botany Department, Kumaon University, S.S.J. Campus, Almora. The ethno-veterinary medicinal data are presented alphabetically disease-wise.

## ENUMERATION OF BIOMEDICINES USED AGAINST VETERINARY DISEASES AND DISORDERS

### Bone Fracture

#### Treatments

To treat fractured bones, different methods are employed by villagers.

1. Paste of two plants, e.g. *harjojan* (*Dendrobium amoenum*) and *dhyar lagual (Vitis himalayansis*) is plastered around fractured bone and bandaged using splints of wood of *Debregeasia salicifolia* until the cure is obtained.
2. Paste of bark of *chamarhmau* (*Carpinus viminea*), soaked *urad* (*Vigna radiata*) and fresh rhizome of *haldi* together with egg yolk is applied on bone fracture and is bandaged.
3. Paste of bark of *chamarhmau*, paste of *urad* (soaked in water) and paste of pine needles is mixed and applied on bone fracture and bandaged using splints made up of *bans* (*Dendrocalamus strictus*).
4. Paste prepared from soaked seeds of *urad (mas)* and *dhyar lagul* mixed with some long hair of human or animal is applied on the fractured bone and bandaged using splints of *bans*.
5. Paste prepared from bark of *chamarhmau*, bark of *tumariya* and stem of *dolu* (*Rheum emodii*) is plastered around fractured bone and bandaged using splints of *Debregeasia salicifolia*.

### Broken Horns

#### Symptoms

Causes bleeding from the injured site; sometimes it gets infected and develops swelling with appearance of pus cells.

Treatments

1. Fresh cow-dung is applied on painful horns.
2. Paste of *haldi* rhizome (*Curcuma domestica*) mixed with *pithyan* is applied on broken horns.
3. Pine (*Pinus roxburghii*) resin is applied on broken horns.
4. Juice or paste prepared from leaves of *neem (Azadirachta indica*) is applied on broken site of horns to prevent bacterial infection.
5. Clean cloth dipped in dilute phenyl is tied on the wounded area.

### Carbuncles/Pimples

Treatments

1. Paste prepared from tender shoot of *ataruwa (Onothera rosea)* is applied on carbuncle or pimples until the cure is obtained.
2. Leaf paste of *pipsos (leucas lanata)* is also applied on pimples.

### Loose Motion (*Chhipari*)

Symptoms

1. Cattle stops drinking and eating.
2. Animals become lean and thin.
3. Stool turns solid or semi-solid.
4. Animal feels sign of restlessness and discomfort.

Treatments

1. *Tumariya gha* pounded with grains of *jau (Hordeum vulagare)* is given orally to the cattle.
2. Dried powder of *lal mirch (Capsicum officinarum)* with limewater is given orally to animal, three times a day till relief. As a precaution, at least one hour before this prescription, 100 gm of *gur (Saccharum officinarum)* should be given.
3. Fresh leaves and young twigs of *Zanthoxylum alatum* are ground into paste and then mixed with dried powder of *lal mirch* and finally this mixture is kept inside *maduwa* flour *(Eleusine coracana)*. The sandwich is given to the cattle thrice a day for three days.

### Constipation (*Kabjiyat*)

Treatments

1. Powder prepared from *ajwain (Carum coptcum)* mixed with wheat (*Triticum aestivum)* flour is fed to animal.

2. Juice made from *Plumbago zeylanica* and *timur* (*Zanthoxylum alatum*) is also given to animal.

DAMARI (SKIN DISEASE): Three types of *Damari* are known in this region:

1. *Suk damari* or *sukhi damari* (stool becomes solid).
2. *Chheeru damari* or *geeli damari* (stool becomes loose).
3. *Simai damari* (boils and blisters appear on the skin).

In all these types of *damari,* other common features that appear are:

1. Skin becomes reddish and dries up and dung smells foul.

### Treatments

1. Paste prepared from black *bhatt (Glycine soja)* along with dried powder of *haldi* is given to the animal.
2. Wheat *(Triticum aestivum)* or cleaned rice *(Oryza sativa)* and seeds of black *bhatt (Glycine soja*) are soaked in water and made into paste; this paste is also given.
3. Paste prepared from *ganjarhu (Stephania glabra),* whole plant of *doob* grass (*Cynodon dactylon*), fresh rhizome of *haldi (Curcuma domistica)* and seeds of black *bhatt* are given to the animal particularly in *suk damari* twice a day for seven days.
4. Crushed stem of *gurch (Tinospora cordifolia)* is given to the animal till cured.
5. A mixture of powder of 22 dried fruits of *lal mirch* (*Capsicum annuum*), nine dried flowers of *laung* (*Syzygium aromaticum*), 13 seeds of *kaali mirch* (*Piper nigrum)* with water is given orally on first, fourth and seventh day.
6. Paste of black *bhatt* and *ganjaru* leaf is given orally once or twice a day for a week.
7. Seeds of *tater* (*Oroxylum indicum*) along with the paste of black *bhatt* are given twice a day for a week.
8. Paste of black *bhatt* with *lahsun* (*Allium sativum*) and a pinch of red sterile soil are given orally to the animal.

### Precaution

Seeds residue or seeds coat of *masoor* (*Lens culinaris*) are not given to animal during *damari.*

## DIARRHOEA

### Symptoms

1. Loose stool (dung).

2. Loss of appetite.
3. The animals become weak.

Treatments

1. *Lassi* with some salt, grounded leaves of *dhania (Coriandrum sativum)* and juice of lemon (*Citrus limon*) is given to the animal.
2. Wheat (*Triticum aestivum*) flour is given with first pudding of rice.
3. Rice husk, grains of *Echinochloa frumentecea,* flour of *jau* grains (*hordeun vulgare*) and ripe fruit of *kaddu (Cucurbita maxima)* are given in diet.

### Dog Bite

Treatments

1. Dried red *pepper (Capsicum annuum)* made into powder is applied locally on the wounds.
2. Wounded portion is burnt with the help of burning wooden stick of *baigain (Solanum melangena).*

### Eczema or Scabies

Symptoms

1. Appearance of different size of blisters on skin followed by itching.
2. Skin becomes thick and reddish.

Treatments

1. Juice of onion *(Allium cepa)* mixed with milk or curd along with sulphur powder is applied on affected area.
2. Black *bhatt (Glycine soja),* gram *(Cicer arietinum)* and salt are given in diet.

### Food Poisoning

Symptoms

1. Stops feeding.
2. Sign of anxiousness and impaired movement.

Treatments

1. Citrus *(Citrus limon)* juice boiled in water is given orally to the animal thrice a day.
2. Paste prepared from fresh rhizome of *adrakha (Zingeber officinale)* and leaves or seeds of *dhania (Coriandrum sativum)* mixed with *lassi* are given to the animal orally.

3. Powder of dried *aam* peels *(Magnifera indica)* and fruit extract of two *nimboos (Citrus limon)* along with water is given to the animal orally.
4. A mixture of powder of *methi (Trigonella foenum-graecum), gur* (product of *Saccharum officinarum*), powder of *ajwain (Carum copticum)*, powder of dried *soonth (Zingiber officinale)* is given to the animal orally.

## Foot and Mouth Disease

### Symptoms

1. Continuous secretion of mucus from mouth and hoofs (cleft of feet).
2. Appearance of boils and blisters with sore around and in mouth as well as on foot (cleft of feet). If not treated immediately, pus and maggots formation may occur.
3. Loss of appetite, continuous fever and reduction in milk yield.

### Treatment

1. Paste prepared from root bark of *karunj (Carissa spinarum)* is applied on affected part.
2. Cleft of feet are washed with phenyl and then *kapoor* (a product of *Cinnamomum tamala*) is applied on the affected part of the animals.
3. Red mud is also applied on the cleft of foot.
4. Villagers take their animals for a walk in mud once in a day until cured.

### Precaution

Movement of animals to adjoining villages is prohibited or restricted.

## Galghotu

### Symptom

Muscular swelling develops on the throat of animals, which causes obstruction in the passage of throat, and the animal faces problems in breathing and eating.

### Treatment

A red-hot iron is applied with jolts for a bit of movement on swollen portion until cured. Only an expert gives this type of treatment.

### Haematuria (Blood Mixed Urine)

#### Treatment

Plant juice of banana (juice prepared from whole plant of *Musa paradisiacal,* e.g. underground stem, pseudo-stem and leaves) is given orally to the animal many times a day.

### Impaction and Tympany

#### Symptoms

1. Stops eating and excreting.
2. Feels uneasy.
3. Nose and mouth dry up.
4. Indigestion and accumulation of gas in the rumen.

#### Treatments

1. Mustard oil (*Brassica campestris*) or *desi ghee* is given to the animal.
2. Leaves of *akhrot (Juglans regia)* and *chalmori (Oxalis corniculata)* are pounded and given.
3. Paste of leaves of *dhania (Coriandrum sativum)* mixed with *lassi* is given to the animal.
4. Leaves of *rameshwar* grass is fed to the animal.
5. Fresh juice of *nimbu (Citrus limon)* is also given.

### Internal Wounds

#### Treatments

1. A pinch of *fitkari* (alum) mixed with milk is given to the animal.
2. Lukewarm salty water is applied as a fomentation on the affected parts.
3. Paste of seeds of *bichhu (Urtica dioca)* mixed with sugar is applied locally.
4. Powder of *charas* (resinous product of female flower of *Cannabis sativa*) mixed with resin of *chir (Pinus longifolia*) is applied at the site of internal wounds.

### Mastitis

#### Symptoms

1. Heaviness and inflammation of the udder/mammary glands. Also blockage of milk capillaries.
2. Stops eating, reduces milk quantity, does not allow to touch the mammary glands due to pain.

### Treatments

1. Paste of *thanelle* plant is applied on udder/mammary glands 2-3 times a day for 4-6 days.
2. Juice extracted from the fresh leaves of *shahtut (Morus serrata)* is applied locally on affected parts.
3. A mixture of paste prepared from fresh rhizome of *haldi (Curcuma domestica)* and clean *rice (Oryza sativa)* is applied on mammary glands 2-3 times a day for 4-6 days.
4. Ash prepared from dried plants of *Kaddu (Cucurbita maxima)* mixed with butter is applied on udder.
5. Fresh and pointed *doob* grass *(Cynodon dactylon*) is used to open the blocked pore of the udder.

## *Mauni*

### Symptoms

Only goat is infected with this disease. Blisters develop on the mouth of the goat. If not treated immediately, it bleeds; inflammation and pus cells appear all over the mouth.

### Treatments

1. Charcoal made into a paste is applied 2-3 times a day on infected part of the mouth of the goat.
2. Cooked *jhungar (Echinochloa furmentacea)* is also applied locally.
3. Any cooked material along with human spit is applied throughout the affected parts of the mouth of the goat.
4. Paste prepared from *mauni* plant is applied locally.

## Neck Sore/Yolk Sore

### Symptoms

1. Cracks, blisters and boils appear on the neck.

### Treatments

1. Paste prepared from any dead animal's horn is applied on neck sore till it is cured.
2. Paste prepared from the lip of dead pig is applied on the wounds.
3. *Chamgadar's* (bat) blood is applied on the neck sore.
4. Frog's (toad) blood is also applied on the neck sore.
5. Fresh *Urtica dioca* leaves are made into poultice and swabbed gently on neck sore.

### Prolapse Uterus

#### Symptoms

1. Uterus remains in the state of prolapse; due to this, the animal feels uneasy and stops eating.

#### Treatments

1. Sufficient water, grass or fodder are given in diet.
2. Uterus is pushed inside with the help of cleaned leaves of *timul (Ficus roxburghii)* or banana (*Musa paradisiacal*).
3. If frequency of prolapse of uterus increases then villagers tie a bag filled with ½ or 1 kg paddy (*Oryza sativa*) on the vagina of the animal.

### Peterygium (*Ankh Mein Fool Parna*)

#### Treatments

1. Fine powder of *pithyan* (product of *Curcuma domestica*) is stuffed in a *naktur (Phragmites karka)* blowpipe and the eye is smoked.
2. Juice of the fruit of *mehal (Pyrus pashia)* mixed with salt is put inside the eye.
3. In some cases, extract of the bulb of the *pinnar (Urginia indica)* is given as eye drop for 3-4 times a day.

### Redness of Eyes (Conjunctivitis/Pink Eye)

#### Treatments

1. Aqueous extract of the *chuthar (Berberis asiatica, Berberis chitria)* is given as eye drop for 2-3 times a day until cured.
2. Aqueous extract of the fresh rhizome of *haldi (Curcuma domestica)* is mixed with dilute alum solution and is sprinkled in the eyes.
3. Aqueous extract of the fruit of *mehal (Pyrus pashia)* is sprinkled in the eye.
4. Fine powder of *haldi (Curcuma domestica)* is stuffed in *naktur (Phragmitis karka)* blowpipe and the eyes are smoked.
5. *Kaddu* (*Curcurbita maxima*) is given to animal in diet.

### Retention of Placenta

#### Symptoms

Placenta gets retained after birth of young one; animal stops feeding the young one, abnormal behaviour due to pain.

### Treatments

1. Fresh juice obtained by crushing whole plant of *kapunaya* (*Strobilanthes sp*) is given to the animal. Juice of the root of the said plant is also given.
2. Leaves of *rameshwar* grass are fed to the animal after childbirth for expulsion of placenta.

## Sprains

### Symptoms

1. Swelling and inflammation at the sprained site.
2. Cattle unable to move.

### Treatments

1. Clay soil or soil of anthills is applied locally.
2. Mixture of paste prepared from the seeds of *urad (Vigna radiata)* and cleaned rice *(Oryza sativa)* is applied on sprains.
3. Fresh rhizome of *haldi (Curcuma domestica)* pounded with *doob* grass *(Cynodom dactylon)* and mixed with a pinch of calcium oxide is boiled. Lukewarm decoction is sprinkled at the sprained site.
4. Fresh needle of *Pinus roxburghii* mixed with ash and pinch of salt is boiled. The solution or decoction prepared in this way is sprinkled gently on sprained site for 10-15 minutes.
5. A glass of lukewarm milk along with a teaspoon full dried *haldi (Curcuma domestica)* powder is given to the cattle twice daily.
6. A fresh twig of *bichhu (Urtica dioca)* is tabbed gently on the sprains.
7. Pine resin is also applied on sprains till cure.

## Sterility

### Treatments

1. Leaves of *jau (Hordeum vulgare)* are pounded with cooked grains of *madira (Echinochloa frumentacea)* and soaked *methi* seeds *(Trigonnel folnum-gracecum),* one administered orally once or twice a day for a month.
2. Cooked or boiled *maduwa (Eleusine coracana)* flour along with a pinch of salt is given.

## Wounds

### Treatments

1. Paste of the whole plant of *Rubia cordifolia* is applied locally on the wounds.

2. Leaf paste of *peoli (Reinwardhia trigyan)* is applied on wounds.
3. Powder of *charas* (resinous product of female flower of *Cannabis sativa*) is applied on wounds.
4. Young leaves of *chaulai* (*Amaranthus sp*) ground with soaked seeds of *urad (Vigna radiata)* are applied on wounds.
5. Paste of *bichhu (Urtica dioca)* seeds mixed with sugar (product of *Saccharum officinarum)* is applied on the washed wounds.

## CONCLUSION

1. The present investigation has brought to light some popular and frequently used prescriptions obtained from 62 plants, five animals, birds, minerals (soils, calcium oxide) and chemicals (phenyle, sulphur powder, alum) available for twenty-five ailments and disorders of domestic animals.
2. Most of the uses (marked with *Δ* in Table 1) were found to be new when compared with those reported in published literature on veterinary medicine from India (Jain 1999). Further, the use of 15 potential plants (marked with √ in the Table 1) species are recorded for the first time.
3. Most of the remedies recorded in this study consist of only one species and some with a mixture of species and additives to enhance their efficacy to cure diseases and majority of diseases and disorders are treated by samples of leaves, grains and fruit.
4. Decoction paste, aqueous extracts, infusion, powder and mixture of plants or plant produce, etc. are the common methods employed by local practitioner for the preparation of herbal drugs.
5. In majority of cases, fresh plants and plant parts are used for alleviating pains. Certain plants (marked with asterisk * in Table 1) have manifold properties or possess efficacy to cure different diseases and disorders.
6. *Galghotu* is the only disease where no herbal medicine is used; hence it is treated mechanically. Similarly prolapse of uterus is also treated mechanically.
7. There is a need to popularize these treatments as they are cheap and effective but before doing so proper analysis of medicinal plants is essential to establish the authenticity and efficacy of these treatments.
8. The study will provide basic data for further studies aimed to conservation of traditional medicine and economic welfare of rural people in the study area.
9. Such traditional knowledge is a wealth for human being and has value in the context of today's Intellectual Property Rights scenario.

## ACKNOWLEDGEMENTS

The authors are thankful to Prof. G.C. Joshi, Head, Department of Botany, Kumaon University, Almora for providing facilities to work and to Prof. D.P. Agrawal for valuable suggestions and encouragements. The cooperation extended by local healers or knowledgeable persons of the study area is gratefully acknowledged.

## BIBLIOGRAPHY

Farooquee, N.A. and A. Nautiyal. 1999. 'Traditional Knowledge and Practices of Bhotia Pastoralists of Kumaon Himalaya: The Need for Value Addition', *Interational J. Sustain. Dev. World Ecol.*, 6(1): 60-70.

Gaur, R.D. *et al.* 1992. 'An Ethnobotanical Study of Uttar Pradesh Himalaya in Relation to Veterinary Medicines', *J. Indian Bot. Soc.*, 72: 139-44.

Issar, R.K. 1981. 'Traditionally Important Medicinal Plants and Folklore of Uttaranchal Himalaya for Animal Treatment', *J. Sci. Res. Pl. Med.*, 2: 61-66.

Jain, S.K. 1999. *Dictionary of Ethnoveterinary Plants of India*. New Delhi: Deep Publications.

Khanna, K.K. *et al.* 1993. 'Unknown Traditional Uses of Plants as Veterinary Medicines from Uttar Pradesh', *Proced. Nat. Acad. Sci. India*, 63 (4).

Mathpal, H. and P.C. Pande. 2000. 'Kumaon Himalaya ke Vinayak Kshetra Main Paltu Pashuon ki Paramparagat Chikistsa Paddhati', *Parvatika*. Ranibag: Lok Chetna Manch evam Mountain Forum.

Pande, P.C. (in press), 'Kumaon Himalaya Main Prachalit Pashu Chikitsa Avam Pashuon Se Sambandhit Anya Gyan' in *Traditions and Traditional Knowledge of Central Himalaya*, P.C. Pande and N. Joshi (eds.). Dehradun: Bishan Singh Mahendra Pal Singh.

Pande, P.C. and G.C. Joshi. 1999. 'Kumaon Himalaya ke Pashu-Chikista Aadi Main Pairh-Paudhon ka Upyog' in *Ethnobotany of Kumaon Himalaya*, P.C. Pande, *et al.* (eds.). Jodhpur: Scientific Publishers. Page numbers?

——. 2001. 'Cultivated Plants of Kumaon Himalaya Used for Medicinal Purpose' in *Himalayan Medicinal Plants: Potential and Prospects*, S.S. Samant. *et al.* (eds.). Nainital: Gyanodaya Prakashan.

Pande, P.C. *et al.* 1989. 'Ethnobotany of Kumaon Himalayas' in *Himalayas: Environment, Resources and Development*, N.K. Sah *et al.* (eds). Almora: Shree Almora Book Depot.

Pande, P.C. and Mamgai. 2001. 'Kumaon Mein Masi Ke Najdeek Bhumka Pani Kshetra Mein Parmparagat Pashub Chikitsha', *Swadheen Praja*, 8:4, 9:4, 12-13:3.

Pande, P.C. and M. Chandra. 2001. '*Kumaon Ke Bugeshwar Kshetra Mein Pashuon Kee Paramparagat Chikitsa Paddhati*' in *Uttaranchal Ke Anchal Se*, C.M. Agrawal (ed.). New Delhi: Indian Publishers Distributors.

Shah, R. 2001. *A Survey of Ethnoveterinary Medicine for Domestic Animal*. M.Sc Dissertation, Kumaon University, Nainital (Unpublished).

Tewari, K.C. *et al.* 1998. 'Uttarakhand Himalaya Mein Pashu Chikista Mein Sthaniy Zadhi Butiyon Ka Upyog' in *Proced. of National Symposium on Constraints and Opportunities in Himalayan Region*. P.C. Herbola (ed.). Mukteshwar: Indian Veterinary Research Institute.

Table 1. Plants Used In Different Diseases And Disorders

| ***Name of Plants*** | 1 | 2 | 3 | 4 | 5 | 6 | 7 | 8 | 9 | 10 | 11 | 12 | 13 | 14 | 15 | 16 | 17 | 18 | 19 | 20 | 21 | 22 | 23 | 24 | 25 |
|---|---|---|---|---|---|---|---|---|---|---|---|---|---|---|---|---|---|---|---|---|---|---|---|---|---|
| *Allium cepa*[Δ] | | | | | | | | | + | | | | | | | | | | | | | | | | |
| *Allium sativum*[Δ] | | | | | | + | | | | | | | | | | | | | | | | | | | |
| *Amaranthus sp.*[Δ] | | | | | | | | | | | | | | | | | | | | | | | | | + |
| *Azadirachata indica* | | + | | | | | | | | | | | | | | | | | | | | | | | |
| *Berberis asiatica*[Δ] | | | | | | | | | | | | | | | | | | | | | + | | | | |
| *Berberis chitria*[√] | | | | | | | | | | | | | | | | | | | | | + | | | | |
| *Brassica compestris* | | | | | | | | | | | | | | + | | | | | | | | | | | |
| *Cannabis sativa*[*Δ] | | | | | | | | | | | | | | | + | | | | | | | | | | + |
| *Capsicum annuum*[*] | | | | + | | + | | + | | | | | | | | | | | | | | | | | |
| *Carissa spinarum*[Δ] | | | | | | | | | | | + | | | | | | | | | | | | | | |
| *Carpinus viminea*[Δ] | + | | | | | | | | | | | | | | | | | | | | | | | | |
| *Carum copticum*[Δ] | | | | | + | | | | | | | | | | | | | | | | | | | | |
| *Cicer arietinum*[Δ] | | | | | | | | | + | | | | | | | | | | | | | | | | |
| *Cinnamomum tamala* | | | | | | | | | | | + | | | | | | | | | | | | | | |
| *Citrus limon*[*Δ] | | | | | | | + | | | + | | | | + | | | | | | | | | | | |
| *Coriandrum sativum*[*Δ] | | | | | | | + | | | + | | | | + | | | | | | | | | | | |
| *Cucurbita maxima*[*Δ] | | | | | | | + | | | | | | | | + | | | | | | | | | | |
| *Curcuma domestica*[*] | + | + | | | | + | | | | | | | | | + | | | | | + | + | | | | |
| *Cynodon dactylon*[*Δ] | | | | | | + | | | | | | | | | | + | | | | | + | | + | | |
| **Debregeasia salicifalia** | + | | | | | | | | | | | | | | | | | | | | | | + | | |
| *Dendrobium amoenum*[√] | + | | | | | | | | | | | | | | | | | | | | | | | | |
| *Dendrocalamus strictus*[Δ] | + | | | | | | | | | | | | | | | | | | | | | | | | |
| *Echinochloa frumentacea*[*√] | | | | | | | + | | | | | | | | | | + | | | | | | | + | |
| *Eleusine coracana*[*√] | | | | + | | | | | | | | | | | | | | | | | | | | + | |

| Name of Plants | 1 | 2 | 3 | 4 | 5 | 6 | 7 | 8 | 9 | 10 | 11 | 12 | 13 | 14 | 15 | 16 | 17 | 18 | 19 | 20 | 21 | 22 | 23 | 24 | 25 |
|---|---|---|---|---|---|---|---|---|---|---|---|---|---|---|---|---|---|---|---|---|---|---|---|---|---|
| *Ficus roxburghii*√ | | | | | | | | | | | | | | | | | | | + | | | | | | |
| *Glycine saja*$^{\Delta}$ | | | | | | | | | + | | | | | | | | | | | | | | | | |
| *Hordeam vulgare** | | | | + | | | + | | | | | | | | | | | | | | | | | | |
| *Juglans regia*$^{\Delta}$ | | | | | | | | | | | | | | + | | | + | | | | | | | | |
| *Lens culinaris*$^{\Delta}$ | | | | | | + | | | | | | | | | | | | | | | | | | | |
| *Leucas lanata*√ | | | + | | | | | | | | | | | | | | | | | | | | | | |
| *Mangifera indica*$^{\Delta}$ | | | | | | | | | + | | | | | | | | | | | | | | | | |
| *Mauni plant* | | | | | | | | | | | | | | | | | + | | | | | | | | |
| *Mours serrata*√ | | | | | | | | | | | | | | | | + | | | | | | | | | |
| *Musa paradisiacal** | | | | | | | | | | | | + | | | | | | | + | | | | | | |
| *Oenothera rosea*√ | | | + | | | | | | | | | | | | | | | | | | | | | | |
| *Oroxylum indicum*$^{\Delta}$ | | | | | | + | | | | | | | | | | | | | | | | | | | |
| *Oryza sativa**$^{\Delta}$ | | | | | | + | | | | | | | | | | | | | + | | | | + | | |
| *Oxalis corniculata* | | | | | | | | | | | | | | + | | | | | | | | | | | |
| *Phragmites karkav* | | | | | | | | | | | | | | | | | | | | + | | | | | |
| *Pinus roxburghii** | + | + | | | | | | | | | | | | | | | | | | | | | + | | |
| *Plumbago zeylanica* | | | | | + | | | | | | | | | | | | | | | | | | | | |
| *Pyrus pashia**$^{\Delta}$ | | | | | | | | | | | | | | | | | | | | + | + | | | | |
| *Rameshwar gha* | | | | | | | | | | | | | | | | | | | | | | + | | | |
| *Reinwardtia indicav* | | | | | | | | | | | | | | | | | | | | | | | | | + |
| *Rheum emodivi* | + | | | | | | | | | | | | | | | | | | | | | | | | |
| *Rubia cordifolia*$^{\Delta}$ | | | | | | | | | | | | | | | | | | | | | | | | | + |
| *Saccharum officinarum** | | | | + | | | | | | + | | | | | | | | | | | | | | | + |
| *Solanum melogena*$^{\Delta}$ | | | | | | | | + | | | | | | | | | | | | | | | | | |
| *Stephania glabra*$^{\Delta}$ | | | | | | + | | | | | | | | | | | | | | | | | | | |
| *Strobilanthis sp.* | | | | | | | | | | | | | | | | | | | | | | + | | | |

| *Name of Plants* | 1 | 2 | 3 | 4 | 5 | 6 | 7 | 8 | 9 | 10 | 11 | 12 | 13 | 14 | 15 | 16 | 17 | 18 | 19 | 20 | 21 | 22 | 23 | 24 | 25 |
|---|---|---|---|---|---|---|---|---|---|---|---|---|---|---|---|---|---|---|---|---|---|---|---|---|---|
| *Syzygium aromaticum* | | | | | | + | | | | | | | | | | | | | | | | | | | |
| *Thanella plant* | | | | | | | | | | | | | | | | + | | | | | | | | | |
| *Tinospora cordifilia* | | | | | | + | | | | | | | | | | | | | | | | | | | |
| *Trigonela foenum-graecum** | | | | | | | | | | + | | | | | | | | | | | | | | + | |
| *Triticum aestivum** | | | | | + | + | + | | | | | | | | | | | | | | | | | | |
| *Tumaria gha (?)* | | | | + | | | | | | + | | | | | | | | | | | | | | | |
| *Urginea indica* | | | | | | | | | | | | | | | | | | | | + | | | | | |
| *Urtica dioca** | | | | | | | | | | | | | | | + | | | + | | | | | | + | + |
| *Vigna radiate** | + | | | | | | | | | | | | | | | | | | | | | | | | + |
| *Vitis himalayensis* | + | | | | | | | | | | | | | | | | | | | | | | | | |
| *Zanthoxylum alatum** | | | | + | + | | | | | | | | | | | | | | | | | | | | |
| *Zingiber officinale* | | | | | | | | | | + | | | | | | | | | | | | | | | |

* Plants showing manifold properties.
√ Potential use of plants recorded for the first time as veterinary medicine.
Δ New uses of known medicinal plants.

**Key**

1= Bone fracture, 2= Broken horns, 3= Carbuncles/Pimples, 4= Loose motion, 5= Constipation, 6= Skin diseases, 7= Diarrhoea, 8= Dog bite, 9= Eczema or Scabies, 10= Food poisoning, 11= Foot and Mouth disease, 12= *Galghotu*, 13= Haematuria, 14= Impaction and Tympany, 15= Internal wounds, 16= Mastitis, 17= *Mauni*, 18= Neck sore/Yolk sore, 19= Prolapse uterus, 20= Pterygium, 21= Redness in eyes, 22= Retention of placenta, 23= Sprains, 24= Sterility, 25= Wounds.

Table 2: Statistical Analysis of Plants Used in Diseases and Disorder-Wise

| *Name of Disease and Disorder* | *WP* | *RT/TU/ RH/BL* | *RB* | *S* | *SH* | *SB* | *RE* | *LF* | *GR/FR* | *SD* | *FL* |
|---|---|---|---|---|---|---|---|---|---|---|---|
| Bone fracture | 2 | 2 | * | 3 | * | 2 | * | 1 | * | 1 | * |
| Broken horns | * | 1 | * | * | * | * | * | 2 | * | * | * |
| Carbuncles/Pimples | * | * | * | * | 1 | * | * | 1 | * | * | * |
| Loose motion | 1 | * | * | 1 | 1 | * | * | 1 | 3 | * | * |
| Constipation | * | * | * | * | 2 | * | * | * | 1 | 1 | * |
| Skin disease | 1 | 3 | * | 1 | * | * | * | 1 | 3 | 3 | 1 |
| Daiarrhoea | * | * | * | * | * | * | * | 1 | 6 | * | * |
| Dog bite | * | * | * | 1 | * | * | * | * | 1 | * | * |
| Eczema or Scabies | * | 1 | * | * | * | * | * | * | * | 2 | * |
| Food poisoning | * | 1 | * | 1 | * | * | * | 1 | 2 | 3 | * |
| Foot and Mouth disease | * | * | 1 | 1 | * | * | * | * | * | * | * |
| *Galghotu* | * | * | * | * | * | * | * | * | * | * | * |
| Haematuria | 1 | * | * | * | * | * | * | * | * | * | * |
| Impaction and tympany | * | * | * | * | * | * | * | 4 | 1 | 1 | * |
| Internal wounds | * | * | * | 1 | * | * | 2 | * | * | 1 | * |
| Mastitis | 2 | 1 | * | 1 | * | * | * | 1 | 1 | * | * |
| *Mauni* | 1 | * | * | 1 | * | * | * | * | 1 | * | * |
| Neck sore/Yolk sore | * | * | * | * | * | * | * | 1 | * | * | * |
| Prolapse uterus | * | * | * | * | * | * | * | 2 | 1 | * | * |
| Pterygium | 1 | 1 | * | 1 | * | * | * | * | 1 | * | * |
| Redness in eyes | 1 | * | * | * | 2 | * | * | * | 2 | * | * |
| Retention of placenta | 1 | * | * | * | * | * | * | 1 | * | * | * |
| Sprains | 1 | 1 | * | * | 1 | * | 1 | 1 | 1 | 1 | * |
| Sterility | * | 1 | * | * | * | * | * | 1 | 2 | 1 | * |
| Wounds | 1 | * | * | * | 1 | * | 1 | 3 | * | 1 | 2 |
| **TOTAL** | **13** | **12** | **1** | **12** | **8** | **2** | **4** | **22** | **26** | **15** | **3** |

***Abbreviations***

WP=Whole plant, RT=Root, TU=Tuber, BL=Bulb, RH=Rhizome, RB=Root bark, S=Stem and products, SH=Shoot, SB=Stem Bark, RE=Resin, LF=Leaf, GR=Grains, FR=Fruit, SD=Seed, FL= Flower.

# 11

# Wood-carving in Uttaranchal

Krishna Bisht

## INTRODUCTION

The craft of wood-carving is a traditional heritage of the people of Uttaranchal, but now this is gradually disappearing. Mahila Haat (MH) conducted a study called "Wood-Carving in Uttaranchal" to analyse the status of the woodcraft, the conditions of crafts persons and to find out ways for revival of this dying art.

In the process, the resource persons, MH team, and others travelled extensively into the interiors of Kumaon and Garhwal Hills. The villages en route to Kailash Mansarovar, such as Gunji, Garbayang, Kutti, Pangu; villages in Champawat, Lohaghat, Tauns Valley in Garhwal and others were covered. MH directly communicated with the crafts persons who are now very few in numbers and recorded their interviews during the study.

During our fieldwork we found that the craftsmen who were engaged in the art of wood-carving were in a very sorry state. The number of craftsmen involved in this economic activity has declined considerably and there are very few left now. On the one hand, we found out that the local craftsmen were unemployed because of the modern concrete housing architecture, on the other hand there was no local demand for wood-carving. Whatever traditional carving is left, is either being sold to Nepal or is being used as fuel wood. Our collection of photographs and slides has become valuable because these pieces are soon going to disappear. MH has an exclusive collection of more than 100 photographs of wood-carving which exhibit the elegant and rich workmanship of the people who were engaged in this craft.

We also found out that some people who were not local craftsmen were producing similar designs on a smaller scale, were giving it an antique touch and then exporting such products. But the original local craftsman does not benefit out of such endeavours because the opportunities are not within his reach because they are inhabitants of inaccessible interior areas of Uttaranchal.

## WOOD-CARVING IN DIFFERENT PARTS OF UTTARANCHAL

### Beas Chaundaas Valley

Beas Chaundaas and Darma Valleys, situated in the northern part of district Pithoragarh on the borders of India, Nepal and Tibet are famous for their cultural opulence. The lifestyle of the natives of this area is different and challenging compared to other parts of Kumaon because of the cold climate and insignificant agricultural activity. Wool craft and trade with Tibet have been the major occupations of this area. The economic condition is fair due to trade but life is very arduous and full of dangers. The sign of prosperity can be seen in the beautiful carvings done in their houses on wooden doors, windows, enclosures, and pillars. The wood-carving tradition here is at least 350 years old.

A team of MH went to this area for research. The journey began from Almora to Bageshwar, Chaukori, Askot, Dharchula and then to Tawaghat where the motor road ends. After that the journey on foot began. It took 15 days to reach Kutti from Pangu village. The natives of this area gave lots of information about the conditions in the past.

Businessmen (Shauka tribe) of this area used to trade with Tibet and that was the means of living for them. Garbayang *mandi* (market) was popular from the point of view of trade. These villages flourished mainly due to the trade with Tibet.

But trade activities of Shauka's of Kumaon and Marcha's of Garhwal stopped after the Chinese occupation of Tibet. The arduous and courageous journeys came to an end. A drastic change came in the lives of the inhabitants; wool trade was badly affected and the people dispersed widely. The natives of the villages on the border began migrating in search of employment. Wool and woodcrafts started degenerating and villages were deserted.

However, there are a few villages in this valley where magnificent art of wood-carving is still alive. When MH team studied the status of wood-carving and the socio-economic conditions of different villages of Beas Chaundaas Valley, it was discovered that Pangu, Sirkha, Bundi, Gunji, Naanbi, Rongkong and Kutti villages are still famous for wood-carving. The houses here are 100-400 years old. The doors and windows are kept intact in their original form. People have not even painted them but now these houses are in a state of disrepair, as proper care is not being taken.

The wood-carvers came from Munsyari, Champawat, Lohaghat and Almora to these villages. A few artisans live in the adjoining villages of Gala. Their ancestors used to practise this craft. But due to poor wages and as it is a time consuming craft, these folks are no more engaged in wood-carving. Moreover, migration is another cause for the degeneration of this craft.

### Champawat Lohaghat Area

In the thirteenth century Chand kings ruled Champawat and its surrounding areas. These kings took special care of the temples and the craftsmen. In those times many water reservoirs, called *naulas* in the local dialect, were built. The Chand kings called masons, carpenters and some Muslim workers from Rajasthan, Manihar and other areas. They were provided lodging facilities at Champawat, Lohaghat and surrounding areas. These people later on settled in this area itself.

Kumaon region has a number of temples, and the temple architecture style indicates that they must have been constructed between the seventh and eleventh century AD. In that period the work of stone carving had reached its acme.

The stone carving in various temples – Maha Mritunjaya temple of Jageshwar, Kuber and Dandeshwar temples of Bageshwar and Baleshwar temple of Champawat – speak volumes of this art and also point to the fact that skilled stone carvers must have lived here. The Shiva temple of Baleshwar has now been declared a heritage temple by the Archaeological Survey of India. It is evident from the 84 erotic figures in the temple of Baleshwar that sexual themes were not under any taboo. At the same time several water reservoirs were also constructed here.

Most of the houses have slanting roofs made of slate. The villages where wood-carving is found are 100-200 years old. The accurate time when these houses were built can only be established by the carbon dating, but people feel that these were built during the period of Chand kings. Wood-carving is found in the houses of Champawat and adjoining villages, Lohaghat, the Meena Bazaar of Lohaghat and in the villages like Rajpura, Chaurimaanes, Pati, Varakot, Khilpani, Digalichaur, Khalag, Kilura, Majhera, and Lamaaee, etc.

In most of the houses the woodwork is limited to designs of leaves-flowers. In many houses of village Khoona, where majority of inhabitants are from Muslim community, motifs of Hindu religion are also found apart from leaves-flowers. Serpent, dragon, Lord Hanuman, peacock, soldier sitting on a chair and fighting warriors are also carved in some houses. These pictures depict that all these must have been carved by Hindu artisans; their imaginative motifs are worth appreciating.

## UTTARKASHI AND CHAMOLI

Holy places like Gangotri and Yamunotri are located in the district Uttarkashi. During our research in Uttarkashi it was found that the temples rather than the dwellings were more adorned with wood-carving. Beautiful woodwork was found in the temples. It was also clear that the architecture of temples in Garhwal is different from the temples of Kumaon. Three-storey temples such as Someshwar and Bhadra Kali temples are found here.

Exquisite examples of wood-carving are seen in the Tons Valley, ahead of Purola. The wood-carving here is quite similar to that of Himachal Pradesh. The dress, language and culture apparently are similar to Himachal. Besides the wooden statues and masks of goddesses, wooden litter for the goddess is a speciality. The barns, used to store cereals, are also embossed with carvings.

The carving done on the doors of the houses in district Chamoli is bewitching. Figures of Lord Hanuman, Surya or Om word are engraved on the doorway of some houses. The double-storey umbrella of the temple of Shri Badri Vishal is made of wood with fine carvings done on it.

A few beautiful illustrations of wood-carving are also kept in the museum at Srinagar University, Garhwal.

## CRAFTSMEN OF WOOD-CARVING

In Uttaranchal, almost all the village-based blacksmiths make carving tools and the carpenters themselves make lathis of tools and wooden hilts. All the craftsmen have inherited the skills of wood-carving from their fathers and grandfathers and later on they developed the art in accordance with their taste and interests. There are not any training centres to learn carpentry and wood-carving in Uttaranchal.

Wood carvers hold a special position among the different artisans. Overlooking the post-Independence social scenario of craftsmen, it is evident that they were ranked fourth in the caste order. Despite the social conservatism regarding the norms of touchability, other castes did not have any ill feelings or discrimination towards this section of society in Uttaranchal. In recent times, the caste system has emerged as a political issue; as a result distances between castes have been created. It was found during the research that wood-carving has been mostly done in houses belonging to wealthy families, but in a few cases it was also seen in the houses belonging to middle class families.

Nowadays, the demands for wood-carving are very limited; the number of craftsmen has decreased and their work is limited to carpentry. Artisans have left the traditional work of wood-carving and have opted for other occupations. A carpenter gets 80-90 rupees per day but there is very little work available for him. They are engaged in this work for not more than 15 days in a month hence their economic condition is weak, so to earn livelihood they work as labourers and also cultivate their small fields. The young men want to change their occupation but at present they are unable to foresee any other employment opportunities. The present day education system diverts them from their traditional occupations and prepares them to take up white-collar jobs that are not available.

The craftsmen who were able to display their art are still proud of their achievements. They were honoured in the society, but today's craftsman does not get an opportunity to show the glory of his craft because the modern houses are no more built in the traditional style in Uttaranchal. Since 1980s the houses are constructed with a RCC ceiling, doors and windows are either made of iron or wood without any carving. The artisans of Uttaranchal excelled in making *patal* (sloping roof of stones) but do not know the techniques of constructing cement ceiling. This fact was referred to many times during our study that the designs, raw material, labourers and artisans coming from outside Uttaranchal are in demand. Today the whole brigade of craftsmen of wood-carvers is standing on the crossroads: what would be their future? Most of the villages of craftsmen were found in a poor state.

Almost all the craftsmen opined that good earnings could be made only if there was work. If the government or other organizations could help in providing training in this craft, or help in marketing the finished goods then their condition could improve. Besides this the craft of wood-carving can be refined if workshops and training centres for wood-carving are opened.

## FUTURE OF WOOD-CARVING

Before discussing the future of wood-carving, it is necessary that we describe below the reasons for the gradual degeneration of this art in Uttaranchal.

If we compare the present day Uttaranchal with that of the period before 1970, we see a vast difference in the socio-economic structure. Moving back in time, we find that the villages had an identity, a distinctiveness of their own. At that time, the social framework was such that every caste excelled in certain vocation and each served the society with its skill. A farmer cultivated fields, ploughman ploughed the fields and artisans and masons constructed beautiful houses. All these occupations were limited to their own society. Because of this reason we find the wood-carvings in Uttaranchal confined to local houses, temples, etc. The artisans of wood-carving have not given it a commercial mould; the wood-carving manifests their fervour for art and craft. To give a beautiful and artistic shape to the place of dwelling, to adorn the temples and express religious and decorative motifs through their wood-carvings was a part of their lifestyle. The wood-carving of the state of Gujarat, Rajasthan, south India, UP, etc. is very beautiful, intricate and commercial. Even today the woodcraft articles made by the craftsmen from these places are exported, while people of Uttaranchal have not developed their craft to this level.

As soon as modernity and fast paced life made its way to Uttaranchal, the traditionally designed houses and the artisans, masons and buildings were also influenced by the change. Everything came from outside to the mountains and because of this reason local craftsmen began losing their base in their work area. It is very difficult for them to earn livelihood from this work. They do not get the opportunity to demonstrate their art. After Independence everybody got equal rights to education and job opportunities were open for them so the new generation was not compelled to follow their forefathers and continue the traditional work. Instead, they preferred to study and work somewhere else but today's generation cannot get jobs easily. Moreover, traditional work is also not available for them because there are no possibilities to integrate the traditional art and craft in our education system. Therefore our traditional skills are not developing and are fading away; hence the craft of wood-carving is on the verge of extinction.

As mentioned earlier, the wood-carving of Uttaranchal was not commercial at all; it was done to embellish temples and houses with auspicious words with deep meaning and images. The new generation can be trained in this. A course module can be developed in the industrial training institutes, training in wood-carving to interested youth can be imparted through workshops, and the craftsmen can also provide training. In these training schools, apart from teaching them the skill of wood-carving, they should be informed about the importance of different trees, wood and the climatic conditions in which they grow. They should also be informed about the importance of forest, environment and their conservation.

Today carved wooden showpieces can be developed. Different shapes of gods and goddesses, jewellery boxes, wall hanging, ashtray, penholder, flowerpot, etc. of wood can be carved and sold. Training in product development can also be imparted. These artefacts can be sold in Uttaranchal since it is a tourist destination. However, the government and NGOs should help the craftsmen in marketing.

If the different government departments, schools, colleges, universities, *panchayat ghar*, hospitals, tourist rest houses, etc. apply traditional architecture and wood-carving in construction of their buildings then many people will get employment and the traditional style of construction will also make the buildings earthquake resistant. The craftsmen should be trained from time to time so that they can excel in their work.

All the construction should be done in the traditional style in Uttaranchal but we should never forget that the forests are the basis of this craft. If we do not conserve and protect our forests then the future of this craft shall be bleak, hence it is necessary to plant more and more trees. These forests should be used for local requirements; whoever cuts a tree shall plant ten trees. Such should be the policy and for this the local people will have to develop a bond with the forest. The efforts that have been made towards this should be intensified.

With all these efforts, the future of wood-carving can become bright and this craft can be saved from extinction.

# 12

# Traditional Knowledge in Environment Management
## A Participatory View

Reema Pant

### INTRODUCTION

Don't walk in front of me: I may not follow
Don't walk behind me: I may not lead
Walk beside me: Be my friend

The exploration into the atomic and sub-atomic world brought to the scientists, a painful realization that the basic rules, thoughts, ideology and to a certain extent even our approach was inadequate to understand the atomic world. Today this no longer remains an intellectual's problem but has permeated down to the level of the common man. The world today is undergoing a crisis of perception. Humanity today is trying to search its identity, which it lost somewhere with the advent of the Industrial Revolution.

We need a paradigm, a farsighted vision which can reduce if not revert the mess we have created in our lives and rekindle the torch of traditional knowledge in a modern perspective.

Traditional knowledge may be defined as the experiences of our ancestors sieved through generations. This set of knowledge is as old as the evolution of the man himself. The ancient man had probably realized the supremacy of nature and developed a lifestyle, which merged him with the nature and both shared a relationship of interdependence.

However, the age of classical science brought dramatic change in the lifestyle of mankind. Once mild and nature worshipping human race became atheist, suddenly the love for nature vanished and greed overcame its entire personality. The silent protests and laments of the ever-forgiving earth fell on deaf ears. The indiscriminate and unmanaged use of natural resources till date has made us a classical example of a world struggling between nature and livelihood. We have to return back to the lap of our mother but with little more sophistication. Now we have to blend the modern scientific findings with the existing traditional knowledge and rebuild our lives.

Traditional knowledge is holistic; it is not compartmentalised like modern science. Our ancestors had an insight and they knew that we could live in peace if we harmonize with nature. Like creation, they accepted destruction with same respect as a law of nature but devised techniques to prevent major losses. In the urbanized world, the traditional knowledge sadly has been buried in the sands of time, and the only bearers of this dying flame are the remnants of the tribal populations.

## SOME ATTEMPTS AT ENVIRONMENT MANAGEMENT

Till date the intellectuals and authorities knew of the approaching crisis but they had more important issues to think of and so the nature was left to tackle the situation alone. Now the authorities with the help of non-governmental organizations and local population are trying to revive the traditional systems to preserve the biodiversity and cultural heritage of these very few pristine areas.

Rajasthan, which is a stronghold of large tribal population, has initiated this step by forming India's first people's parliament. This body ensures protection of water catchments, encourages organic farming and conserves forests and wildlife. A lot has changed for the people in this tribal belt since then. Still the question that arises is how far will this effort continue without malice?

The problem lies in the execution. Laws may be passed and the court may order the authorities to enforce them. In practice, how much will actually be done to clean up the mess accumulated over the years due to faulty policies and careless implementation will need to be ascertained.

In our own state, that is Uttaranchal, the fragile ecological balance has been tampered with by excessive anthropogenic interferences. The situation has come to a stage that the culturally and ecologically rich state has patches of bare rocky structures once called the green Himalayas. The local community of Uttaranchal for long had remained isolated from the rest of the country and had developed a sustainable system to survive, exploiting the natural resources without taxing the earth. Traditionally, the village communities had identified certain forest patches as sacred. These patches usually with a perennial spring and economically important trees have high religious sentiments.

These sacred groves not only provided people with pure drinking water but also were a source of fodder leaves and compost for agriculture. The removal of dry leaves and twigs was permissible but plantation of young saplings of the *deodar* trees was mandatory. This ritual, however unusual it may sound, had immense conservation value. It maintained a simple sustainable living pattern with no major damage to the ecosystem. But the initial intervention of the British for their selfish purposes and later the shallow and short-sighted decisions of the concerned authorities failed to understand the depth of the tradition and broke the chastity of this land.

Excessive felling of the trees for economic reasons without proper regeneration plan led to denudation of the forests and disappearance of the wildlife. This accounted for landslides and climatic fluctuations. To replenish the felling, pine plantation was carried out on mass scale, further damaging the natural balance.

Biodiversity cannot be preserved without the participation of the local people and inputs from their traditional methods of conservation. Practice of sanctification of certain grooves was revived again by the locals when they felt that judicial activism had failed them. The problem lies in the implementation. We cannot expect a person with a westernized perception to sit remotely and dictate solutions for problems faced by the local people. Hence, problems should be addressed by employing the strengths of indigenous techniques and that of community participation. And when the problem at hand is as sensitive as ecology then there is no room for compromise.

Another example where traditional knowledge and modern science have blended to solve the problem of people is of salinity of water in the state of Gujarat. Here the problem was that saline groundwater was polluting stored rainwater ponds managed by the local village women. To combat the problem, women with the help of a non-governmental organization working in the area constructed new ponds and lined them with low density polythene. This experiment has been so successful that it could be used as an example to conserve water even in places where lining the pond with cement is not possible for a variety of reasons.

## CONCLUSION

Today when technology has given us the options, we must initiate the process of ironing the self-created differences between modern and traditional systems of science. We must learn from the mistakes made by the developed countries that just dumped their traditional wisdom and thought that modern science had answers to all their troubles.

This can, therefore, be said that the earth needs us and we are dependent on it. There is a strong need to start a new kind of literacy mission: mission of eco-literacy. In an attempt to undo our mistakes we have to work together to reduce the effects of catastrophe. Charity begins from home, so why wait. A scheme has to be crafted incorporating all living and non-living systems for building a sustainable programme. We need to work out a way that allows a smooth flow of energy. Selfish gains have to be given up for attaining a common goal. Each one of us needs to start this work within our capacities at the earliest.

# 13

# The Craftsman as Mythicist

Shampa Shah

## INTRODUCTION

"Thanks to an imaginary breakthrough, reality follows suit. Nature imitates narrative" writes Levi-Strauss while relating the instance of a difficult childbirth, for which a shaman (a traditional healer) had to be summoned. This shaman then narrates to the woman, the story of a man imprisoned by a demon, subsequently rescued by a handful of chivalrous arms-men. That is the way he resolves the difficulty with the help of a story. The prisoner emerging free from the cave of the demon inspires similar sense of liberation in the expectant mother and thereby in the child to come.

Over a decade, my association with the tribal and folk societies has somewhere made me realize that they do not necessarily inhabit the world they are born into. More often than not it is the vivid world of the narrative that they inhabit. The paradoxes of the "given" world and the various problems it poses forces the inhabitants to find their solutions in this other world of their creation, thereby throwing the whole question of "reality" into jeopardy.

Similar to this world of imagination and yet different from it is another world – that of the dream. Gandhi's dream of *Ramrajya* is one such dream, not very distant though and already haunted by the nightmare of the American materialism. Humanity has dreamt many such dreams whose subsequent ruins have also become a part of its memory. Though the dreams we are talking about are essentially concerned with improving the quality of life of this tangible world we are born into, sometimes of transforming it too. This is not a challenge to its fate but its very nature of being.

Nevertheless, the history of these dreams is on record for anyone to see, and moreover this discourse focuses not on these dream worlds but on the narrative world that was mentioned above.

## RELATIONSHIP BETWEEN THE NARRATIVE WORLD AND THE PRACTICAL KNOWLEDGE OF THE HUMAN BEING

Here I would like to dwell upon the relationship between the narrative world and the knowledge of the people of their existence and environment. Different persons narrated these narratives to me. Craftsman Shri Pyarelal Poyam narrated the first of these narratives, Gond myth of creation. Badadev felt like creating something. He rubbed his two hands together and gathered some dirt. Thereafter he started making some forms with it, cow, horse, lion, deer, duck and hen; his hands just would not stop. When it came to man, he created as many kinds of faces as he could, so much so that it mounted up to a crowd and created chaos. Badadev looked down and saw water everywhere below him. Where was the earth? Where to keep all these creatures? Badadev did not feel like rolling them back to dirt. The responsibility to go looking for the earth fell on the crow. After three nights and four days of non-stop flight, a stump on the water surface caught its eye. The exhausted crow had barely settled down on it when a voice was heard, "Who is sitting on my claw?" The voice belonged to Kakramal Kshatriya (the crab).

On hearing the reason for the crow's visit, Kakramal said, "But the earth has sunk to the nether world, and Keechakmal (the earthworm) is constantly nibbling at it". After that Kakramal descended to the nether world and caught hold of the culprit. Keechakmal asked, "What will I eat if I give up the earth?" At which Kakramal strangled him so that he vomited the earth then and there. The mark of Kakramal's claw can still be seen on Keechakmal's neck. The crow thus brought the earth back in its beak. On Badadev's prompting, Makramal (spider) wove a net suspended over the water body for the earth to rest. And one by one all the creatures were placed on it. Badadev then plucked three of his hair strands and threw them down on the earth. They turned into the three trees of mango, *kasi* and teak. Ash from the fire-altar was sprinkled on them and soon there were trees everywhere. Badadev then gave his pickaxe to man and asked him to fell the dried trees and make something out of it. Whatever he made thus ensured the sustenance of his race thereafter.

Man immediately set to work with his pickaxe on the dry wood of the tree. But every time he struck the wood, *phadki*, the woodpecker from above pecked its beak in imitation too. Man was distracted. One by one he cut down three trees and to no avail. Not a single one of the pieces had come straight; all were crooked. In his rage man threw his pickaxe at *phadki*. It flew away and so did his pickaxe. Hungry and exhausted, the man reached Badadev.

Badadev however could not hide his annoyance, "How is it that all the other animals are able to fend for them and not you? Why don't you exercise your brain? If the wood is getting crooked again and again, there must be some secret there that you should try to find out." Man returned and in disgust struck the ground with the crooked wood. No sooner did the wood hit the ground than *basin kanya* or lady bamboo came out and from inside appeared the *Anna Devi* or the grain goddess.

The Gond woman taking a cue or two from the termite's house, constructed the *lillaar kothi* (granary) so that grain for the whole world could be stored in it. It is a belief among the Gonds that when the constellation is in the shape of the pickaxe and the plough is about to disappear in the sky, it is time for sowing. Two days later, the reappearing of the same *Nangar Kotela* constellation in the sky signifies the ushering of the monsoons.

This evolution myth of the Gonds carries within it a whole world-view besides many other signifiers. The idea of a granary to safely keep all the world's grains and the Gond woman's ingenuity in designing it calls for a closer look – the termite hill if one looks at it is made in such a way from the inside that there are many circular ways for the rainwater to flow out. Apart from it, it has separate compartments for the termite as well as grain storage, where the water cannot reach. The *lillaar kothi* or the clay granary's structure apart from being based on this particular design, in addition, serves architecturally as a partition or a door within the space of the Gond tribal house.

This knowledge of the termite hill structure, of the constellation in the sky, of ash as fertilizer, of the crab-claw mark on the earthworm's neck, of the story of evolution and its crucial links with water, all this goes on to prove an essential livewire link with the environment. The urge for story-telling is not just a wish to engage in a dialogue with a fellow human being, but in fact with the whole of the living and non-living world. And the beginnings of this wish are left too far behind for us to trace. To quote Tolkien one can very well express this view, "To ask what is the origin of stories is to ask, what is the origin of the language or of the mind itself"?

Life in its innumerable manifestations is ever ready to surprise us at every corner. By the time one begins to comprehend one's face, ten more raise their heads like the Ravana. Why this earth? Why this life on earth? Why this sky arching above? Why these insects and pests? Who are we? Where do we come and where will we go? Psychologist Carl Jung says, "Myths symbolise not cosmic phenomena but subconscious urges which if not expressed, can destroy us".

The potter Shri Sahadev of Bastar narrated the second narrative, the Halbi myth, to me. In Bastar district of Chhattisgarh, Doomadev is much revered. In the small village of Pendrawand, there is a lake with steps all around.

Story goes that a tribal lad and girl met on these steps once and fell in love. Their falling in love however was preceeded by quite a few unusual happenings. For instance, the trees burst into blooms absolutely out of season; tiger and deer were seen drinking side by side and so on. But after sometime, no one knew what happened between the two; the girl was seen by many sitting and sobbing alone on the *ghats* for days on end. She just wouldn't listen to anyone as she continued with her crying and finally one day jumped headlong into the lake. When the boy came to know this, he followed suit and so did their near and dear relatives, friends as well as the big and small animals of the forest. Ever since then, the lake is known as the abode of the Doomadev. The village folk tell that even today in the month of *Bhado,* or the period of August-September, a sad *bendri* or she-monkey, can sometimes be seen sitting on the same *ghats* cupping her face in her hands as if lost in deep thought. People of Bastar offer clay images of this *bendri* at the shrine of Doomadev even now.

This enigma called life and the incomprehensible misery, parting, snapping and ends it contains within, all seem so inexplicable. Is there a way to stop the time clock from ticking? Perhaps not. Only it just might be possible to blanket it a little, so as to be able to live. Such questions seem to have little to do with the common man and his everyday life; and seem more relevant for the philosopher, the thinker or the creative mind. However, this last category of the "Creative mind" is vast. In fact, whenever someone is asked who are you, what do you do, a story is about to be born. Is it not that our own identity stays coiled inside us as a discourse, that constantly tries to bring together the various unrelated pieces in life to create some sense. If Levi-Strauss talks of myth as "Machines for the suppression of time", Tolkien calls it "our yearning for the Great Escape called death".

The third of such narratives, Bhil myth of origin, was narrated by the painter Shri Pema Fatya of Jhabua. The myth of the Pithora Kunwar popular in the Jhabua region of western Madhya Pradesh talks of a prosperous kingdom going to pieces owing to a certain curse that made the people forget laughter. The whole rhythm of life was affected by forgetting something as basic and simple as laughter. All rejoicing and festivity, marriage celebrations, birth and death everything came to a standstill. The water in the well rotted, the rainbow coloured earth turned to waste and life itself stagnated like the water in a ditch. This story talks of the delicate balance, the interlinkages and their interspersed threads in a unique way. How in the absence of the necessary expressions of the happy and sad shades of life, the surface prosperity is left with nothing to protect the citadel from crumbling. It is a suspended bridge that this story weaves in the air in the midst of life's paradoxes.

## IMPORTANCE OF MYTH IN THE DEVELOPMENT OF HUMAN RACE

W.D. Flaherty writes, "A myth is like a palimpsest and we must decipher each layer with a different code book". Elaborating upon this very strange and seemingly disjointed structure of the myth, Levi-Strauss had observed that all mythologies reflect an eclectic method of construction, and he has duly demonstrated that "myth makers like bricoleurs piece their cosmologies together with the cultural scraps that are at hand".

Perhaps the seeming illogic of the myth is also there because we choose to look at it always through the one set frame of our logic. The happenings falling outside our known territory of experience tend to appear untrue, ridiculous and revolting to our reason.

Arnold Toynbee, the historian, speaks of Homer's *Iliad* (written around the Trojan War), "It has been said of the *Iliad* that anyone who starts reading it as history would find it full of fiction but anyone who starts reading it as fantasy would find that it is nothing but history."

If one undertakes a comparative analysis between the various mythologies or folk discourses vis-à-vis the classical discourses, many new significations and meanings will surface in light of which human relation will acquire a new dimension. It is possible that the long held conventions of different origins give way to fresh common meeting grounds as much as it is possible that each gets isolated in its uniqueness, turns ethnocentric and plays havoc with the possibility of any dialogue whatsoever.

The trouble is that in the absence of any such myths or discourses, what we are left with are dry facts, absolutely incapable of holding and nurturing life. And if this discourse is made the basis on which truth rests, it nevertheless leads us to a blind alley of dogmatism.

Writing on the shared mythical consciousness and history of England and Ireland, Richard Kearney points towards a significant pitfall, "We need to keep our mythological memories in critical dialogue with history. And by extension, every culture must go on telling stories, reinventing its inherited imagery, lest its history congeal into dogma".

What therefore are the notes that can be said to resonate in the mythic consciousness of the folk and tribal world of this country? What are the strains that make each of the tribe special and distinct from the other and at the same time string them together? This however is a matter for serious research that attempts at probing deeper into the heart of the matter, beyond the pitfalls of easy generalization. However, within the scope of the myths mentioned in this paper, it might be interesting to look at the concept of space and time in the realm of tribal mythology in particular.

If on the one hand it acknowledges the limitless, the inexhaustible, on the other, it invariably talks of the eternal. Any story whether of the blacksmith or the potter or any other creation myth, does not begin at the very beginning "when there was nothing". The narrative hides within it the knowledge that the earth was immersed in water before it sank to the nether world. If not man himself, the sun, the moon, the bug inside the fruit or the tortoise in the water is bound to have existed since time immemorial.

However, time is also stretched only as much as it can be saved from turning into a scary bottomless pit. It has to be comfortably fitted into the given or the available, so that the world seems as if it was born only the day before, and by virtue of that is close and familiar. For instance, the pickaxe thrown at *phadki* still appears in the sky as the *Nangar Kotela* constellation every monsoon; the earthworm still carries the mark of the crab claw; and the earth still stands poised on the back of *horo,* the tortoise for the Santhals who remember him with every tremor of the quake, saying that perhaps the weight is becoming too much for *horo* and he is moving his toe. The Gond people of Amarkantak have not forgotten Narmada's humiliation till date when her marriage was stalled by a deceitful conspiracy and even now, every time a marriage procession crosses the river they remember to ask for her forgiveness.

Similarly, the treatment of space is peculiar in its divided yet at the same time undivided aspects. In the *Pithora* painting of the Rathwas of Gujarat, for example, there is a division of the human and the divine world on the plane of the fresco, but the Milky Way is made on the side of the humans. Besides this, the people attending Pithora Kunwar's marriage range from a one-legged man to a girl with fan-like ears that might exist as they say on some planet somewhere. The space as we see is often extended to hitherto unknown frontiers, only to bring them back closer, as if in the warmth of an embrace.

## CONCLUSION

Arundhati Roy says, "The storyteller tells stories of the gods, but his yarn is spun from the ungodly, human heart".

So is the case with these stories; those are woven more around the human than the divine. Opening innumerable windows on the human world, they seldom look upon the narrow lanes of reason. Neither do they seem obliged to choose between any "either or". The tortoise floats on the water with the earth precariously balanced on its back and to prevent its falling off; the goddess Jahir Era has tied its legs firmly to a peg. But where is this peg rooted? It is somewhere of course and yet perhaps nowhere. The tortoise is tied and at the same time floating. This is the mythic spacc, a whole parallel world in itself, open like the *lillaar kothi* through which one can pass as if through an open door. It is not just any granary, but one where food for the entire humanity is stored away safely from the wind, water, storm, hail or fire for the tougher times ahead.

# 14

# Developing Uttaranchal in the Light of Traditional Knowledge

Ila Shah and Manikant Shah

## INTRODUCTION

"Dwell on the past and you'll lose an eye. Forget the past and you'll lose both eyes" (A Russian saying).

We could find a similar expression in the traditional sayings of almost all the communities around the world. We can also say that the saying was never as true as it seems today, for despite the intense material advancement that we have made and the unlimited access to speedy information we have, we are nevertheless faced with problems and circumstances that threaten the very existence of life and the planet itself. For all the resources (that is how in a commercial sense we refer to the nature's bounty now) and the time and energy saving skills, generated by our advancement that we have at our disposal, we find it ever more so difficult to surmount the problems of our day-to-day living, regardless of the boundaries of race, ethnicity and nation states. Hence, it may not be inappropriate to say that we in our frantic act of trying to surmount the problems, tend to aggravate them as though blinded by both eyes. Thus, now we should pause for a while and ponder as to what were those ways that helped us sustain ourselves in the past. But what is the past we are referring to? Surely, it is not the record of what happened in the past – all that we would find in history. They are the systems of perception and knowledge by which the people in the past conducted their lives. These processes were developed and nurtured in interaction with the immediate physico-climatic surroundings of the communities that provided them with a sustainable living, devoid of the sense of scarcity, exploitation and competition for survival. Because of this very reason, more and more people around the world are turning to look at these processes, which have become known as the Traditional Knowledge Systems (TKS).

The United Nations University has defined the TKS as:

> Traditional knowledge or local knowledge is a record of human achievement in comprehending the complexities of life and survival in often unfriendly environments. Traditional knowledge, which may be technical, social, organizational or cultural, was obtained as part of the great human experiment of survival and development.

The implications of the definition are clear. TKS are the record of human achievements either individual or social in close interaction with the immediate environmental settings. Now, lately there are many nomenclatures in vogue signifying processes that are similar in perception but different with regard to what specifically they include, such as indigenous knowledge, local knowledge, endogenous knowledge, folk knowledge, etc. Though they are widely used as synonymous to TKS but the difference between them has been shown by Antweiler (1998). Further he points out that the positive potential of traditional and local knowledge for the local development process, however, remains widely unused and scientific knowledge always implies ignorance of other types of knowledge. To quote Siverts would be appropriate here, "The process of acquiring insight produces awareness of one's own way of life as something worthwhile, and the mastery of skills breeds" self-esteem. Thus knowledge is created in combination of utilitarian and symbiotic practice, not in vacuum (1991:308).

This understanding of the concept of TKS is very apt in the context of Uttaranchal, which has a distinct socio-economic and cultural life pattern since historical times. Here we do indeed find that the local knowledge domain was overshadowed and suffocated by the modern ways of knowledge and behaviour. On the one hand, the arrest of the pace of potential development and the lack of people's initiative could well be attributed to this phenomenon; and on the other hand, more and more interventions of the government with policies based on promoting the faulty notions of "scientific" attitudes and methods largely ignore the local treasure house of knowledge that could bring about development in a spontaneous manner without any strains.

## TRADITIONAL KNOWLEDGE AND MODERN KNOWLEDGE

Before coming into prominence, of the modern science as a knowledge system based on reductionism, objectivity and empiricism (after the Renaissance), it were generally the value based, non-materialistic and holistic knowledge systems that held the sway. And that was the case all around the world whether east or west, north or south. It is not that the material pursuit was totally absent in these societies but history tells us that people holding viewpoints similar to the modern knowledge systems were probably shunned as barbarians in Greek and other civilizations. They were held in the same stead eastwards. It was perhaps out of experience that they must have realized that in the long run, the materialistic approach would lead them nowhere as if was quite limited in scope and ephemeral. So they resorted to an approach that took them beyond the material and sensate experiences to the one that was based upon faith, faith that man was just a small part of a greater whole, which was as alive as he himself. This made him see God and life in everything and everywhere whether living or dead in appearance. Such a viewpoint that promoted community feeling over and above the individual became ingrained into the wide traditional knowledge base. Modern scientific knowledge systems with an appeal to the senses and their pleasures promoting individualism, competition, materialism and commercialism threaten the very bases of faith upon which traditional knowledge systems are built.

Jackson (2002) says,

> Present day science in its essential features has been created by mathematical physicists, beginning with the work of Galileo in the 17th century and extending up to Einstein in the 20th century. Its defining concept is material objects in motion. But this concept is derived from only one part of the totality of human experience – that of the physical universe. So great has been its success in creating a machine culture, that it has, in the minds of everyone, become the ultimate explanation for all phenomena.

Indeed, if we look closely we will find that traditional knowledge and modern scientific knowledge are not two different or contradictory approaches to understand and act within a given environment, rather they are complementary. Goonatilake (1999) very aptly remarks that modern science and knowledge seem to have run out of their agenda. Therefore, it is necessary that we mine the traditional knowledge for contemporary uses, though it is debatable whether traditional knowledge can be transplanted into the modern set-up entirely devoid of the thought processes it was found in. In reality, modern knowledge is restricted to the experience gained through the senses whereas TKS goes beyond and takes into account even the non-empirical phenomena. In our evolutionary make-up, both approaches are required. But we must ensure that from the sense experiences we should graduate to the experiences that are beyond the senses, for then only we can have experiences of the whole and our actions can then have a lasting and fulfilling impact.

## USE OF TRADITIONAL KNOWLEDGE IN THE CONTEMPORARY WORLD

At a time when the world is caught between two opposing forces of the rapidly expanding global monoculture of the multinational companies on the one hand and the emphatic assertion of regional aspirations and considerations on the other, the thinking men are vigorously contemplating a reasonable way out that might rid the earth of the scourge its people face.

There are many voices heard, there are some which find faults with existing systems and there are others which are prone to reconsider the alternatives we ignored in the quest of material well-being. Most potent are the latter voices, which in all rationality acknowledge the diversity inherent in the unity of the universe. They are no more averse to the ways of the good old days. They are not afraid of even looking into the traditional knowledge systems of the people and communities in the past. They remind us that such traditional systems were holistic in approach and were quite sustainable in contrast to our present knowledge systems, which are suffused, in acute reductionism. That the traditional knowledge systems have stood the test of time and can also be relevant today. This faith is borne out by the very fact that Chinese, Japanese and Indian medicines are already beginning to compete against the modern medicine systems. Moreover, Goonatilake (1999) has cited many examples from Thailand, Africa and many other countries where people and governments are falling back on the traditional knowledge systems for their development. Focus is being turned towards the traditional knowledge base of small communities around the world for matters of regional development. Nader (1996) draws our attention towards this direction extensively referring to the works of sociologists, anthropologists, philosophers and scholars.

Traditional knowledge system within small communities is claiming the attention of thinking men today. With the realization that the contradictions of the present day world tend to frustrate most of their efforts to mitigate or resolve them, they try to seek the remedy in the traditional knowledge systems and perhaps rightly extol it as ancient wisdom.

## TRADITIONAL KNOWLEDGE AND THE DEVELOPMENT OF UTTARANCHAL

Dreze and Sen (1998) argue that, "The achievements of even the limited objectives of the current reforms will depend crucially on conscious and organized pursuit of the social means on which the economic performance and results are frequently conditional". The authors here are speaking about the socio-economic development of a region or a community. The social means cannot be entirely divorced from the traditions in which the society has been nurtured. This holds true for Uttaranchal as well, which has been and still is primarily a traditional society. Its traditions are richly reflected in the religious observations and rituals involving the entire lifespan between the birth and the death of an individual, individual and social behavioural attitudes, eating and dressing choices and habits, precautionary and curative health practices and activities relating to the fulfilment of their individual and social needs. Because of this richness, the traditional knowledge of the area holds potential for the rapid socio-economic development of the people.

Uttaranchal, a mountainous area in the Central Himalayan region, has a distinct socio-economic and cultural pattern and its mention is found in the ancient texts of India. People and communities have inhabited this land since long past who built up a cultural edifice that was consistent with the surrounding environment and their thought patterns. Diffusion through the north and the south must have played their parts but local initiatives, thoughts, needs and wants must have decided what to adopt. The thought patterns so becoming a part of the native's existence are identified as the "lesser tradition" in comparison to the "greater tradition" relating to the wider Indian consciousness. Since Uttaranchal has been referred to as the abode of gods and constant flow of pilgrims took place over the ages, the "greater tradition" must have had a deeper influence upon the "lesser tradition" forming a unique cultural pattern that it has.

In almost every sphere of traditional life in Uttaranchal we find a reservoir of traditional knowledge. At the present juncture of our material progress, it may not be a good idea to talk of reverting back wholesale to the culture of the past for that is neither practical nor desirable. But technology is one thing that can easily be revived and adopted in the present times without much strain in the society. In reviving these technologies we can obtain many benefits with regard to employment and sustainable development. Many of such technologies were intentionally discouraged and deliberately destroyed by the British for fear of competition. Others buckled under the pressure from the new materialistic thought. Such technologies include *gharats* (the watermills), copper works, iron works, ornaments making, housing and architecture, wood-carving, paper making, etc. Some of the technologies, which can be used in the present time, are as given below.

## SOME TRADITIONAL TECHNOLOGIES

### Gharats

One of the remarkable technologies that the people of Uttaranchal utilized in harnessing the natural resources was by way of the *gharat*s. Grain milling was the most widespread use of *gharats* in the Himalayas. Constructions similar to *gharat*s and working on a similar principle are known in the West as watermills. Stowell (1992) tells us how profitable these mills were to the owner and how in absence of a clear policy Sir Henry Ramsay laid down rules against these mills favouring irrigation. Sapru (1924 and 1925) gives due importance to these watermills in the lifeline of people of Almora and of Tehri Garhwal districts.

Traditional *gharat*s have been used for centuries. However, in recent years, *gharat*s have started to fall into disuse due to various contributory factors. The State, especially the British, did nothing other than collecting water tax from the *gharat* owners. The design of traditional watermills is centuries old. Because of having extremely low output, these mills do not provide enough profit to the mill-owners. Increasing the output of these mills by developing efficient mill design would undoubtedly bring significant increase. This feeling has encouraged the technologists to improve the existing design of the *gharat*. There are potentially two kinds of improvements which could be worked upon the *gharat*s. The first would result in increasing the output of milled grain and the second would result in generating power from these *gharat*s. The State can easily benefit immensely from protecting and reviving the use of *gharats*. The government might have to give due protection to the *gharats* and also review the water policy by which the *gharats* could use the water unhindered. The *gharats* are immensely helpful in water conservation too by checking the rapid run offs.

### Iron and Copper

There are people who are speculating and trying to find out, wherefrom the "second urbanization" was supplied with metals like iron and copper. For, these metals are undeniably necessary for any civilization to prosper. One of the areas that hold the imagination of these thinkers happens to be Uttaranchal. Indeed iron and copper works have long been associated with Uttaranchal. Especially today, when we talk of iron or copper wares we do not forget to mention the *iron krahai* (deep frying pan) from Champawat that does not rust and the copper utilities from Almora. Nowadays it is primarily the imported iron and copper from outside upon which the artisans work here. But earlier both the metals were mined and smelted here, as late as the beginning of 1900s. The ores and the goods produced were of a high quality, which even the British feared as a threat to their economy. Atkinson (1996) while quoting from a set of written orders and instructions to a mineralogical surveyor writes,

> The existence of iron and copper ores in considerable quantity has already been ascertained but as the working of these metals might injuriously affect important articles of British import it is not designed and your attention should be occupied in detailing any practical arrangements for that purpose.

Going further in the *Gazetteer* it becomes clear that the British may have deliberately destroyed this trade. The government might have to review its forest and mining policies that may help regenerate such works; for the government fears that opening the mines to the people may be detrimental to the environment is perhaps not well founded. The government could even fix some kind of a quota for extracting the minerals and the ores that does not make up for exploitation but provides employment in the area.

### Wood-carving

The wood-carvings, adorning the old houses, in Uttaranchal that are still intact are breathtaking. But the skilled workers shaping the wood in this fashion are no more to be found. Though Indian market imports wooden artefacts and furniture from abroad yet despite our rich heritage in working on wood does not attract any attention or interest, which would even generate employment and economic activity. Many such examples of traditional technologies of Uttaranchal could be cited which if regenerated could to some extent rid the people of their apathy and contribute to the economic activity of the area. We need to give this a serious consideration.

## OTHER FORMS OF TRADITIONAL KNOWLEDGE

Besides the technologies, traditional knowledge inherent in religious, social and cultural aspects of life could also be used to advantage, to ensure a sustainable development with the active participation of the people of the state. But before we could make any use of these we must face the challenges of globalisation on one hand and the highly centralized functioning of our bureaucracy on the other. With these, our needs and wants have considerably changed. Ignoring the production and employment scene here, our interests have come to rest upon the global market necessitating imports from international markets with further eroding any opportunities here. This has even given rise to various social ills, unthought-of, that we now witness around us.

## CONCLUSION

Regenerating the traditional knowledge systems ensures an active and spontaneous peoples' participation in the development process that frustrates the government and non-government schemes in the present. For, unless the people identify with the process it is hard to enlist their committed support.

In this light it becomes extremely pressing for us to study, research, document and learn from the TKS' inherent within our own regional society. Such knowledge may accelerate the pace of our development without having to waste resources upon the circumstances of unrest and indifference and in controlling the calamities brought about by our own mindlessness.

To conclude, the following statement by Le-Bon (1960) seems the most appropriate,

> Civilization is impossible without traditions, and progress impossible without the destruction of those traditions. The difficulty, and it is an immense difficulty, is to find a proper equilibrium between stability and variability.

## BIBLIOGRAPHY

Antweiler, C. 1998. 'Local Knowledge and Local Knowing – An Anthropological Analysis of Contested Cultural Products in the Context of Development', *Anthropos*, 93:4-6.

Atkinson, E.T. 1996. *The Himalayan Gazetteer*, Vol. I, Part I. Dehradun: Natraj Publishers.

Dreze, J. and A. Sen. 1998. *Indian Development*. Delhi: Oxford University Press.

Goonatilake, S. 1999. *Towards a Global Science – Mining Civilizational Knowledge*. New Delhi: Vistaar Publications.

Le-Bon, G. 1960. *The Crowd: A Study of the Popular Mind*. Viking Press.

Jackson, M.G. 2002. 'Plants and Soils: Liebig's Legacy and Beyond', *Asian Agri History*, 6 (1).

Nader, L. (ed.). 1996. *Naked Science: Anthropological Enquiries into Boundaries, Power and Knowledge*. New York: Routledge.

Sapru, H.N. 1924. *Report on the Industrial Survey of the Garhwal District of the United Provinces*. Allahabad: Government Press.

——. 1925. *Report on the Industrial Survey of the Almora District of the United Provinces*. Allahabad: Government Press.

Schumacher, E.F. 1973. *Small is Beautiful – A Study of Economics as if People Mattered*. London: Blond and Briggs Limited.

Stowell, V.A. 1992. *A Manual of the Land Tenures of the Kumaon Division (Hill Tracts)*. Allahabad: Government Press.

15

# Indigenous Knowledge of Wool Dyeing and Making of Fermented Foods and Beverages by the High Altitude Bhotia Community of Kumaon Himalaya

Nehal A. Farooquee, Babul Roy and C.P. Kala

## INTRODUCTION

Wool and woollen products are an integral part of the human society, especially in the colder regions where they are required throughout the year by the inhabitants. Various indigenous practices have been associated with the woollen-based products, and one of the important practices is the colouring and dyeing of wool using natural vegetation. Higher reaches of the Himalayan regions have been the homeland for various types of societies adapted to the climatic conditions of extreme cold, and hence they have to depend upon heavy woollen garments. The Bhotias of Munsyari and Dharchula areas of district Pithoragarh residing in the border regions of Kumaon Himalaya are well-known for their traditional expertise in making a range of woollen garments and materials, besides processing and colouring of wool (Atkinson 1882; Pant 1935; Bhandari 1981; Farooquee and Saxena 1996). Till 1962, these people were involved in trans-border trade between India and the erstwhile Tibet Import of wool from Tibet was the backbone of their woollen-based traditional cottage industry (Farooquee 1994 and 1998; Sharma and Rikhari 1995). After the Indo-China conflict of 1962, the import of wool from Tibet has been stopped and their traditional woollen industry got a severe setback. But over a period of time they established trade links with other regions like Nepal and other parts of India. Besides this, they also harness their local wool production (Dabral 1964; Raipa 1974; Sanwal 1985; Hoon 1996; Farooquee and Nautiyal 1999). Use of natural vegetation for colouring is in practice in the Bhotia society. This study explores the indigenous methods of dyeing and colouring in the wool-based traditional cottage industry in the higher Himalayan region, and analyses the ongoing trends of this art.

## METHODOLOGY USED FOR THE STUDY

Based on the qualitative information collected during the surveys in 1992-94 regarding the natural resource patterns and dependence of the Bhotia society on their immediate environment in the high altitude regions of Dharchula and Munsyari, villages with traditional mode of production and knowledge systems were identified. Extensive surveys were made in the traditional high altitude villages of Munsyari in 1999 and in the beginning of 2000 to identify and explore the indigenous methods of wool dyeing and colouring. The information on the indigenous knowledge of natural dye making was acquired through participatory field research methods such as semi-structured interviews, field inspections, field observations and participation in their social life and events. Market surveys were also carried out a various shops of Munsyari to understand the consumption patterns of synthetic dyes, to quantify the trends of transactions of synthetic dyes and to project the future prospects of such knowledge systems.

## INDIGENOUS KNOWLEDGE OF DYE MAKING AND WOOL COLOURING

Plants have provided an important source of pigments and tannins for millennia. While tannins have been used in preserving animal skins, plant pigments have been used in dyeing textiles, wool and fibres in different societies across the world (Harborne 1984). Useful plant pigments have been isolated from many different plant families, and from almost all plant parts–bark, leaves, seeds, fruits, stems and roots-to yield a wide range of colours, from yellow to crimson and purple to black. For example, throughout Ghana, useful pigments have been isolated from more than 100 plant species (Cotton 1997). However, in this region only a few selected plant species were used to make dye for their woollen products. The indigenous method involves use of various plant parts of different plant species ranging from herbs to large trees (Table 1) to make base colours, viz., three different shades of yellow, *akhroti-rong* (light brown) and pink, apart from the natural white colour of the wool. A number of intermediate colours and their shades are produced by mixing of these base colour dyes into different combinations. For example, the colours obtained from *tatori, akhrot,* and *dolu* plants are used together to produce a bright red pigment. In this way, a whole range of different colours are produced to suit the aesthetic requirements. The other commonly used plants in the making of dye by this community are *sayama* and *kilmora.*

Table 1. Plants used in wool processing and for dyeing

| *Plant* | *Name* | | *Purpose / Part used* | *Colour* |
|---|---|---|---|---|
| | *Local* | *Botanical* | | |
| Tree | *Reetha*<br>*Akhrot* | *Sapindus mucoraceae*<br>*Juglans regia* | Washing – Fruit<br>Dyeing – Bark<br>Fruit<br>Root | -<br>Light violet<br>Intermediate shade<br>Dark violet |
| Shrub | *Kilmora* | *Berberis asiatice* | Dyeing-Root | Yellow |
| Herb | *Dolu*<br>*Sayama*<br>*Tatori* | *Rheum emodi*<br>*Rumex nepalensis*<br>*Rheum sp.* | Dyeing-Root<br>Dyeing-Root<br>Dyeing-Root | Yellow<br>Yellow<br>Pink |

Indigenous knowledge also extends to identify the appropriate time to collect the required plant part for making a dye. For example, in the case of walnut, the best time to collect required part for making quality dye is after the flowering of the tree. During the flowering stage, it is believed that plants absorb more water so all the qualitative contents remain in a dilute condition. Scientific rationale may be linked as identification of proper time and season to suit temperature requirement in the cold climate of high altitudes. Developing isotherms on phenological based events was a past practice in Europe. As flowering in walnut (winter deciduous tree) occurs during March-April, an early harvesting will cause heavy loss of nutrients than when it is harvested after flowering. This loss of nutrient may damage the tree and subsequent regeneration through seeds. Required plant parts are collected accordingly and after sun-drying stored for future or off-season use.

The work relating to the production of woollen products is shared by both the sexes, however, women have the greater share of work in this activity. The womenfolk in the Munsyari region are the real custodians of knowledge regarding the making of natural dyes. The elderly women generally collect the plant materials for the making of natural dyes, and either they themselves prepare the dyes, or the younger women of the family prepare the dyes on the advice of the elder women. Similarly, the Bhotia women also hold the knowledge of making different shades. Right from the shearing of wool to the marketing of finished products, work is divided into different sequential stages based on the internal adjustment of the family (Table 2). Dyeing of wool is done either before spinning if into threads or after threading. Usually woollen threads are preferred for dyeing rather than un-spinned raw wool. Raw wool is normally either black or white in colour, and for the purpose of dyeing only white colour wool is used to give different shades of colours. Before dyeing, the woollen material is washed and dusted thoroughly for proper dyeing. The indigenous method of washing the woollen threads by the fruits of *reetha* is used extensively.

Table 2. Sexwise work distribution in the making of woollen products

| *Activity* | *Decision-making* | *Performed By* | *Time Taken* |
|---|---|---|---|
| Wool Shearing | Men | Men | 30 minutes per sheep |
| Carding of wool | Women | Both | 1-2 hours per kg |
| Washing of wool | Women | Both | 2-3 hours |
| Drying of wool | Women | Women | 6 hours |
| Brushing of wool | Women | Women | 3-4 hours per kg |
| Spinning of wool | Both | Both | 5-6 hours daily |
| Making of dyes | Women | Women | 5-8 hours |
| Dyeing of wool | Women | Women | 2-3 hours |
| Designing | Women | Women | 5-6 hours |
| Weaving | Women | Women | 6-8 hours daily |
| Knitting | Either | Both | 4-5 hours daily |
| Marketing | Either | Both | As required |

Collected or stored plant parts are processed to make a dye. The method for making dye from various parts (root/bark/fruit shell) of walnut is done in different stages. Collected fresh material is first ground into a soft mass or paste, which is later on mixed with water to make the dye solution. This solution is later heated until it rises to its boiling point. In the case of using root portion, for dyeing of 1 kg of wool, approximately 6 litres of water is boiled with approximately 50-60 gm of fresh root. The plant material quantity becomes half when the same part is used in dry form. When the solution rises to its boiling point, the woollen material to be dyed is slowly put into this solution, and is stirred thoroughly for a long time so that the solution reaches the entire material. Stirring is usually done with the help of a wooden stick (stirrer) for about half an hour or until the desired colour is achieved. In case of difficulties in colour fixation due to the presence of impurities in the woollen materials, a little amount of common food salt is added to the solution for the desired colour and perfect finishing. Once the desired dyeing has been achieved the woollen material is removed from the boiling pot and is allowed to cool and dry in shade. Direct sunlight is avoided for drying to retain the brightness of the colour. The method of making dye from other plants is not much different from that of walnut, except that the appropriate vegetative part and their quantity used differ from plant to plant.

## MAKING OF INDIGENOUS FERMENTED FOOD AND BEVERAGES

The making and use of fermented food and beverages using local food crops and other biological resources is very common amongst the highlanders of The Himalaya, though the name of the products and the base material vary from region to region. The people of Laddakh make local beverages from barley called *chang*. The people in Kinnaur call it *ghanti* which is made from fermented musk. In Sikkim and Darjeeling finger millet is the main substrate for their local beverages called *kodo ko jaanr* (Rizvi 1983; Bajpai 1987; Tamang *et al.* 1996). In Kumaon region it is called *chakti* in Dharchula and *daru* in Munsyari. The traditional Bhotia method food fermentation and beverage making was designed in such a way that it utilized those available crops, which did not make their main food stuffs. The commonly used fermented drinks of this community are *jann* and *daru*; and the fermented food is *sez* (the semi-fermented rice) which is taken as light snacks.

### Preparation of *Balam* (Starter Culture)

The traditional catalyzing agent used in the preparation of fermented food and beverages is called *balam*, which is not prepared by all villagers in the society. The alpine grazers called *anwals* have specialized know-how in the preparation of this starter culture. It is made of wheat by mixing a number of herbs and spices. First, the raw wheat is washed in water and is sun dried, later this is ground into flour and then it is roasted over fire and removed before it becomes brown in colour. The roasted flour is then mixed with spices like clove *(Chinnamon zylenica)*, cardamom, black pepper, leaves of wild chilies and seeds of *pipal* (*Ficus religiousa*). In this mixture, powder of old *balam* is also added. The appropriate quantity of required ingredients in the preparation of *balam* is shown in Table 3. The addition of old *balam* powder is a must; without this, production of fresh *balam* is not possible. The mixture so prepared is then thoroughly mixed in the required quantity of water and is rolled into a thick paste. Dough of this mixture is then pressed between palms to make *balam* balls of the required size. These balls are then dried in shade and stored for future use for an indefinite period of time.

Table 3. Ingredients required in the making of *balam*

| *Name of the ingredient* | *Processing* | *Quantity required* |
|---|---|---|
| Wheat (*Tritium sativum*) | Flour | 1 kg |
| Clove (*Cinnamon zylenica*) | Powder | 5–10 gm |
| Cardamom | Powder | 5–10 gm |
| Pepper (*Piper longum*) | Powder | 20–30 gm |
| Old *balam* powder | Powder | 40–60 gm |
| *Pipal* seeds*(*Ficus religiosa*) | Powder | 3–4 gm |
| Mirchi gash* | Powder | 2–3 gm |

*These are not often used.

### Preparation of *Jann* (Local Beer)

*Jann* is a traditional soft drink of the Bhotias of Munsyari and it contains very low concentration of alcohol. It is commonly prepared from rice; however, it can also be made out of good number of substrates of both cereals and fruits (Table 4). Some of common cereals from which *jaan* can be made are rice, wheat, *jau* (*Hordeum vulgare*), *koni* (*Setaria italica*), *china* (*Panicum milicaceae*), *oowa* (*Hordeum himalayans*) and *chuwa* (*Amaranthus*). Similarly, amongst the fruits, apple is the most desired and is also very delicious. But *jann* prepared from *koni* is considered to be the best in quality. The quality of *jann* is best judged by its taste (sweetness), smell and strength.

Table 4. Preference of cereals in the preparation of *jaan*

| *Cereals* | *Most common* | *Best quality* | *Less preferred* |
|---|---|---|---|
| Rice (*Oryza sativa*) | * | | |
| *Koni* (*Setaria italica*) | | * | |
| Wheat (*Aestivum sativum*) | | | * |
| *Jau* (*Hordeum vulgare*) | * | | |
| Oowa (*Hordeum himalayans*) | * | | |
| Chuwa (*Amaranthus sp.*) | | | * |
| *China* (*Panicum milicaceae*) | | | * |

The most commonly used rice *jann* was earlier prepared almost in every household in this society, but now its preparation and consumption have declined. In the making of rice *jaan,* first rice is cooked or boiled for about half an hour or until it becomes soft and edible. The cooked rice is drained off the excess water and spread on a flat container allowing to be cooled quickly. The cooked rice is then thoroughly mixed with *balam* powder. The quantity of the *balam* powder required is proportionate to the quantity of rice to be fermented (Table 5). This mixture is then kept in an airtight container (the mouth of the container is sealed usually by piece of cloth) and is kept in a dark and warm place for fermentation. In cold conditions, the rate of fermentation is slow as compared to warm. But for a good quality *jann*, slow fermentation at low temperature is a required condition. The process of fermentation takes place in the absence of oxygen, and usually after a week of fermentation *jann* is prepared. However, for a better quality of *jann*, the fermentation period is extended as long as possible but not more than a year. Importantly, longer the period of fermentation, the lesser the undigested remains of rice, and in that case the quantity of *jann* produce is more. After the completion of fermentation, the *jann* so produced is filtered with the help of a sieve. The filtrate is a whitish liquid, which is abandoned or used as animal fodder. Earlier, when they used to migrate to their winter settlement in lower valleys, before their migration they prepared *jaan* material and left them for fermentation. For six months of winter, their entire settlement got submerged under snow, and as a result of the internal heat generated due to the external pressure of ice from the top, the *jaan* fermentation was slow but steady. On their return to the place again in summer, the people found their *jann* ready for drink, and *jann* produced in this way is considered to be the best in quality.

Table 5. Yield rate of local beverages using rice as a substrate

| *Beverages* | *Input* | | | | *Yield Rate* |
|---|---|---|---|---|---|
| | Rice | Balam | Jaggary | Fuel wood | |
| *Jaan* | 5 kg | 40 gm | - | - | 3-4 litres (partially fermented)<br>6-7 litres (fully fermented) |
| *Daru* | 5 kg | 100 gm | 2 kg | 10-12 kg | 3-4 litres |

Similarly, the preparation of *jann* is same from other cereals like *koni*, wheat, *jau, oowa, chuwa* and *china*. Like rice, first the seeds of any of these cereals are boiled in water until they become soft and edible. Then they are mixed with *balam* powder and the rest of the stages of storing and fermentation, and finally yielding of *jann* is the same. Only in the case of *jau*, the seeds are partially ground before boiling, which enables quick fermentation and optimum yield. *Jann* is also prepared from fruits like apple, banana, pumpkin and orange. Apples are first cut into pieces and then are mixed with *balam* powder for fermentation. The rest of the method is the same, except in the case of orange, where either the juice or the complete fruit after peeling is mixed with *balam* powder and fermented for yielding *jann*. Banana is used without removing its outer skin. The preparation of *jann* from pumpkin is slightly different, where a small cut is made in a large sized pumpkin in such a way that the cut piece is again fitted back to its place. First the seeds and loose tissue contents of the fruit are removed through the opening, and boiled rice or other substrate mixed with *balam* powder as usual is poured into the empty space of the fruit. It is then sealed again by placing back the cut piece in its place. The process of fermentation takes place inside; as a result, along with rice, the inner soft tissue of the fruit also gets digested and thus is produced *jann* in due course of time.

### PREPARATION OF *DARU* (ALCOHOLIC DRINK)

*Daru* is the distilled liquor containing ethyl alcohol at a much higher concentration than other alcoholic beverages. Rice and jaggery are the common substrate used for preparation of *daru*. Apart from rice, the cereals like *koni, chuwa, oowa* and wheat are used in the preparation of *daru*. However, unlike in the case of *jann* the taste (i.e. quality) of the *daru* does not vary according to the type of substrate used. Therefore, choice of substrate does not matter in the preparation of *daru*. The most commonly available and cost effective materials used in the preparation of *daru,* are rice and jaggery.

Cooked rice on becoming cold is mixed with the powder of *balam*; the proportion of *balam* powder required in preparation of *daru* is much more than what is required in *jann* preparation (Table 6). This mixture is then kept in an airtight container for fermentation, and is kept preferably in a warmer place. To ensure the warmth, the container is covered with woollen cloth or else it is kept near the cooking hearth; direct heating is, however, avoided. After about a week of fermentation, when the mixture is in a semi-liquid condition, it is distilled in a distillation vessel. The distillate is the *daru,* which is collected in bottles. The undigested residue called *chak,* is dirty white in colour; this can be used again for preparation of *daru* by fortification with jaggery and fresh *balam* powder. This way *chak* is recycled or reused in *daru* preparation. However, this is not used for more than three times, and then it is given to animals to eat.

Table 6. Comparative fermentation process of *daru* and *jann*

| *Characteristics* | *Jann* | *Daru* |
|---|---|---|
| Optimum temperature | Room temperature 10°C–15°C | 30°C to 40°C |
| Fermentation nature | Anaerobic | Anaerobic |
| Fermentation container | Porous earthenware | Non-porous metallic ware |
| Fermentation rate | Slow fermentation is preferred (6-10 months) | Rapid fermentation; completed within 2 to 3 days under optimum temperature (30° to 40°C) |
| Taste | Vary according to the substrate used. | Constant irrespective of substrate used. |
| Yield | Ethyl alcohol < 10 per cent plus carbohydrate, amino-acid, vitamins, etc., depending upon the substrate used. | Ethyl alcohol invariably to the quality of the substrate used. |

### Distillation and Colouring of *Daru*

The traditional distillation method is still practiced in this region. The indigenous distillation set, which is quite simple, has three parts – *parar, jokhal* and *tal,* as called in the local dialect. The *parar* is a big saucepan like container with flat bottom, and *jokhal* is a flat wooden device like a dish having an elongated channel with a hole at the centre, and is indigenously prepared by the people. The *tal* is a simple cooking vessel, but the neck of the *tal* and the bottom of the *parar* is of such size that they hold the *jokhal* perfectly. This whole set is put on fire. On being heated, the alcoholic vapour first evaporates and then comes up through the central hole of the *jokhal.* But on coming in contact with cold bottom of *parar,* the vapour gets condensed into liquid. This liquid is collected in a container and this distillate is the alcohol. The *daru* collected in first three to four bottles during the process of distillation contains very high percentage of alcohol and is always diluted before consumption. The alcohol content gradually reduces and finally only water evaporates. Traditionally *daru* is graded into three categories: the initial few bottles containing high percentage of alcohol is called *paileful;* the last few bottles containing very low contents of alcohol is called *piskani* and a few bottles in between them containing moderate contents of alcohol are rated good for consumption. For making the *daru* attractive in appearance, a small quantity of turmeric is hung right at the mouth of the distillation set through which the distillate is collected. This makes the liquid a light but brilliantly shining yellow in colour.

### *Sez* (Semi-Fermented Food)

The traditional semi-fermented food used by the Bhotias is called *sez.* It is made from rice and is mostly used as snacks. In most cases, *sez* is extracted while preparing of rice *jann.* In the case of *daru* preparation, the intermediate stage yielding *sez* is very unstable. Thus whenever extraction of *sez* is required, the fermentation process has to be slowed down. To that effect, only a small quantity of *balam* powder is mixed with the substrate. Under slow fermentation it becomes easy to intervene into the process and remove the *sez* easily. Once *sez* has been removed, fresh *balam* powder is added to hasten the process of fermentation so that *jann* or *daru* could be yielded.

### Production of *Jann*, *Sez* and *Daru* from a Common Cycle of Fermentation

All the three different categories of fermented beverages and food can be prepared from a common fermentation cycle only when rice is used as substrate. As stated above, from boiling of rice to keeping it in an airtight container, process is same for *jann.* After one or two days of fermentation, the *sez* is ready for consumption. The required quantity of *sez* could be removed at this stage. After that, the container is again kept airtight for another five to 10 days for further fermentation, then *jann* is produced. *Jann* is removed by filtration, i.e. by passing the content through a sieve or a piece of cloth. In the remaining mixture, jaggery and fresh balls of *balam* at a ratio of one ball per kg jaggery is added for the preparation of *daru.* The jaggery is boiled and cooled, and is mixed with *balam* powder. This is then added to the mixture and kept for fermentation in a tin container. Earthenware is not used in *daru* preparation. The container set for fermentation is made airtight and kept in a warmer condition. *Daru* is produced within three to four days of fermentation.

## CONCLUSION

The relationship between indigenous knowledge of natural dye making and import of raw wool from outside at a low price, and value addition to this in the form of coloured woollen products to earn profit and revenue out of it is an established fact, and an example of sustainable development through traditional knowledge. The emergence of this knowledge system was due to the interactions and keen observation of their environment, and a realization that their system was capable of meeting most of their requirements for their sustenance. The way this society carved a niche in the making and selling of woollen garments is their ingenuity and adaptation to the emerging circumstances in the region. However, the collapse of this practice was due to the strong intervention of economic and scientific forces, which have damaged such self-sustaining systems in the name of development. As in the case of Munsyari, where linking of roads and communication in the name of development brought changes, such as the expansion of market systems, which made a number of synthetic dyes in a wide range of colours and shades available in these remote local markets. In view of the wide availability of colour choices through synthetic dyes, the traditional natural dyes, which offered only a limited range, suffered a severe setback. As a consequence, the artisans slowly switched over to the use of synthetic dyes, resulting into their growing faith on outside products over their own. The availability of factory-made wool in a wide range of colours and shades at a much lower price, further discouraged the traditional wool industry of the region and gave final blow for its extinction.

## ACKNOWLEDGEMENT

The authors are thankful to Dr. S.S. Samant in the identification of plants and to Mr. Jagat Singh Martoliya for his assistance in the field survey.

## BIBLIOGRAPHY

Atkinson, E.T. 1882. *Gazetteer, North West Province: The Himalayan Districts of the North Western Provinces of India Vol. III.* North Western Provinces & Oudh: Government Press.

Bajpai, S.C. 1987. *Lahaul-Spiti: A Forbidden Land in the Himalayas.* New Delhi: Indus Publishing Company.

Bhandari, J.S. 1981. 'Structure and Change among the Borderland Communities of Kumaon Himalaya' in *The Himalaya: Aspects of Change,* J.S. Lall and A.D. Moddie, (eds.). New Delhi: Oxford University Press.

Cotton, C.M. 1997. *Ethnobotany: Principles and Applications*. West Sussex.: John Wiley & Sons.

Dabral, S.P. 1964. *Uttrakhand ke Bhotantic.* Garhwal: Vir Gatha Prakashan.

Farooquee, N.A. 1994. *Transhumance in the Central Himalaya: A Study of its Impact on Environment.* Ph.D. Thesis, H.N. B. Garhwal University, Srinagar, Garhwal.

——. 1998. 'Development and the Eradication of Traditional Resource Use Practice in the Central Himalayan Transhumant Pastoral Society', *International Journal of Sustainable Development and World Ecology* 5(3): 43-50.

Farooquee, N.A. and A. Nautiyal. 1999. 'Traditional Knowledge and Practices of Bhotia Pastoralists of Kumaon Himalaya: The Need for Value Addition', *International Journal of Sustainable Development and World Ecology* 6(2): 60-67.

Farooquee, N.A. and K.G. Saxena. 1996. 'Conservation and Utilization of Medicinal Plants in High Hills of the Central Himalaya', *Environmental Conservation* 23(1): 75-80.

Harborne, J.B. 1984. *Phytochemical Methods: A Guide to Modern Techniques of Plant Analysis.* London: Chapman and Hall.

Hoon, V. 1996. *Living on the Move: Bhotias of Kumaon Himalaya.* New Delhi: Sage Publications.

Pant, S.D. 1935. *The Social Economy of the Himalaya.* London: George Allen and Unwin.

Raipa, R.S. 1974. *Shauka Simavarti Janjati.* Dharchula: R.A. Brothers.

Sanwal, R.D. 1985. *The Social Stratification in Rural Kumaon.* New Delhi: Oxford University Press.

Sharma, S. and H.C. Rikhiri. 1995. 'The Bhotias: The Disruption in Lifestyle of a Nomadic Community in the Indian Central Himalaya', *Nomadic Peoples* 36/37: 167-74.

Tamang, J.P. *et al.* 1996. 'Indigenous Fermented Food Beverages of Darjeeling Hills and Sikkim: Process and Product Characterization', *Journal of Hill Research* 9(2): 401-11.

16

# Traditional Methods of Storage and Conservation of Fodder Plants in Kumaon Himalayas

Hema Joshi

## INTRODUCTION

The Kumaon region of the Western Himalayas with its wide physiographic, climatic and biotic diversity is endowed with a remarkably rich flora and fauna. The climate of this region exhibits a distinctive periodicity. The cold season starts from late November and has its peak in January; the summer season stretches from March to May and the monsoon (rainy season) covers the whole area by the mid June to the mid – September.

This periodicity in climatic conditions is reflected in the seasonality of the vegetation. Since the main subsistence in the villages of Kumaon is based on agriculture and animal husbandry (which constitute the vital base of the society), the efficient livestock production, good supply of fodder and protection (management and development) of grasslands assume a great significance in the lives of the people. The largest numbers of fodder plants occur during the rainy season. For use in winter or a season of long continued drought when growth of fodder species is reduced or checked and the supply of fodder from the natural sources is reduced to a minimum, preservation of fodder in sufficient quantity is undertaken by the people. Various techniques are used for appropriate animal health care, high animal productivity, for supply of fodders and feeds and for the raising of superior grasses, leafy fodder and legumes.

This is done consciously to nurture an integrated system of social development where management of pastures and ecological balance of the region are maintained. And at the same time, ecological potential of the region is also harnessed to its full to meet the needs of the people.

Although considerable amount of work has been done on the grasses and grassland management of the area (Bor 1960; Mishra 1964; Meherhomji 1965; Dabadghao *et al.* 1973; Yadav and Singh 1974 and 1977; Singh and Billore 1975), but no such study has been done on the various methods employed by the villagers of Kumaon for the efficient use and preservation of fodder plants. Therefore, in this paper, an attempt is made to present some common methods/techniques used by the local people.

## METHODS OF DATA COLLECTION

Villages of Kumaon were surveyed and the various modes of preservation, utilization and management of fodder were recorded using various field research techniques such as interview, discussions with local people and direct observation. Cross-questioning with knowledgeable and elderly persons of the different villages verified the documented information. The common fodder used includes grasses, tree leaves, leguminous plants, nuts, rice, wheat straws and other agricultural by-products.

## TRADITIONAL METHODS OF FODDER STORAGE AND MANAGEMENT

### Silage

The majority of fodder grasses flourish during the rainy season and some of the best kinds flower immediately after the rainy season. It is well known that the stems and leaves of grasses attain their maximum nutritive value during the period of flowering. So some people cut rainy season grasses and preserve it for future use as silage.

In some villages, which are subjected to periodical drought, fodder is preserved in the form of compressed silage. It is not only economic and safe but also a nutritious food.

### Stacking

The stacking of hay, which is a compressed form of storing fodder, is undertaken to provide a sufficient quantity for use during the winter months. Many grasses when stacked retain their nutritive properties for 1-2 years.

During the rainy season palatable grasses are cut and tied in bundles and arranged in a specific conical manner on a tree. This conical structure commonly called *luta* has a special significance. It protects the grasses from moisture, pathogens, insects, rodents, etc. In this form grasses can be preserved for several years (2-4 years). *Luta* making is an indigenous technique. In the absence of a tree, a wooden pole or a log is used and *luta* is prepared accordingly. The grasses are arranged in conical manner around the log.

Sometimes tied bundles (stacks) of grasses and straws are arranged in a specific manner on the agricultural field and kept on roofs of houses. This is used for short term consumption.

In some villages straws of wheat, rice, etc. are kept inside caves to be used for longer periods.

Fodder grasses are allowed to grow in areas protected from grazing during the rainy season (i.e. from mid-June to mid-September). These protected grasses are cut, spread and sun-dried. Thereafter small bundles are made and stored on roofs, open fields, wastelands, caves, cowshed, trees, etc. in the form of *luta*.

### Periodical Protection of Pastures

Many outlying grass tracts are utilized by driving the cattle to such places for grazing purposes. Many grazers habitually migrate with their herds to distant localities during the different seasons of the year. This protects the nearby grasslands and other vegetation from overgrazing. Periodical protection of fodder plants has a direct advantage.

In many places cattle are allowed to graze for a few days/weeks (moderate light grazing) in the open. This avoids unscrupulous destruction of vegetation by uncontrolled grazing or overgrazing. Heavy grazing often leads to deterioration of the pasture while medium grazing results in greater diversity and productivity. Intensity of grazing also influences the quality of fodder grasses. Moderate grazing increases the net primary production of fodder through enhanced tilling and increased diversity.

Rotational grazing is also practised in many places to preserve natural vegetation from deterioration. It is a system of controlled grazing and has much advantage as the vegetation is offered a chance for better growth; young and nutritious grasses become continuously available as feed during the grazing period; seedlings and saplings of trees are not damaged or browsed by cattle since sufficient feed is available for them. Rotational grazing also increases the carrying capacity of grasslands. Continuous grazing at controlled rates based on the carrying capacity is one of the best ways to maintain ranges under conditions of sustained high productivity (Mann and Ahuja 1974).

### Periodical Cultivation

Cropland also contributes to the supply of cattle feed in the form of agricultural by-product and stubble grazing.

After March burning treatments are given to sloping grassy areas. It promotes the release of nutrients particularly nitrate, increases soil fertility, bacterial activity and growth of new palatable grasses.

Some grasses thrive under cultivation as winter grasses. These would come to flowering stage at a time when the winter would admit of their being made into excellent hay and certain amount of valuable fodder would be rendered available throughout the summer.

### Fencing of Grasslands

To protect the nutritive palatable grasses from heavy, continuous grazing and browsing, permanent grasslands, if available, are properly protected with cattle-proof fence. Stonewall fences are also constructed.

Forest floor vegetation is harvested for hay and the forest floor is used as grazing land (during winter and dry conditions) in many places.

## CONSERVATION OF FODDER TREES

A major reason of ill-treatment of natural vegetation in this area is due to scarcity of fodder resources. The several methods the people use to conserve the trees are:

- The fodder trees are cultivated at various places such as wastelands, border of crop fields, etc.
- Villagers never cut the apical branches of these trees while collecting the fodder.
- At places farmers cultivate several traditional varieties of fodder trees, shrubs (in waste places, open areas, in fields) which are better adapted to tolerate diseases, drought and other environmental conditions. Women have a special role in the protection of biodiversity of fodder grasses, shrubs and trees.

# 17

# Folk Sciences in the Folklore of Uttaranchal

Alakhnath Upreti

## INTRODUCTION

Science does not begin with Newton or Galileo but from the time the first human being appeared on this planet. Early human beings also made scientific observations and historic devices to transmit knowledge and science to posterity. It was done through legends, myths and folklore.

Science cannot just be a branch of knowledge conducted on objective principles involving the systematized observations of experiments and phenomena, especially, concerned with the materialistic functions of the physical universe. We find the folk science now, more accurate, more harmonious and more humane in social relations. Similarly, in traditional folk sciences of Uttaranchal we are amazed to witness more accuracy in understanding of the concrete phenomena that guided the people in the multilateral realm of human life. In this part of the hills, there are several such examples like the crow making its nest on upper/middle/lower part of the trees depending on the severity of the coming winter. Further, the different types of crowing by crows are thought to be way of deciding whether that particular moment or phenomenon is auspicious or inauspicious. Materialistic basis of the folk science developed through trial and error and was a Heuristic method (tradition).

## WESTERN SCIENCE VERSUS TRADITIONAL KNOWLEDGE SYSTEM

Let us start with the myths of the western science, which seem to dominate all scientific activities and claims.

Western science seems to monopolize logic, rigour and rationality in all knowledge acquiring processes. Anything outside its domain becomes non-science. It is seldom realized that traditional knowledge systems (TKS) preserve the wisdom gained through millennia of experiences, direct observations and word of mouth. Development projects based on techno science or western science are pushing the TKS towards extinction.

If we have a look at some of the folklores of Uttaranchal we soon come to realize that this is nothing but the arrogance of western science because there are so many facts of life, both social and natural, which are embedded in these folklores which are part of the folk science.

In Kumaoni folklore there are a number of references where appearance of a particular bird or flowering of a particular plant are taken as a mark of the beginning of new season.

The *Nanda* folklore (*anthu)* is a story of curse and blessing upon pine and oak trees respectively. It is basically nothing but the description of the respective ecological properties of these trees.

Geological observation has also become a monopoly of western science. But there are numerous examples of accurate geological observations in the garb of legends and myths, e.g. the braiding of the Satluj is recorded in the story of Vashishtha who tried to commit suicide and the river was divided into hundred channels. Similarly, the recession of the sea is also recorded in the legend of Parshuram who through his *Parshu* pushed back the sea. This knowledge was transmitted to posterity by the word of mouth garbed in the form of legends and myths.

Therefore western science need not judge this knowledge system with its yardstick, for folk knowledge was generated through millennia of observations, experimentations and trial and error and it is more eco-friendly system of knowledge in which human beings are a part of their environment. Therefore in TKS there is no exploitation of nature, but there exists a symbiotic relationship between human beings and nature in contrast to modern mindset where there is a large scale exploitation of nature.

## SCIENTIFIC OUTLOOK IN FOLKLORES OF UTTARANCHAL

### States of Mind

It is well known that the western science did not believe in the existence of the unconscious and subconscious states of mind till it was recognized by Sigmund Freud in 1939. But the existence of the unconscious state of mind was well known in different cultures. In India it was well known long before Buddha's birth in the yoga-philosophy. It is the awakening of this unconscious mind which is the basis of *jagar* therapy.

The meaning of *jagar* is "to awaken". In the *jagar*, the *jagaria* with his chants over folk-music awakens the unconscious mind of the medium. This medium is called *dangaria* or *gantua*. The *dangaria* is conditioned by the changing tunes sung by the *jagaria* and soon the *dangaria* comes in contact with the unconscious that is the state of trance. The person (the medium) who gets conditioned is the victim of social oppression and to give vent to his\her feelings the person dances in the form of a deity. In order to consummate a *jagar* descent of the spirit into a human being is a must. Then this medium becomes a God. This spirit can narrate amazing facts of past and present life. *Shiv* and *asur* are probably the native inhabitants and the killing of *mahishasur* is the event prevalent in the different folklore. Probably it is a narration that represents the struggle between the invading Aryans and the local natives. Therefore *jagar* on one hand is the science of probing the unconscious and on the other hand it is also a resource reference to the past history.

Since folklore tradition is based on the word of mouth and memory hence it is given a perpetual life and continuity. Besides, it is also a dynamic tradition where the folk singer also adds, alters and interpolates events and personages in the course of time. The *ramola jagar* (which shows different styles of singing) is a good example of this.

The folklore view of salvation is simply living full life with full enjoyment; only those who die prematurely do not attain salvation therefore they become ghosts. To liberate them, they have to descend in the human body; unless this descent is achieved the *jagar* is considered incomplete. It is very interesting to note that the spirit descends into a living human being and thus the person who possesses this spirit becomes a God and is worshipped accordingly. Now it becomes possible to enshrine the spirit in a stone and it is thus liberated from its eternal wandering. Haru Khem and Gorill are recognized as god today but they were historical personages to begin with, thus the process of deification can easily be seen in the folk-tales. *Garuri* tales are related to curing of diseases. Through these songs the diseases are eliminated by removing *airi* and *vish* (poison).

Myths and folklores represent an attempt of our interests to form a scientific base of our knowledge for the coming generations. For example the geological history of Kashmir Valley is protected in the folk story of *Satisar*. The scientific knowledge is hidden in the story of Vashishtha.

Another aspect of the folklores is that they are primarily the windows through which we can peep into the unconscious. Havell (1950) forcefully condemned the scientific outlook in which the unconscious is totally ignored. Jung agreed with Havell.

For further details we can go through many folk legends like *Ramolas* and *Gorill* and their *tantra mantra* practices where we can find the traces of science peeping through it.

### Description of History through *Jagar*

The unconscious has another important aspect of the *jagar* being a genuine source reference to the past history, which the *dangaria* (medium) narrates unceasingly, while in the state of trance. In this way the *jagar* narrations can be equated with old copper-plates which give information about the past. For instance, the famous *jagar* of Kumaon region is the *Nandadevi jagar*, in which the story of bravery of a Katyuri king is sung by the *dangaria.* In 1398 when Taimoor attacked Kumaon, the forces of the Katyuri king Brahmdev near Roorkee stopped him. Every year in the *jagar* performed at Ranibagh in Nainital district, folk singers from Katyuri village tell the story of queen Jijarani, wife of Preetam Dev of Katyuri dynasty and thus show their regards to past heroes. The folk tune and folk music are the soul of *jagar* shows.

### Religion

Through the medium of the dreams probably the knowledge of the future events was achieved. Rudra knows through her dreams that Gorakh Nath is going to impress her brother. In the world of folklore, the world of dreams and that of imagination appear closely intermingled. Haru Khem, Gorill and Golu Devta were all historical characters but now they have been deified as gods. Thus the process illustrates how people with their imagination create the deities. In this way it is the man who creates the god, not the god who create the human being.

### Futility of Horoscope Reading

A famous proverb in Kumaoni *kundli ke dekhani munali dekhani* which means that instead of running after the astrologer to read one's horoscope to know the future course of life events, one should really depend on the use of one's brain and common sense to deal with life. This proverb is a warning against constant and useless reference to one's horoscope (which is always carefully preserved but mostly turns out to be false). Illiterate people of these hills, like elsewhere, so unquestionably believe the prediction of horoscope that they regard the things predicted by the astrologer to be the truth.

### Community Living

It appears that the *tantric* cult was quite dominant in Kumaon region of Uttaranchal. Guru Gorakh Nath is one of the powerful leaders of the *tantric* cult. Heroes like Jhangu Ramola received training under him. He is also probably responsible for the foundation of the *nath* sect; members of this cult bury their dead even today. Nine *naths* are mentioned in the folklores. The *nath* cult being closer to the people is dominated by magic spells, co-operative events, primitive elements, etc. The Ramola brothers were famous for their extraordinary valour that was supposed to be based on their *tantric* power. It is also mentioned that *tantric chakra* was completed by Siduwa Ramola through which he used to call upon fairies.

### Personality Development

*Jamana bati kamana* means that when a plant starts quivering as soon as it sprouts above the ground, it is sure that it will wither. This proverb is applied to a boy or a girl who learns bad habits from the childhood and is sure to be ruined in the future.

### Habit and Nature

*Chaumasa ka jara raja ko kara.* Fever during the monsoon season is like a tax levied by the king. This means that if one suffers from ill-health during this season, it becomes very difficult to overcome, and in the process a lot of money is spent much to a person's dislike. Likewise if a tax is levied by the king, you have to pay it up – whether you like it or not.

### Agriculture

There is a saying in Kumaoni that *barkhe hyun tako samala gyun.* This means that if there is a heavy snowfall, then the bumper crop of wheat will be yielded. This is actually applicable to high altitude regions. When the rain falls at this height it does not stop and washes down the slopes, so fields are not able to retain the water. But when there is heavy snowfall the snow melts slowly and gradually and is soaked into the ground causing a better crop. In this way, effect of snowfall and wind direction on the wheat fields is wisely explained.

Similarly there is another saying *mala kheti bala raja* which means that as the strength of the region depends upon its army so the agriculture of village depends upon the manure. This explains the value of organic farming as opposed to that of chemicals.

### Farming System

Traditional farming system of Uttaranchal region is generally called *barahanaja* which actually means twelve (or more) grains. In this method of farming, twelve grains including millets, legumes and oil seeds are grown together which is a very scientific way of growing a wide variety of nourishing and nutritious food in the hilly areas where people have very small plots of cultivable land. It also makes sense to grow a number of mixed crops together as these crops can grow upon each other and thus maintain the fertility of land. For example, there is a tradition of growing *madua, chaulai* and legume seeds together in hilly areas of Uttaranchal. There are many advantages of this traditional farming system. Some of them are given below:

- The leguminous creepers use the stem of *chaulai* as the natural support so there is no need to put an extra support for legumes.
- *Madua*'s roots grip the soil firmly and prevent soil erosion.

These locally grown grains are very nutritious and are potent help in certain ailments. For instance –

- *Madua* is a rich source of calcium, phosphorous, iodine and vitamin B-1 and is a good nutritious food for children suffering from malnutrition
- *Chaulai* is a rich source of iron and protein.
- *Kulth* or *gahat* is very useful in the treatment of stones.

Thus *barahanaja* is a very scientific and sustainable method of growing a wide variety of nutritious food for the villagers of Himalayan region. This traditional farming system is now on the verge of extinction due to government policies and lack of awareness among the people. Several movements, like Save the Seed Movement, are promoting the traditional farming system. The movement is trying not only to retain this advanced method of farming against the onslaught of unthought of and aggressive system of monoculture based on the use of chemical fertilizers, but it is also trying to save a variety of local crops and their seeds. The idea behind this movement is to retain the sovereignty of the farmers and the richness of local crops that are less susceptible to pests and diseases and are eco-friendly.

## CONCLUSION

The kinship community of these hills revolves around the blissful ecology of folk sciences, but the western-oriented hegemonic modern science ridiculed the native folk science as a barbaric trash not worth investigation. In essence, the advent of modern science was conditioned by the rapacious rage for exploitation and plundering. This further alienated human beings from their folk bearings and they were thrown into the clutches of different modern exploitative systems like capitalism, imperialism and fascism. The hegemonic western science is promoting a lifestyle and mindset, which is mercilessly destroying the earth and its inhabitants. The depletion of ozone, the melting of the polar glaciers and the impending nuclear and bio-weapon's catastrophe is the culmination of this alienation of modern science from its progenitor.

The humane folk science is very much rooted in the soil, but we have been forced to abandon this due to overarching pressure of unwise development. Though we sometimes shed some superficial tears but we are really not doing substantially enough to revert and check this gross mistake. Hence, this alienation is leading us towards consumerism and the destruction of animate and inanimate life on the earth.

To forestall this doom we need to negate the existing hegemony of western science, which fosters a mindset of exploitation, and adopt a world-view that helps us to go back to our folk roots.

# 18

# Role of Informatics in Traditional Knowledge Systems

Durgesh Pant

## INTRODUCTION

The history of humankind can be taken as a superset of data and information. The events, which took place in the past, become a source of data and information for the future. With the passage of time, past events provide information subject to meaningful interpretation. The processed information, which gives meaningful output in its complete form, can be addressed as informatics. It can, therefore, be inferred that human civilization revolves more around informatics than anything else.

It would not be improper to state that human history represents the history of informatics. Information is not a buzzword. It is rather an ancient road than a modern highway. Man has survived over this super-quantum of time by the preservation and bequeathing of this very information from one generation to another, which he has gathered through experimentation, observation and trial and error. It is also certain that every human group, tribe had some specific knowledge, which was based on the experiences of their generations. The information gathered and assimilated by these groups over hundreds of years turned into a knowledge base. This knowledge used to be multidimensional. The knowledge base created and generated by our previous generations has been termed as traditional knowledge system (TKS).

During the past hundred years, with the advent of modern technologies, the traditional information started diminishing gradually as people did not see any utility of such information. In the past few years, however, some people have realized the importance of TKS; hence has been felt the need to gather, store, collate and retrieve such important information. This will help in curbing the loss of such valuable information.

The objective of this paper first is to put forward a framework of informatics which could lead to creation of a super-knowledge base system by gathering, storing and collating such information by the use of modern technologies so that one can retrieve important information as and when required. Secondly, it is to emphasize the fact that losing the information, which has been compiled by many generations, would be an irreparable loss to humanity in terms of time, energy and evolutionary process.

## FRAMEWORK

Since information is the backbone of the TKS, we are really interested in ensuring that the informatics helps in preserving and retrieving this vast array of rich knowledge, as at no point in time can humanity afford to miss out the information, which it has accumulated over the entire period of evolution. The previous generations must have garnered some crucial experiences in order to survive against the multiple vagaries existing on this planet, which we inhabit today. Following are the various steps of the proposed framework.

### Collection of Traditional Knowledge

The first step towards this endeavour is collecting the information about traditional knowledge. The components of collecting information are enumerated as under:

### Study Area

The study area may be a village, a block, a district, a region, a state, a country, etc. Besides, it can be limited up to a particular tribal population.

### Type of Data Collection from the Field

Since the topic is multidisciplinary, the sources of data collection are also diverse. To name a few we have to gather information related to medicine including veterinary medicine (ethno-gastrology), food, fodder, fibre, household goods, musical instruments, fuel, oil seeds, narcotics, beverages, magico-religious belief, dyes, staining materials, clothing, plants-in-art, decoration, taboos, festivals, biodiversity conservation, sacred groves, agriculture and domestication of plants by our ancestors, gene banks, architecture of houses and temples, traditional technologies related to architecture, metallurgy, water harvesting, biotechnology, germ plasm collection. All such information is to be stored making use of multi-media applications.

### Methodology

Not much work has been done on such a topic and because it is a congregation of many fields, methodology will have to be worked out after a survey of the study area selected and also after clearly marking out the fields from which traditional knowledge is to be retrieved. Depending on the type of study, frequent field trips are necessary, to consult the persons of the study area for collecting the samples, data, etc. Before studying the area, one should know the history, anthropology and language of the particular ethnic group under study. Besides this, the person carrying out the study should be well acquainted with subjects like Botany, Chemistry, Economics, Ecology, etc. The information gathered is to be stored in the form of a database, which will cover wide range of fields depending on the type of the study undertaken.

### Storage and Retrieval of Traditional Knowledge

Although humans are adept at processing information stored in their memories but analog information stored external to the mind or in human brain is not processed easily. Modern information technology greatly facilitates the manipulation of analog information by representing it as digital signals, i.e. as the presence or absence of energy (electricity, light or magnetism). Information represented digitally in two-state, or binary form, is often referred to as digital information. The conversion of analog information to digital one is known as digitialization.

Storage of TKS in the form of digital signals is a must so that it can be processed and retrieved and is easily available for the future generations. For this, a specific integrated package can be developed. This will include the needs of different diversified fields consisting of attributes of different divergent experiential knowledge base systems prevailing in different parts of the world. This intelligent interactive software package can be given data/ information individually or collectively. This input can further be validated by the system and if found correct, can be incorporated.

Simulation techniques can also be applied for this traditional knowledge system. This can be put into use in case of bio-informatics systems where experimentation can only be carried out on computer systems, not on living beings. One of the effective ways of storing and retrieving is the use of expert systems, which is a new category of service-oriented information system. It is named so because its database stores a description of decision-making skills of human experts in some narrow domain of performance, such as medical image interpretation, taxation, brickwork design, configuration of computer system hardware, trouble-shooting malfunctioning equipment or beer brewing. The motivation for constructing expert systems is the desire to replicate the scarce, unstructured and perhaps poorly documented empirical knowledge of specialists so that others can readily use it. Expert systems, which provide expert information, would be developed all across the globe for the proper utilization of past knowledge base. There is also a need to design and develop expert systems integrated with the super-software TKS system (Richard 1984; Holsapple and Whinston 1989).

## Domains of Informatics for TKS

1. Creation of a super-database of existing experiential knowledge.
2. Use of computer system for simulation purposes to authenticate the use of TKS with respect to the applications of present times and under varied situations.
3. There is need for a comprehensive software package that could process information related to different traditions spread among different ethnic, tribal groups making use of distributed processing over a network operating environment. The processing of information is possible of areas as wide and complicated as medicine, architecture, navigational aspects, weather forecasting, astronomy, animal husbandry, disaster management, metallurgy, and other multiple areas. The information available can be intelligently processed.
4. Use of bio-informatics in relation to TKS.
5. Creation of video and audio aids related to TKS using multi-media.
6. Putting the TKS on the web.
7. Testing and validation of authenticity of existing experiential information.
8. To bring about cohesiveness among different societies, cultures, linguistic groups across the frontiers of the nations of the world.
9. Informatics can further be used for checking the bio-piracy as well as taking the information on patenting of different materials or objectives. This can further be ascertained by implementing intellectual property rights.

## IMPORTANCE OF PRESERVING THE TRADITIONAL KNOWLEDGE

The "paradigm shift" (Kuhn 1962), which is a keyword in the scientific world today, gives emphasis on eco-sustainable harmonic society. Traditional concept of scientific progress is believed to be a gradual, cumulative acquisition of knowledge based on rationally chosen experimental frameworks. Instead, the paradigm determines the kinds of experiments scientists perform, the types of questions they ask and the problems they consider important.

A shift in the paradigm alters the fundamental concepts underlying research and inspires new standards of evidence, new research techniques and new pathways of theory and experiment that are radically incommensurate with the old ones. This mammoth task is possible indeed only by restoring our traditional knowledge base system.

Further by preserving TKS we would be able to find many technologies in our tradition, which need to be tapped for the benefit of people as well as to save our environment, as most of these technologies are eco-friendly and sustainable. One such technology crying for attention in Uttaranchal and elsewhere is cross-flow watermill known as *gharat/panghat/panchakki,* etc.

## CONCLUSION

The history of humanity also signifies the history of informatics. This is important because history is known and recorded in terms of information. Man dies but information remains.

The earlier generations used to live in harmony with nature. They had a tremendous binding with the basic elements of the nature. For them, nature was ultimate. Their information base was also in congruence with nature's attributes. There was a total symphony and synchronization with nature. Over the entire voyage of human history, the role human beings played was more of nature worshipper rather than of a conqueror. Informatics with eco-friendly attitude would prove to be the correct combination and a true representation of this interdependence that was the very basis of the life of our ancestors. Therefore the traditional knowledge of the system has to have its catalytic base firmly rooted in the understanding of nature.

Use of informatics can contribute to a great extent for providing quality information. The TKS system integrated with informatics would pave the way towards a better understanding of the world. The knowledge that the human society has accumulated over its entire journey of evolution must not dissipate, rather it should continue from the point where it was left off by our predecessors, so that the knowledge base of traditional societies is not lost and we are not forced to start once again from scratch.

## BIBLIOGRAPHY

Capra, F. 1982. *The Turning Point: Science Society and the Rising Culture*. London.

——. 1997. *The Web of Life: A New Synthesis of Mind and Matter*. London: Fontana Paperbacks.

IGNOU Study Material. 2001. *The Information Society*, UNIT 1. New Delhi.

Date, C.J. 2001. *An Introduction to Database Systems*. Delhi: Pearson Edition.

Forsyth, R. (ed.). 1984. *Experts System Principles and Case Studies*. London: Chapmen & Hall.

Hanken, A.F.G. 1981. *Cybernetics and Society: An Analysis of Social System*. Kent: Abacus Press.

Holsapple, C.W. and A.B. Whinston. 1989. *Business Expert Systems*. Delhi: Galgotia Publication Pvt. Ltd.

Hwang-Kai, F. and A. Briggs. 1985. *Computer Architecture and Parallel Processing*. New Delhi: McGraw-Hill Book Company.

Kuhn, T.S. 1962. *The Structure of Scientific Revolution*. Chicago: University of Chicago Press.

Toffler, A. 1990. *Power Shift*. New York: Bantam Books.

19

# *Brahmakamal* and Uttaranchal

Nirmala Koranga

## INTRODUCTION

The Uttaranchal Himalaya, a part of Western Himalaya, is one of the richest and the most fascinating zones of the Himalayas with diverse and unique biotic forms distributed over sub-tropical to alpine zones. *Brahmakamal* (*Saussurea obvallata* DC), the state flower of Uttaranchal, belongs to the genus *Saussurea* DC of *Asteraceae* which is represented in India by 61 species. Out of the 61 species occurring in India, 24 species are represented in Uttaranchal state.

The paper is an attempt to highlight the importance traditionally given to the *Brahmakamal* by the people in Uttaranchal in their religious/ritualistic observances, ethno-medicinal practices, and their fairs and festivals. This importance is even narrated in their folk songs and folk tales. But the ruthless plucking and collection of flowers by local people and tourists coupled with habitat destruction has endangered the species. The impact of over-exploitation of *Brahmakamal* in the natural alpine ecosystem is discussed here and strategies for its conservation and sustainable utilization are suggested.

## MYTHS RELATED TO THE *BRAHMAKAMAL*

Etymology of the word *Brahmakamal* (Brahma-creator of the universe, *kamal*-lotus) reflects that it is the lotus of Brahma. In Hindu Mythology/Cosmology creation is attributed to the trinity of Brahma-Vishnu-and Mahesh. It is told that a lotus blossomed forth from the navel of Vishnu through which Brahma emerged and produced progeny on earth who were primarily ascetics, the *Rishis*. The Himalaya is regarded as the abode of Lord Brahma, therefore the Central-Western Himalayan zone of which Uttaranchal is a part came also to be known as *Brahmarshidesh*. In the early *Brahmanical* period (after *Vedic* period) therefore, the *kamal* found in *Brahmarshidesh* came to be known as the *Brahmakamal*. Indeed, the *Brahmakamal* is one of the most attractive flowers distributed in these higher altitudes.

A legend narrates that the heroes of the *Mahabharata*, the Pandavas, came to Pandukeshwar in Garhwal during their exile. Draupadi, the wife of the Pandavas, while bathing in the river Pushpavati, noticed a beautiful lotus like flower (*kamal*) floating in water. She requested Bhim, one of her husbands, to bring her more of those flowers. Draupadi then offered the flowers to Lord Brahma. Hence, the name *Brahmakamal*. Much similar mythological lore is there in Uttaranchal as well as *Puranic* literature regarding the *Brahmakamal*.

## CENTRALITY OF THE *BRAHMAKAMAL* IN UTTARANCHAL

### In Terms of Magico-Religious Beliefs

In the remote villages of Uttaranchal people believe that there are many diseases caused by evil sprits; and that the flowers of *Brahmakamal* protect the family from these. Therefore, dried up *Brahmakamal* is usually hung by communities in their houses on high altitudes. Local exorcists also use this flower for warding off evil spirits.

### In Terms of its Description in Folk Songs

*Brahmakamal* has found its place in one of the most popular folk songs of people of Uttaranchal.

*Swarg Uttrarakhand bhumi*
*Narain phool jaiso phool brahmakamal....*

The Uttaranchal region is like the heaven where the king of flowers, *Brahmakamal* in the likeness of Narain, the Lord himself is found. This tells that *Brahmakamal* is taken in high esteem in Uttaranchal. Likewise, there are many folk songs describing the *Brahmakamal*.

### In Terms of its Uses

Ethno-medicine: The Bhotias and other villagers of Garhwal districts use the *Brahmakamal* to cure hydrocele. The bracts are removed and flowers are roasted and mixed with the flour of *Hordium vulgare* (barley). In a similar manner there are various other medicinal uses of the flower in the local as well as the other medicinal systems.

Decoration: Many villages near the habitat of *Brahmakamal* decorate their houses with its garlands. The shrines of Badrinath, Kedarnath, Gangotri, Yamnotri and many other temples are also decorated with the inflorescences of *Brahmakamal.* Shepherds returning from high mountains put a *Brahmakamal* in their cap, which is indicative of their proud visit to its holy habitat.

Local Festivals: *Brahmakamal* is an integral part of many festivals among Garhwalis. Of these *Nandastami* and *Shardudu* need special mention. The *Shardudu* festival starts with the women bringing pots of curd to the village temple which are worshiped with a *Brahmakamal* by the village priest. The curd is then transferred to a big pot locally known as *panchayati bartan*. The male members of the village now appear on the scene dancing with *doli* of god on their shoulders. The ceremony ends with the distribution of curd to all guests and villagers. Lastly, one *Brahmakamal* is gifted to each guest. *Nandastami,* known as the festival of *Brahmakamal* is observed in the month of September in and around the village Auli in district Chamoli. The village people decorate special umbrellas with *Brahmakamal* and even the guests are welcomed with *Brahmakamal*. The villagers perform their traditional folk dances after worshipping the sacred flowers. The colourful festival ends with the distribution of *Brahmakamal* as a symbol of happiness and prosperity. At Kedarnath, the priests bless devotees with flowers of *Brahmakamal*.

## CONCLUSION

As thousands of plants are removed by the local people in the region in order to make offerings at various shrines and also for the local festivals, the spread area of the *Brahmakamal* has drastically diminished. These are even sold for Rs. 2-5\- per inflorescence at some places. Tourism is another major threat to the species. At Hemkund and other holy places, the tourists pluck *Brahmakamals* out of curiosity and ultimately discard them. Owing to this, once commonly available, the flower has now become an almost rare occurrence.

One of the possible ways of conservation of this species would be to introduce controlled or managed extraction/harvesting of the flower. Places where *Brahmakamal* is found could be divided into 2-3 plots and only the local people given permission to collect *Brahmakamal* from these plots on a rotational basis. It is only then that sustainable utilization of the species can be achieved and its central place in the lives of the Uttaranchalis maintained.

## BIBLIOGRAPHY

Gaur, R.D. and J.K. Tiwari. 1987. 'Indigenous Medicinal Plants of Garhwal Himalaya (India): An Ethnobotanical Study of Medicinal and Poisonous Plants of the Tropics', *International Botanical Congress:* 139-142.

Jain, S.K and A. Saklani. 1991. 'Observation on the Ethnobotany of Tour Valley Region in Uttarkashi District of the North-West Himalaya, India', *Mount Res. Dev,* 11(2): 157-161.

Saklani, A. 1995. 'Brahmakamal' in *Vanaspati Adhyatma: Vishwas Vigyan Aur Tathya,* R.K. Dubey. Lucknow: Shubham Prakashan.

Saklani, A. and R.R. Rao.1996. 'Role of Brahmakamal (*Saussura obvallata* DC) in the Life and Culture of Uttaranchalis', *Ethnobotany,* vol. 8.

Shah, N.C. and S.K. Jain.1988. 'Ethno-Medico Botany of the Kumaon Himalaya, India', *Social Pharmacology,* 2(4) 359 -380.